JAMES CLEUGH   16862

LOVE LOCKED OUT

A survey of love licence and
restriction in the Middle Ages

HQ
14
C54
1963

SPRING BOOKS

Université de Sudbury | University of Sudbury

London/New York/Sydney/Toronto

PRINTED IN EAST GERMANY.

Original edition 1963
by Anthony Blond Ltd
© Copyright 1963 James Cleugh

This edition published 1970 by
The Hamlyn Publishing Group Ltd
London/New York/Sydney/Toronto
Hamlyn House, Feltham, Middlesex, England

SBN 600 02216 1

CONTENTS

I	INTRODUCTION	7
II	ARTISTS	20
III	HOLIDAYMAKERS	
	i. Dancers	37
	ii. Mummers	45
	iii. Flagellants	51
IV	THE FOOL CULT	
	i. The Fool Proper	57
	ii. Students as 'Fools'	75
V	COWLS AND COIFS	83
VI	WITCHCRAFT	107
VII	WHOREDOM	131
VIII	BATHERS	154
IX	DANSE MACABRE	173
X	PRIVILEGE	
	i. Lords of Misrule	198
	ii. The Case of Gilles de Rais	211
	iii. Epilogue	223
XI	EASTERN GLAMOUR	228
XII	PORNOGRAPHY	246
XIII	CENSORS	272
XIV	CONCLUSION	294
	SELECT BIBLIOGRAPHY	311
	INDEX	313

LOVE LOCKED OUT

I Introduction

SOME two hundred years after the execution of Jesus of Nazareth an earnest young schoolmaster of Alexandria, who had been studying Christian theology under the Greek scholar Clement in that city, castrated himself. The operation was quite familiar to the surgeons of the day. They had an effective apparatus for performing it in quick time with the least possible trouble to the patient. He would usually be a slave required for attendance on young ladies or in households where a lot of nubile female labour was employed. But the subject might occasionally be a criminal convicted of rape.

One such surgical instrument, about a foot long, was fished up from the Thames near London Bridge in 1840. It is an elaborately worked bronze clamp adorned with the heads of gods and goddesses and certain symbols of fertility and virility. The two shanks were originally hinged at one end, where there is an oval ring through which the penis would be passed. The scrotum and testes were then drawn up between the serrated surfaces on the inside of the shanks. When the clamp was closed they could be removed with a rapid knife-slash. The penis was thus left intact and the wound duly cauterised and sutured. Details of the structure and decoration of this tool can be inspected in the Romano-British Room at the British Museum, where it is preserved.

The ancient Romans distinguished three categories of those whom they contemptuously called 'half-men'. There were in the first place the *castrati*, who had been deprived of all the external generative organs. These creatures, since they could be relied on not to seduce, in the full sense of the word, their charges, cost the most money. They were also the most disagreeable of eunuchs, generally both ill-mannered and fraudulent. They were beardless, squeaky-voiced and long-lived, especially the blacks. If ugly they commanded still higher prices. They were regularly inspected in order to make sure that their lost members, like the limbs and tails of truncated lizards, were not growing again.

The second category, that of the *spadones*, retained the penis but had lost both testicles by excision, as was the case with those on whom the clamp described above was used. They and the third class, the *thlibiae*, with testicles still in place but artificially crushed, were capable of copulation and interested in it, the prostate gland secretion producing the orgasm. They were prized by licentious women. Yet they soon lost such potency as they possessed and very rarely generated offspring. Accordingly, employers who could not afford *castrati* put up with *spadones* and *thlibiae*. Both these two last species wore beards and spoke in deep voices. They were more intelligent than the *castrati*. But as a rule they soon died. The white eunuchs, in all three cases, suffered more from ill-health than the black.

Origen, the Alexandrian schoolmaster referred to above, was nothing if not thorough in all that he did. So it is probable that he rendered himself a *castratus*. But self-inflicted amputations of this nature were rather rare, being confined for the most part to devotees of the goddesses Diana and Astarte and the more excitable candidates for the priesthood of Cybele, the Great Mother of the Gods. Sir James Frazer in *The Golden Bough* has described how these novices hurled their severed members against her image as an act of mourning for her companion, or in some legends lover, Attis, who sacrificed his virility for reasons which vary in the different myths. After emasculation the new priests wore female clothing and ornaments for the rest of their lives.

In the time of Origen the cult of Cybele, together with those of the Persian Mithras and the Egyptian Isis, had far exceeded in the Roman Empire those of the Olympian gods derived from Greece. Origen's tutor Clement of Alexandria was largely bombinating in a vacuum when he called attention to Christianity and led one of his best pupils to decide that its doctrines

INTRODUCTION

demanded the total abnegation of sexual potency. But Clement himself, to do him justice, never actually said such a thing. He concentrated mainly, so far as women were concerned, on urging them to abjure thin or coloured fabrics in their garments, as well as all jewellery and such cosmetics as eyebrow-soot and white lead for the cheeks. For at this period, while a pagan emperor ruled, women were still socially important. They were as determined to remain so as the Christians were to demote them.

Origen, who afterwards regretted having gone the whole hog in this way, became in due course one of the most eminent, if also most controversial, Fathers of the new Church. He was really less ferocious than his older contemporary Tertullian, a married priest, and less of a misogynist than Jerome, a saint who, after beholding visions of 'bevies of girls' in his hermit's cave, only grudgingly allowed marriage because, he said, it produced virgins, the most admirable beings in the world, he considered, if they kept themselves to themselves. They were the natural 'brides of Christ', he affirmed. So seduction of them made Christ a cuckold and the ex-virgin an adulteress.

By the time of St. Cyprian, elected bishop of Carthage in the middle of the third century, however, there seem to have been some virgins who tried to have it both ways. For that illustrious cleric found it necessary to forbid their remarkable practice, called agapetism, from a Greek word meaning other than carnal love, of sleeping with men yet claiming to preserve their chastity. Cyprian ordered these young ladies, as soon as they made any such announcement, to be examined by midwives before being compared with the mother of Christ.

Various theories had been started at that period to account for the miracle of immaculate conception, afterwards denied point-blank by St. Augustine, which made her a virgin. Some authorities maintained that she had been impregnated through the ear by divine beings specified alternatively as the Holy Ghost, the Archangel Gabriel or the First Person of the Trinity. Others asserted that her son, whose divinity was not, incidentally, admitted by all Christians until towards the end of the century, had been born of her breast or navel.

Meanwhile legends multiplied about the duly authenticated virgin martyrs. St. Agnes, stripped for the brothel at the age of thirteen by her persecutors in 303, miraculously produced an instantaneous growth of hair which covered her whole body, enough to repel any would-be ravisher. St. Gorgonia refused to be touched by a doctor, since the lightest contact with any male of any sort instantly brought to her mind all the detestable horrors of the act of defloration, befouling the ideal of Christian purity advocated by St. Jerome. So great was his influence just then and for long afterwards that a convention arose and still exists of depicting the Redeemer Himself as much like a virgin as possible, with blonde tresses and peach-bloom complexion.

The narrator of an anonymous MS. credibly dated about A.D. 100, but also assigned to one Hermas, brother of a second-century Roman bishop, appears as one of the earliest representatives of the Christian virgin-cult. He is left by a shepherd at nightfall in the company of twelve maidens who, when he asks where he is to sleep, tell him, like true 'agapetists': 'You are to sleep with us, but like a brother, not an ordinary man. For you are our brother and in future we shall serve you, for we love you.' 'Then she who seemed to be the leader kissed me and so did all the rest. Then these virgins laid their linen undergarments on the floor and made me lie down on the clothing amongst them. Next they prayed, and I with them. And I remained with them, praying, until two o'clock of the morning. Then came the shepherd and said to them: "I hope that ye abused him not." And they answered: "Ask him." I told the shepherd: "Lord, it gave me pleasure to spend the night with them." '

Sly as this retort may appear to modern ears, it is probable that the phrase is quite solemnly meant, as a recommendation to asceticism. But Cyprian, when informed by a nun that she had done likewise and was still a virgin, pronounced that she was nevertheless guilty if she had sinned with parts of her body, the mouth for instance, not leading directly to the womb. For, said he, virgins can be contaminated in many ways, though it is only the female generative organ itself which can afford proof of defilement.

Such 'chaste' marriages were a feature of the period from the second to the tenth Christian centuries. An Anglo-Saxon queen was actually canonised for refusing intercourse with her husband. The abbess Ebbe, one of the last virgin-saints in England, on sighting a body of Danish raiders from the convent wall, cut off her nose and upper lip in the hope of evading rape and ordered all her nuns to do the same. But the savage heathens, quite indifferent to this disfigurement, nevertheless deflowered every single woman in the place.

St. Athanasius the Great, however, who did not write the 'Athanasian Creed' as used to be supposed, couldn't stand 'agapetism' when applied to himself. After six years of persistent solicitation by his young housekeeper he simply fled, early in the fourth century, from his episcopal residence at Alexandria, not being able to bring himself, in the kindness of his heart, to dismiss the girl.

Origen, from whom Athanasius learnt much, was made of sterner stuff. But the older Egyptian did not practise the opportunism of either the arrogant, guilt-ridden Numidian, St. Augustine, tormented by the murky past which had preceded his appointment as bishop of Hippo in North Africa, who reminds one of D. H. Lawrence, or St. Chrysostom, Archbishop of Constantinople at the end of the fourth century, who carried on a love-hate relationship for years on end with the fat but ultra-smart empress Eudoxia, a far from good-natured blonde of Teutonic lineage. Chrysostom was of the same opinion as Clement of Alexandria and his own contemporary and colleague St. Gregory of Nazianzus in Cappadocia (329-c. 389), who forbade Christian women to 'build towers of other people's hair on their heads' (like certain fashionable ladies of 1963 A.D.) and to adopt the languid affectations of 'actresses, dancers and harlots'.

The self-castrated eunuch of Alexandria was the only one of the Fathers to carry to its logical conclusion, in his own physical person, the idea that the good man, he who can expect an eternity of bliss after death, must be sexually passive, especially if he has to teach classes of both boys and girls. Naturally, the third-century bishops disliked Origen. They suspected him of heathen hysteria. But this born educationist, after once acting on the impulse of a crazy fanatic, seems to a modern mind to have achieved a much sounder theological position than they did.

The conception which so appealed to Origen of Alexandria had not been unknown in pre-Christian times. Other oriental religions, as noted above, had suggested it. But neither the earlier nor the later Hebrew prophets troubled themselves much about concubinage, an automatic custom throughout the East among those who could afford it. The apocryphal Ecclesiasticus (fl. c. 150 B.C.) had certainly written: 'From a woman was the beginning of sin and because of her we all die.' But this dogmatic assertion merely proved that the author, like many classical Romans and Greeks, as well as the small sect of pre-Christian Jews called the Essenes, detested human females of any kind.

Origen seems to have borrowed the notion of sexual desire as the root of all evil, not from the sayings of the founder of his religion, who never proclaimed such a thing, but from a very different person. For some thirty years after the execution of Jesus a little bald, bandy-legged and beetle-browed renegade Jew, of Greek lineage, surpassing eloquence and powerful personality, had been dashing about Asia Minor declaring that the dead Nazarene, now resurrected in heaven, had been sent down to earth as a Messiah, to redeem humanity from its appalling vices of concupiscence and cruelty.

Saul of Tarsus, in the days when he had been an ardent persecutor of Christians, had proposed marriage to the daughter of the High Priest of Jerusalem. But that young woman had rejected his offer. Shortly afterwards the disgruntled suitor, while jogging along the road to Damascus on one of his zealous missions to wipe out the hated sect, had seen a vision which converted him to its faith and caused him to adopt the Gentile name of Paul. Thereafter his sermons on that creed's behalf, as fervent as those he had formerly preached against it, assumed an aggressively masculine bias. They ended in Rome about the year 62. In that city, so far as Origen knew, Paul the Apostle had been put to death on the usual charge of conspiring against the State.

But by that time his main message, the reiterated cry of 'Flee fornication!' had already impressed quite a number of thoughtful Roman citizens. They were fascinated, like the Essenes and the Greek sage Pythagoras (fl. c. 532 B.C.), by this watchword's absolute contradiction of the most universal preoccupation of human nature, apart from the sheer necessities of eating, drinking and evacuation. The Roman amateur philosophers could not help wondering, as they beheld the misery into which the reckless exploitation of the sex instinct plunged so many people, whether at any rate a drastic reduction of its operations might not make life a good deal more secure and worth living for the majority.

Paul had written in his famous Epistle to the Romans (vii. 23-4): 'I see another law in my members warring against the law of my mind and bringing me into captivity to the law of sin which is in my members. O wretched man that I am! Who shall deliver me from the body of this death?' There was no mistaking the import of this magnificently rhetorical capital sentence passed on the flesh. But more letters followed, even more specifically expressed. 'Now the body is not for fornication ...' (I Corinthians vi. 13). 'He that committeth fornication sinneth against his own body ...' (Id. 18). 'It is good for a man not to touch a woman. Nevertheless, to avoid fornication, let every man have his own wife ... if they cannot contain let them marry: for it is better to marry than to burn.' (Id. vii. 1, 2, 9). The Apostle goes on to recommend his own state of bachelorhood as the most suitable for a true Christian. For (Galatians v. 17) 'the flesh lusteth against the spirit and the spirit against the flesh ... adultery, fornication, uncleanness, lasciviousness'.

'Mortify therefore your members,' he exclaims in Colossians iii. 5, repeating and amplifying the list of synonyms for the sex act that so obsessed him. Such quotations could be multiplied, the key-word 'fornication' recurring again and again. Paul's early disappointment in love had certainly hit him very hard indeed.

Yet for well over a hundred years after his death those who agreed with him that sexual abstinence might improve their prospects both on earth and in heaven remained a small and unpopular minority. A generation or so before Origen took the Apostle's advice so literally one Athenagoras, a Greek apologist for the Christians, was telling the philosophic emperor Marcus Aurelius that although 'we only have wives for the purpose of procreation of children' the community in question did not, as was constantly rumoured, indulge in cannibalism and unnatural vice.

The emperor probably only raised his eyebrows. But the new slogan gained much ground during the next century and a half.

It had fastened irrevocably on men's minds throughout the empire by 325. In that year the Council of Nicaea, one of the two rival capitals of Bithynia, a province lying along the southwestern coast of the Black Sea, defined still further the Pauline theology which had inspired an Egyptian schoolmaster to remove his sexual organs.

Little more than a generation later the State which had silenced Paul the Apostle for ever—no doubt after due legal procedure—pronounced his beliefs to be the official religion of the distracted Roman world. Constantine, its head, had declared himself a Christian in 312. But the old gods, discredited as they were, died hard. Nothing is so conservative as any sort of faith in the supernatural. Well over another century was to pass before Pan, Priapus and Aphrodite, Vertumnus, Vesta and Flora, Mithras and Isis, were driven underground to an extent which justifies historians fond of generalisations in concluding that an entirely distinct epoch of European thought had been initiated. It begins approximately about the year 500, soon after the deposition of the last Roman emperor of the West, Romulus Augustulus.

A rather briefer period of transition took place at the other end of the time-scale. Renaissance ideals are definitely foreshadowed in the early fifteenth century. By its close in 1500 they may be considered to have become so conspicuous as to be almost paramount. Yet at this stage, too, theologians of an older fashion, which had been the decisive moulder of life in Europe for the last thousand years, fought obstinately against the revival of conceptions current in pagan Greece and Rome.

The execution of an Italian monk of genius, Girolamo Savonarola, in 1498, strikingly illustrates the change that was then coming over the European scene, a panorama as sinister in its way, at that time, as the picture which had horrified the first disciples of Paul. Fra Girolamo, like the Apostle, was an ascetic mystic, hot-tempered and eloquent as he. But the friar's intellectual and even aesthetic culture, as well as his scholarship, were far superior to those of the man from Tarsus.

Savonarola detested the strenuously gay organisation men and women of his day and place. He loathed the vigorous festivities and the ostentatious luxury, refined or otherwise, which decorated so prominently the fast growing interest of the age in the civilisations of antiquity. These revels, he noted with bitter indignation, had invaded the venerable Church itself. He denounced them in such forcible terms that he came into conflict with a Pope, Alexander VI, who exemplified in his own person, to put it mildly, the more frivolous side of the new craze for imitating Alcibiades and Julius Caesar.

Alexander vainly endeavoured to bribe the rebel preacher with a cardinal's hat, then excommunicated him. But Savonarola was by then practically dictator of Florence, where he had scored his most scarifying oratorical triumphs. He not only defied the Holy Father, whom he rightly stigmatised as very far from holy. He also risked the fury of the art and pleasure loving Florentines, not for the first time, by a great 'bonfire of vanities'. The fuel included, in addition to personal adornments, certain valuable books and works of the finest craftsmanship, which the friar considered indecent. He was arrested, mobbed, tortured and burnt at the stake.

It is impossible to withhold sympathy from this high-minded but exasperating man, in some ways the Matthew Arnold of his age and an obvious precursor of the Reformation. But his personal charm, learning and integrity could not save him from forces in irresistible flood against the bigotry of a millennium. It will be a main preoccupation of the present text to suggest the evidence for the rise, progress and ultimate victory of this revolt, largely concentrated in the sexual field, where the clerical rulers of medieval times had shown such oppressive intolerance.

There had always been signs of insurrection even in the 'Apostolic Age' of the second century. Not every convert to or fellow-traveller with Christianity then regarded copulation as a disreputable function like micturition or excretion. Nor did all Christians meditate on birth solely with reference to its location, as did St. Augustine in his reminder that 'we are all born between urine and faeces'.

As time went on the isolated attempts to unbar the door thus savagely banged upon the material consummation of love grew more and more numerous. Chaucer's contemptuous aspersions, towards the end of the fourteenth century, on the 'archedeken

... that boldely did execution in punishing of fornication ... But certes lechours did he gretest wo ...' (*Frere's Tale*, 2 sqq.), only represents the culmination of a long process of resentment of interference by clerics in their charges' private lives. As the fifteenth century dawned the rebels may fairly be said to have forced the lock.

Human nature is now known to have evolved from bestial. Man's disposition shares with that of wild animals a deeply based and ineradicable objection to restraint. The combination of this native refractoriness with an equally native urge to coition not restricted, as in brutes, to particular seasons, ensured the defeat in practice of the Pauline theory postulating strong sexual feeling as anathema to heaven. The priests had no more difficulty than any modern commissar in obtaining lip-service to their prohibitions. But faith in this aspect of the doctrine they were supposed to uphold could not be congenial to the majority of mankind.

Consequently, such occasional glimpses of common eroticism as are afforded by documents surviving from the Middle Ages show that the casual licentiousness of the pagans in this respect pales in comparison with the lurid performances of medieval humanity. The fanaticism, real or pretended, of the clerical hierarchy in its repression of sexual indulgence led directly to an unprecedented preoccupation with such matters. Perversions of every kind grew rife. The Canon Law Penitentials, which provide for their punishment, list scores of them. Lust masqueraded as religious exaltation far more often than it had in the regularly prescribed sacred orgies of ancient Greece and Rome. Positive mania in this connection, erupting into the very behaviour so reprehended by the Church, came to be excused, even regarded with awe, as 'demoniacal possession'.

On these occasions formerly respectable nuns, for instance, could be seen by visiting ecclesiastics and sometimes even by the public, rolling on the floors of their cells, pulling up their skirts, exhibiting their sexual organs and using the foulest language. A woman so 'possessed' was also liable to make obscene gestures and invite intercourse. Some had been known, in accordance with the principle of psychological ambivalence—every positive begets its corresponding negative—to use a crucifix as an artificial phallus.

Madness, therefore, was often simulated. It was actually adopted by certain persons, usually male however, as a profession. Behind so convenient a veil all sorts of improprieties could be committed with impunity. The Court, castle and abbey 'Fools', in their motley garb, did pretty well as they chose, like revered lunatics in the East today. But perfectly sane monks and nuns, in their closed communities, vowed to a largely impracticable chastity, repeatedly succumbed to its opposite. Punishment itself, in the relatively mild form of flagellation, frequently sharpened appetite. Again, on the sound theory that one should understand one's enemy, the goatish 'Devil' of Christian theology was intently studied, together with the whole lore of witchcraft and 'black magic' related to this figure. Practice followed education. Churches and chapels themselves became the scenes of blasphemous orgies of predominantly libidinous character.

In addition, throughout the so called 'Dark Ages', and indeed beyond them, religious disputes, heresy hunts and missionary activities, in many cases as a cover for purely secular ambition, dragged the continent into incessant warfare, with its inevitable accompaniment of frantic sexual debaucheries, either in the mindless fury of military assault and tyranny or in the despair to which the prospective victims of marauding armies were reduced. The long succession of devastating epidemics, due to the prevailing ignorance of sanitation and the almost universal misunderstanding of the causes and cure of disease, produced the same effect. Even Boccaccio's highly civilised and privileged protagonists, in their retreat from the Black Death of 1348, tended to tell one another distinctly licentious stories to keep their minds off the subject.

The very organisation of feudal society, with its practical enslavement of the many poor to the few rich, enabled the latter to force the former into the position of helpless ministrants to carnality whenever lords and ladies and even abbots and abbesses, to say nothing of kings, queens and bishops, happened to feel like it, which seems to have been pretty often. The weary masses, accordingly, were encouraged to plunge more and more deeply, among themselves, into the only pleasures that didn't cost them anything. For feudal power extended very profitably to the spiritual sphere. The whole clerical hierarchy, from popes and cardinals to lay brothers, again and again used their ghostly authority to satisfy their erotic instincts.

Nor was there in these centuries, at any rate during the first thousand years of the Christian era, any very widespread and easily accessible cultural alternative to concentration upon lasciviousness. Moreover, long before the date (1096) of the First Crusade the infiltration of oriental habits of life from Asia and North Africa had added, through Byzantium, Spain and Sicily, a massive new wave of erotic dissipation to that already in vogue throughout Gaul, Italy and Central Europe. In literature and in law, in the great epics of chivalry and in the ecclesiastical enactments against 'sin', the uses and abuses of the procreative impulse are repeatedly illustrated.

As late as the fourteenth century the pen of an English knight of French extraction, La Tour-Landry, records the following bizarre anecdote of the continuing struggle between gross superstition and reckless immorality.

'It happened that one Pers Lenard, a sergeant, on the night delt flesshely with a woman in church. By a miracle they were tyed fast togedre that night and the morw alle day. People came to see the miracle and all prayed that orible sight might be ended. So the offenders were separated. And they that dede the dede were ioyned to penaunce to go naked afore the procession thre Sondays beting hem self and recordyng her synne tofore the pepille.'

But finally the Christian conception of absolution and its manipulation by a priesthood by no means always incorruptible neutralised for the most part the fear of damnation and everlasting torment which might otherwise have deterred all but the most incorrigible devotees of fornication, pederasty and other manifestations of the concupiscence so implacably, to all appearance, abominated by the clergy. The obligation, however, which the men of God felt to investigate this abomination in the utmost detail produced only too predictable results on both themselves and the laity.

INTRODUCTION

Thomas Wright, who lived in the reign of Richard III, burst into song as follows:

> 'Were I a man that hous helde
> if any woman with me dwelde
> ther is no frer bot he were gelde
> shuld com within my wones.
>
> For may he til a woman wynne
> in privetye he wyl not blynne
> er he a childe put hir withinne
> and perchaunce two at ones.'

One can almost hear the roars of laughter and the clashing tankards that greeted this ditty.

Accordingly, medieval sexuality presents a character very different from that of pagan Europeans on the one hand and that of post-1500 Western civilisation on the other. The rest of the world has of course remained, from the dawn of history down to our own day, on the whole very little affected by Christian ideas. The man of the European Middle Ages, when related to human beings in other continents and at other epochs, appears to have been simultaneously more obsessed by his generative faculties and more unsophisticated in his addiction to them. His gaiety in their exercise has almost always a touch of something like Victorian 'naughtiness', though, if English, he would use this word in a much more pejorative sense than it has acquired today. Such self-conscious 'mischievousness' is entirely alien from the uninhibited minds of ancient Greeks and Romans, the cultivated passions of Orientals in all times and the experimental attitudes prevailing among Westerners after 1500. Medieval perversities and ardours are those of a schoolboy by comparison. They seem constantly aware of a vigilant if possibly also hypocritical and gullible headmaster. This outlook is clearly far from extinct yet over an area still nominally Christian. Even furious atheists, especially northerners like David Lawrence and Theodore Powys a generation ago, continually reveal it. But the kink was far more universal and conspicuous in the days when bishops rode armed to the battlefield and the vast majority of laymen could neither read nor write.

II   Artists

HALF a century elapsed between the date (312) of the emperor Constantine's public championship of the still persecuted sect of Christians and the adoption in 363 of Christianity as the official religion of the Roman Empire. During this period the arts of painting and sculpture in Europe had fallen to as low a level as those of literature and music. Five hundred years at least were to pass before any of these modes of reflecting civilisation revived enough to compare with the much steadier contemporary development of such arts in Asia. Yet even then the Moors and Jews in Spain, the Slavs and Levantines in Byzantium, reached a far higher standard of creative craft than any of the other inhabitants of the continent. Only with the establishment of the so called Romanesque architecture of the eleventh century could the cultural achievements of Christianity in western Europe begin to rival the products of current oriental thought and feeling.

Nevertheless, crude popular illustrations of common social and religious life continued to be turned out in relative profusion, especially in a sexual connection, by both painters and sculptors during the transitional ages that bridged the gulf between specifically heathen and specifically Christian manners. There is little difference in actual style between the obscene frescoes discovered in Pompeii, which date from the first century of the Christian era, and the figures of Christ and the Apostles to be seen on the walls of the catacombs in which the early adherents of the new faith took refuge. It is true that the former were intended to excite festive visitors to brothels and the latter to encourage or console the victims of persecution. But both aimed at an intensification of susceptibility in the spectator. They produced their effects, just as far more sophisticated artists do in our own day, by conspicuous distortion of natural appearances.

Not until the thirteenth century at least did the examples of Giotto and the sculptors and mosaic workers of his period prove that a closer approximation to living forms and the proportions of buildings could raise the coefficient of sentiment, whether in the lustful or the pious, to a higher figure by conveying the illusion of actuality. For by that time a great advance in philosophic and scientific thinking had taken place. It was largely due to the inspiration of a now deeply rooted faith in orderly supernatural control of the visible world. Thus the European mind was by then cleared of a great part of the cruder superstitions of the heathen decadence. Men gained a new respect for the concrete evidence of what was considered the handiwork of heaven.

But long before this change a realism in the erotic field something like that of the archaic classical epoch can occasionally be noted alongside the exaggerations, contortions and rigidities of the current convention. For example, a figure of Daniel in the lions' den was incised—in the fourth century at earliest—on the lid of a sarcophagus preserved in the crypt of the church of St. Maximin in the Var department of Provence. Daniel is naked, with penis and testicles clearly shown. Again, a seventh-century manuscript in the monastery of St. Gratien at Tours, but of Visigoth, probably Spanish, origin is illustrated by a painting of the Flood with similarly nude males.

Two hundred years later, while Charlemagne's short-lived attempt to revive something of the spirit of ancient Rome was in vogue, a manuscript presented to Charles the Bald (823-877), King of the West Franks, is adorned in colour with a picture of Adam and Eve in paradise, divided into several scenes. In that of the Temptation Eve's pubic hair is very prominent, though her other sexual features are minimised. But by the eleventh century the pubis in both man and woman is nearly always covered or effaced. The free and easy classical tradition in these matters had already been crushed by clerical dictation.

The art known as Romanesque took the place of Greco-Roman. In this substitution the clerical dictators, like their secular predecessors and successors, gave instructions that a combination of popular appeal and grandiose majesty should govern the conceptions of their artists. The sculptors and painters responded with notable success. In their carved reliefs and brightly decorated psalters a certain amount of quasi-heathen jocularity and leg-pulling appears. Usurers are ignominiously tormented by demons. Conceited musicians have asses' heads. Adam gives Eve a hiding. Angels twitch playfully at St. Joseph's beard. This saint, incidentally, as a rule bears a glum expression in medieval art. It has been suggested that this is because he had, in a certain sense, been cuckolded. At any rate a carved capital in the church at Clermont Ferrand shows one of the angels in the group teasing him to be full of malice, as he darts a comically sly glance over his shoulder at the sufferer.

The austere St. Bernard of Clairvaux (1090-1153) deplored this sort of thing. But it only annoyed him because, he said, it kept the congregation and the minor clergy from their prayers. Twelfth century worshippers certainly had a good deal to laugh at. They could observe their dignified priests depicted as foxes, wolves, lions, donkeys, bats, pigs, monkeys, stags, crows and rats. They could see, in stone, the familiar burlesque actors of the day sticking out their tongues, showing their backsides and genitals, letting farts, dropping their breeches and running after women. There were plenty of sculptured nudes of both sexes being punished for concupiscence by having their private parts devoured by snakes and griffins. Here and there an actual whore could be seen in these groups, recognisable by her special headdress, a tall hat shaped like a sugar-loaf.

Figures of this kind were both carved in relief and painted on walls or stained on glass. The cathedral apse at Alby in northern Savoy, not far from Geneva, displays a fresco unmistakably representative of sodomites in action. But in church after church, of France particularly, the repressed sexual fantasies of Romanesque artists, few of whom were laymen at this period, break out at unexpected points. In Bourges Cathedral there are radiant Day of Resurrection nudes. The amazonian forms of 'Virtues' invite embraces at Civray. At Parthenay a lady—bust only, however—sits in her bath and a siren flirts with a triton. In Vézelay parish church St. Eugenia opens her robe to prove her sex to her accusers and a demon seizes the breasts of a woman who frantically covers her pudenda with her hand, while a serpent attacks the demon's testicles and the fiend's jaws gape in a frightful grimace of agony. Copulating couples, as at Sonillac, are not uncommon. Nymphs, centaurs and fauns, obvious imitations of classical models, do just what one gathered at school they were always doing.

But such mirrors of both reality and dreams remained until Renaissance times far from exact. They still retained important elements of caricature. The great painters of the late fifteenth and early sixteenth century, Hieronymus Bosch in particular, borrowed these motives time after time. Romanesque work, however, was much more deliberately contrived than its apparent lack of sophistication seems at first sight. The clumsy spontaneity of the earlier period has almost gone. In architectural sculpture, for instance, the frequent representations of a bare posterior, quite disproportionate in its magnitude, does not necessarily mean that the artist was either obsessed by this anatomical feature or even wished others to admire it. In the great majority of cases he is quite clearly joking in exactly the same spirit as a Rowlandson.

Unfortunately this variety of plastic art has not, naturally enough, survived in bulk. Much of it was executed in ephemeral materials and on a small scale. Much was destroyed in warfare, much by accidental catastrophe or through the zeal of reforming ecclesiastics. But the scattered residue, mainly in the great cathedrals but also to an extent in manuscript illustration, is sufficient to enable certain indubitable conclusions to be reached concerning the sexual habits of medieval Europe.

For the cathedral is the most precise record we have, as well as the least prone to defacement, of the preoccupations, ordinary and extraordinary, of the Christians who erected these vast edifices and spent a large part of their lives in them. They arose for the most part in an almost illiterate age. It was only after medieval institutions had declined about the middle of the fifteenth century that books became the normal repository of records of human behaviour and ideas. Moreover, the enormous numbers of people engaged in the construction of these buildings ensured a diversity in their contents far beyond the capacity of even the most multilateral single author.

Nearly all the masons and sculptors employed were monks or

lay brothers, men of humble origin and, whatever their talents, simple and downright character. They were practically slaves compared with the administrative and property-owning classes. They must have had as a rule all a slave's grim contempt for masters no better in the sight of heaven than themselves. They therefore often added to the works they were ordered to carry out certain subsidiary features expressing more or less defiantly rebellious or at least satirical feelings. The general specification had authorised a language in stone or paint which the masses of the people could understand and appreciate. The artists knew exactly how to do this, since they were themselves men of the people. They rightly guessed that their blunt impudence on occasion would be ignored or tolerated by their patrons. For the hierarchy at this date had no misgivings about its omnipotence. It never dreamed of seriously fearing or even resenting such pin-pricks of its complacency. Such taunts by solitary individuals, however many, could never in any case be proved to be more than good-humoured mockery.

There are paintings in manuscripts of the Offices of the Church which show, in addition to the depictions already mentioned of priests with the heads of cunning, ruttish or torpid animals, monks and nuns in the most indecent postures. In one even a Pope—the legendary 'Pope Joan'—appears in the act of parturition during a religious ceremony. She looks most demure and charming, having one hand on her stomach and the other helping a very large new-born infant to emerge from a slit in her gown at the level of the groin. The cardinal immediately behind her, a bishop next him and an abbot or prior with upraised hands indicating astonishment as he stands beside the cardinal seem mystified by rather than censorious of this awful proof of lewdness in the supposedly virginal occupant of St. Peter's chair. The two figures ahead of 'Pope Joan' in the procession, another cardinal and a tonsured chorister, have no idea, apparently, what is happening. They gaze straight in front of them, with the solemnly hieratic expressions appropriate to an important ecclesiastical occasion. It is impossible to avoid the impression that the artist's feelings in delineating this really perfectly scandalous scene were simply those of a quite tender amusement, as of a mother watching her children at play. There is no trace of perturbation at the physical improprieties of the performance.

The boldness, not to say insolence, of such pictorial derision of the all-powerful representatives on earth of a divinity from which there was no appeal suggests at first a widespread scepticism of, indeed a popular contempt for, the official faith. But this was by no means the case. On the lectern of Strasbourg Cathedral the figure of a monk is incised. He holds an open breviary in his hand. But the other hand has pulled up a distressed nun's skirt and is thrust between her bare thighs. The draughtsman no doubt believed in all the articles of the Christian creed. He was sure that God existed, that virtue would be rewarded and vice punished, if not in this world, then in the next. But he must have been equally certain that monks and nuns, even abbots and bishops, were every bit as human as himself, i.e. as susceptible of the common impulses of carnality.

Such instincts, it has always to be remembered, were not then considered shocking even by priests, even by St. Bernard himself. It was only after the adoption by Europeans, largely under oriental influence, of more elaborate conventions of behaviour that public exhibitions of the cruder aspects of eroticism came to be reprobated. It seems pretty clear that Hyde Park on a summer evening in the mid-twentieth century still lagged some way behind what could be seen by daylight in any medieval street or square, probably also in churches at either ordinary or extraordinary services.

In the twelfth century the grotesque humour of such artists as the Strasbourg sculptor was rife in northern France, the Netherlands and England as well as in the Mediterranean lands. But in the colder latitudes it began to assume a more delicate character, typically Gothic in its gentle and ingenuous gaiety. The brutality of Romanesque, its interest in awe and terror, grow much less evident. For by this time the clergy had learnt a lesson in tact. They were already laying less emphasis on their personal sanctity.

Up to the years around 1250 many churchmen of all ranks had been as openly licentious in their everyday conduct as the average layman. Some even gloried in this evidence of their ordinary humanity, since humility was ordained by the most impeccable Christian orthodoxy. Accordingly, congregations at Lyons could behold the late classical motive of Aristotle being ridden by a whore and the Christian one of women on their knees to grinning pigs. At Amiens stone couples could be seen embracing and at Laon bearded and beardless nudes in pursuit of one another like so many satyrs were carefully carved.

Consequently, no one, high or low, could at that time be scandalised by the spectacle in marble, on parchment or in real life of a vomiting or urinating cardinal or a bare-thighed abbess. Manuscripts of the Bible itself were adorned with such intimate revelations. A bishop fondles a girl. One of his colleagues seizes in the same way a monk who is watching the other prelate. A later version of this subject again portrays two bishops. But this time they are entertaining a couple of young women to dinner. Situations of this sort were regarded as inevitable in human beings created by an omnipotent and infallible deity. Sexual organs, one of the Fathers wrote, are mechanisms contrived by God. There is no reason whatever to be ashamed of them or pretend they do not exist. On the contrary, we had better be constantly aware of them, if only to guard against their abuse.

At the church of Notre Dame de l'Épine in Châlons-sur-Marne a sculptured peasant girl holding up her skirt may have been intended to warn the faithful against lust, one of the seven deadly sins. But it might just as well be thought, by either a medieval or a modern mind, to invite the commission of this offence. Another relief, at Strasbourg, of a monk lasciviously adoring a nun, is equally ambiguous. But in some fifteenth-century illustrations such ambivalence seems definitely on the way out. The unmistakably admonitory note sounds less frequently than the frankly facetious or even excited.

The frontispiece of calendars at this period often displays a male citizen with a jester in motley between his legs, perhaps calling attention to the bestriding figure's private parts. The depiction of acts of pederasty and masturbation, as well as ordinary sexual congress, and of some very pleasing harlots, is not at all uncommon in other documents. A tapestry of the Apocalypse at Angers Cathedral includes a vividly attractive 'great whore of Babylon', holding her 'cup full of abominations and the impurity of fornication' as described by St. John the Divine. Yet, from the look of her, she might just as well be toasting us in champagne. Another gay lady, nude this time, crops up in the capital of a pillar at Chartres Cathedral. She is riding a centaur and tugging roguishly at his beard.

In these circumstances the prelates who turned the pages of a missal, breviary or psalter or paused to examine the carvings in a choir can only have smiled indulgently at the occasionally exuberant illustrations in the margins of a sacred text or the references to *luxuria*, as the Fathers generally called concupiscence, in the reliefs on a pulpit or episcopal throne. Such works of art demonstrated a part of life as everyone knew it. The practices suggested would be sinful if carried to excess. But the best way to avoid over-indulgence in them was of course to be thoroughly familiar with their nature as normal phenomena.

The social and moral situation in this respect bore in fact a close resemblance to that of a school in which the pupils draw caricatures on the blackboard of members of the staff. These adult individuals may often be quite popular with the boys or girls. But they would be foolish seriously to resent such evidence, which can never affect their official position, of an irreverence due mainly to the desire for relief from feelings of inferiority. The impulse to ridicule is therefore not at all dangerously vindictive.

At the same time the testimony of medieval plastic art, especially from the eleventh to the fifteenth centuries, does strongly reinforce the impression that the more bolts and bars the higher officers of the clergy added to the door locked against carnal love the more it insisted on flying in at the window, even the stained-glass window.

But the Romanesque and Gothic sculptors and painters did of course produce much work of the highest quality from which the erotic element is either altogether absent or only lightly stressed. The porches of hundreds of twelfth-century churches, the west portals of Chartres Cathedral in particular, contain magnificent examples of architectural sculpture. In painting and mural decoration the dignity and sentiment reach a maturity comparable with those of any later period.

During the thirteenth and fourteenth centuries realism and technical skill improved even further in richness and facility. The harmony of design, the feeling for structural form and in manuscript illumination the deeply glowing hues contrast strongly with the cold restraint, distortion and stiffness, always typical of art in an age of autocratic bigotry, which had marked the output of the early Christian centuries. The superb *Très Riches Heures* possessed by the Duc de Berry is a missal illustrated by themes of everyday life and landscape. These were begun by the three brothers Limbourg in 1416 and completed by another hand in 1485. They show all the signs of a magisterial ease, delicacy and sumptuousness characteristic of a sensuously sophisticated and relatively free civilisation.

It is significant, however, that even here the border vignettes carry grotesquely humorous, though never sexually suggestive, forms, such as that of a bear playing bagpipes, which prove the liberation from theologically prescribed control. For in Italy such comparatively independent masters as Masaccio, Angelico, Botticelli, Leonardo and Mantegna, in Flanders Jan van Eyck and Rogier van der Weyden and in France the miniaturist Jean Fouquet, who had no need to proclaim themselves rebels against puritanism, were already active.

Of the architectural sculpture then prevalent, which later came to be regarded as obscene, a great part represented the tortures of the damned. It is certain that these works were executed in accordance with ecclesiastical orders. For the souls condemned for amorous excesses and perversions seem to outnumber the rest. These unhappy beings have their sexual organs and, in the case of women, their breasts, devoured by demons in the forms of toads, serpents and other beasts, including monstrosities, then regarded by most people as peculiarly terrifying or hateful.

As we have seen, St. Bernard, as early as the eleventh century, protested in vain against licentious jocularity in Christian art. But he also vigorously deprecated, equally without result, the still more sensational presentation of details connected with the punishment of libertines in hell. He declared that these scenes prevented priests, who became absorbed in deciphering their often complex and intricate designs, from attending to their duties during Divine Service.

The majority of theologians, however, approved such carvings. The conventional view was that they were far more effective in preventing sin than any necessarily vague and undramatic visions of eternal blessedness. But towards the end of the fourteenth century, when official clerical puritanism was almost everywhere in retreat, and 'heretics' were multiplying, some artists, especially the illuminators, began to handle these grim topics with a strange levity. The opening page of a collection of penitential psalms, for instance, shows the damned being seized by devils in castles, cities and—sad to say—convents, whence they are hurled down into hell to be devoured by Satan and tortured by his minions. Yet the general impression given by this picture is one of light-hearted, bustling activity.

If this evidence were modern it would mean that the painter at any rate was jeering at Christian beliefs. But such an attitude was scarcely possible in the Middle Ages. To a medieval eye vigour rather than frivolity would be the keynote of the illustration. It would probably frighten most of the penitents. On the other hand the irrepressible slyness of medieval humour, so well authenticated by other testimony, makes it difficult to be sure no malice was intended. It is most likely that the same uncompromising realism which never fails to sketch a grin somewhere in scenes of torment and martyrdom is here at work.

In any case the paternally indulgent Church was fighting its rearguard action with much forbearance so far as decorative art was concerned. The bishops passed for public exhibition in the cathedrals of Chartres, Amiens and Rouen such groups as the already mentioned young couples embracing, pretty girls admiring themselves in mirrors and scenes of flagellation in which that favourite subject of medieval stall-carving, the nude posterior, is usually delineated with great care and detail.

Outside the church of Notre Dame de l'Épine, near Châlons, again, the squatting figure of a woman with raised skirts, urinating, can still be seen. Elsewhere defecation, complete with the deposited excrement, is a frequent motive, especially at the intersections of arches. One of the most extraordinary of these items is preserved in the Cluny museum. It takes the form of a gargoyle composed by the figure of a monk carrying a nun over his right shoulder in such a way that her naked buttocks, most lovingly designed, protrude down towards the street. The monk's right hand draws the flesh of one buttock aside so as to reveal the anal orifice through which, if the gargoyle were in position, the rain-water from the roof would gush.

Such obsessions with the excretory processes of the human body are characteristic also of children in the individual. They go back far into the morning of the Christian era. A searing contempt for the flesh is already discernible in the preaching of Paul of Tarsus. It probably originated the first plastic display of these functions, their delineation being regarded as a salutary reminder of the superiority of the soul.

This preoccupation extended of course to the reproductive act itself. Above the main entrance to a village church in the French department of Deux-Sèvres there can be distinguished a carving of the male and female organs of sex in actual conjunction. The design is flanked on either side by figures of a man and a woman. Their contorted features clearly indicate the experience, that of the copulation orgasm, which they are supposed to be undergoing.

Oddly enough this *département* also affords in another village church examples of solitary onanism, exhibited by two separate figures of women. The well known nineteenth-century author Prosper Merimée considers (*Voyage dans le Midi*, p. 295) that the sculptors, in particular, of the eleventh and twelfth centuries 'when they depicted a certain sin with the crudest naturalism, exactly as it takes place, did so with perfect good humour, not in the least with malice aforethought'. It does not seem to have occurred to Merimée that these frivolities may have been rooted in resentment. But this latter feeling was perhaps in temporary abeyance when a young man was shown presenting his bare backside to a blankly staring young woman. The gesture may be taken possibly as depicting a retort discourteous to some disobliging maiden. Or the man may be understood as merely calling her attention, with proper piety, to the less attractive aspects of human anatomy. It is hard, at this time of day, to decide.

Inversions and perversions, such as sodomy and bestiality, both active and passive, were punishable in the later medieval period by burning alive. But they were not infrequently represented in the sculpture of, especially, gargoyles. The realism of these carvings is often carried to excess in the idiotic simpers of the participants, even of the goats and monkeys. The latter beasts were also occasionally chiselled as squatting in the attitude of masturbation, their semi-human visages expressing a ludicrous solemnity. The entablature of a side door of the cathedral at Orléans has two very grotesque gargoyles, the first in the form of an ape copulating with a woman and the second showing the same woman in the act of giving birth to the result of this performance, a tiny monkey which appears between her legs and is still attached to her vulva by the umbilical cord.

All the same, so far as the rather frequent medieval offence of bestiality is concerned, Christian sculptures and reliefs of this subject differ notably from its common aspect in the plastic art of antiquity. The treatment is remarkably mild in comparison with that of the heathens. To a modern eye the whimsical naïvety of the Christian artist affords an extraordinary contrast with what appears to be the shameless brutality, combined with a cynical sophistication, of the pagan style.

It is this feature of medieval art in general, a kind of tender indulgence or charming sweetness that yet never approaches sentimentality, a profound innocence, so to speak, or childish merriment, in dealing with matters of terrifying or disgusting import, that renders the carving and painting of the European Middle Ages absolutely unique. Perhaps never before or since have the most appalling phenomena of life been faced and depicted with such utter objectivity. For at that time and in those regions no one could doubt that the sublunary world was strictly limited, a mere brief preparation for either an eternity of happiness specifically located somewhere above the visible sky or perpetual misery far down under the soil.

This pure and simple faith began to decay in the fourteenth and fifteenth centuries. A complex of causes was responsible. Increased material affluence, increased knowledge of other civilisations and increased awareness of much apparently triumphant defiance of heaven all played their part in the modification of the old ingenuousness. It was only then that both laymen and priests came gradually to conclude that certain aspects of life could not be tolerated, let alone laughed at. The idea of obscenity, hitherto unknown in Europe, was born.

Almost at once the natural rebelliousness of the human spirit deepened to a positive cultivation of perversity, as opposed to the mere laxity of principle that had preceded it. What had now to be done in secret spread far more widely. It fastened much more inexorably upon both the senses and the mind. Medieval sexual habits rarely sicken the investigator, since they did not sicken the practitioner. But later enormities in this respect aroused more and more horror and fascination in persons conditioned for so long to associate the mechanism of reproduction with guilt and squalor, rather than with the mirth and mockery their Christian ancestors, like their heathen predecessors, so regularly applied to it.

An anecdote of the celebrated painter Fra Bartolomeo di San Marco (d. 1517) illustrates this transition in feeling. He had completed an entirely nude figure of St. Sebastian. It was much admired by other artists. But the priests of the church in which it was displayed were perturbed. Their fair penitents repeatedly ascribed their adulteries to contemplation of Bartolomeo's splendidly virile evocation of masculine beauty. So the picture was withdrawn from exhibition and sold to the King of France.

The point is that a couple of hundred years before this date the ladies would have been very unlikely to think of this excuse. They would have been well accustomed then to casual views of male nakedness. Nor, if they had dreamed up such a far-fetched pretext, would their confessors have believed them. But by 1500 public nudity was already becoming unusual. In 1541 Michelangelo got into serious trouble with Pope Paul IV for showing the sexual organs of the figures in his *Last Judgment*. The short-tempered artist is said to have commented between his teeth: 'The Pope would do better if, instead of trying to correct paintings, he would pay more attention to his job of trying to correct the morals of his congregations.'

Many of the medieval carvings which appear most obscene to modern eyes are to be found, naturally enough, on those parts of a wooden choir-stall known as misericords or misereres. They were small brackets on the underside of the folding seat, designed as a support against which the chorister could lean when he got tired of standing upright as prescribed by canon law. The name 'pities' was given them in recognition of this compassionate function. During long services they would be in permanent contact with the posterior of the occupant of the stall. In France and Italy, consequently, they were decorated in such frankly ribald style that the zeal of later ecclesiastics has left few of them now decipherable.

But misericords carved in Westminster Abbey and some other English cathedrals, e.g. that of Winchester, during the thirteenth century often show nude or semi-nude females mounted on huge cats. They are witches on the way to an orgy. In France, during the next century, similar girls, mostly represented as quite attractive, ride demons of unusually affable and humane aspect. The interest of Christians in witchcraft of course far antedates the Bull of Pope Innocent VIII (1484) condemning this heresy officially.

Other subjects of equal sexual suggestiveness also figured on shadowed or half obscured surfaces almost anywhere. The base of a lamp-standard from a church at Bruges has a relief depicting a maid washing the hair of her mistress. The lady's head is bent so far over the basin that she cannot see the girl complacently submitting, meanwhile, to the libidinous attentions of a gentleman evidently the master of the house.

In France such inconspicuous slabs often showed nudes of both sexes bathing in the same tub. A misericord in the church of St. Nicholas at Amsterdam is carved with the squatting figure of a man excreting coins. He sits beside a naked girl in the same attitude. From her anus a long tapeworm protrudes. An older woman is already winding most of it over a frame, perhaps for the purpose of measuring it. At Evreux Cathedral in north-western France even the somewhat rare perversion of coprophagy itself is illustrated on a misericord. A young woman there lifts to her lips a handful of the faeces which her lover has just deposited. A too frenzied amorous passion, we may perhaps deduce, cannot be less than degrading to a Christian bound to scorn every aspect of carnality.

As noted above, the fifteenth century saw far less public nudity than its predecessors. But if love was not primarily the point, there might be exceptions. A coloured relief certainly to be dated before 1500 and probably designed to serve as an apothecary's street-sign, is preserved in the museum at Bruges. In this picture a doctor and his assistant, with clyster at the ready, stand in the street. Through an open ground-floor window of the house opposite projects the bare fundament of a lady who is evidently to undergo kidney-flushing. It may be a moot point here whether any specifically sexual reference is intended.

But, as already noted, illumination rivalled sculpture in hammering the sex nerve. Byron had every reason to write (*Don Juan*, Canto I.xlvi):

> 'The missal too—it was the family missal—
> was ornamented in a sort of way
> which ancient mass-books often are and this all
> kinds of grotesques illumined. And how they
> who saw those figures on the margin kiss all
> could turn their optics to the text and pray
> is more than I know.'

The missal reader might behold the incestuous Lot raping his daughters, Joseph and Potiphar's wife, a lady of the manor seated before the domestic hearth with her skirts pulled up waist-high, a lover fondling the bare breast of his mistress (hardly an appropriate illustration, in modern eyes, to the adjacent words of the Office of the Purification of the Virgin), nude human posteriors set on legs and surmounted by a face, on the very page at which the missal is to be opened, at a certain point in the liturgy, for kissing, and indecent portraits of the mistresses of wealthy owners. The French Renaissance scholar Henri Estienne (1531-98) swears that some of these pictures, then at least a hundred years old, 'could soften even the austerity of Hippolytus'.

In general the Romanesque painters signalised their rebellion against the solemnity of their clerical tyrants in the eleventh and twelfth centuries by a certain boyish impudence. It involved grotesque postures and grimaces akin to those which have sometimes characterised the twentieth-century's artistic revolt against academicism and its romantic derivatives. Picasso and Dali, Klee and Kirchner, Lautrec and Gromaire, in their deliberate playing down of human and natural dignity, their Shavian mockery of the portentous, were often impelled by similarly impatient restlessness under dictation. Their majestic moods were better suited by the impersonal style of abstraction than by distortion, just as the Romanesque carvers reached supremacy only in the applied mathematics of architecture and monumental sculpture.

But since nothing like the camera was known in medieval

times development could only be in the direction of greater realism, not abstraction. Giotto tried both. But his influence worked only in the former field. Concrete detail came to be the fashion. But the Church was long able to prevent its normal culmination in the extreme sensuousness, even sensuality, of the High Renaissance. In the early fifteenth century Masaccio's nudes would probably have become more than merely classical if he had lived beyond the age of twenty-seven. But the other fifteenth-century heralds of fuller-blooded ideals were more or less consciously forced by ecclesiastical control into mysticism, like Angelico and Botticelli, or a naturalism, such as Jan van Eyck's, that strictly excluded erotic elements.

It was only the advent of Leonardo's superb genius that saved this movement from degenerating into a sterile sentimentality. Michelangelo, who was twenty-five in 1500, reversed the trend of a millennium by bringing the sexual features of the human figure strongly into the foreground of his preoccupations. The same could be said of his northern contemporary Dürer. But the less sensuous Germans and Dutchmen, like Grünewald and Bosch, tended to look back only as far as Romanesque fantasy. They seem to have hated and feared the ancient Greeks as much as Michelangelo adored them. On the whole, by 1500, the specifically Christian reaction had proved a blind alley. For the next four hundred years the future of painting was to be determined by Giorgione (d. 1510), followed by the whole Venetian school, by Rubens and Rembrandt, by Poussin, Watteau, Boucher and Fragonard. No outstanding artist was ever again to forget, or to be bullied into ignoring, the most powerful of human instincts, until the iron hand of social revolution and world-wide war crushed for ever, in the early twentieth century, the natural gaiety of nations.

Sculpture followed much the same development as painting. The beginnings of Romanesque realism in the twelfth century were confined, so to speak, to holes and corners, unable to reach full expression within the rigid framework of an authoritarian theocracy. Then, at the turn of the fourteenth and fifteenth centuries, the robust imagination of Jacopo della Quercia of Siena (1374-1438) devised a splendidly sensual relief of the creation of Eve for the doors of the Baptistery in Bologna. It later inspired

Michelangelo. Jacopo's contemporary Donatello struck the same note about 1430 in his bronze David. Once more the story ends with the complete freedom of Buonarotti. His growl at Pope Paul IV in 1541 sufficiently indicates the new independence of clerical censure, even from the highest quarters, enjoyed by Christian artists in the sixteenth century. In so awe-inspiring a scene as that of the Last Judgment fresco the painter would not allow his honest conception of humanity in the dock to be degraded by the introduction of any equivalent of a loin-cloth, even if the theoretically infallible Vicar of Christ himself ordered it.

The extraordinarily bitter and prolonged opposition to the struggle of painters and sculptors to express the truth about life and human nature had held plastic artists in subjection for nearly fifteen hundred years. But for the last third of this period the tide had been slowly turning. The Church had breathed again after the fiasco of the year 1000, when the world was supposed to come to an end. One of the first results of the chastened ecclesiastical spirit was the carving, painting and building of the men who have made the terms Romanesque and Gothic famous. A great cultural stride forward had been taken. Laughter and carnality were recognised to be of help in shedding an essential light on the dark riddle of existence. The real poetry of a religion which had formerly been interpreted far too prosaically then had a chance to shine.

It was perhaps the artists rather than the politicians and theologians who, in saving themselves, saved the Christian idea for mankind in the second five hundred years of Christendom's maturity. In the first five hundred the statesmen and prelates had rescued their faith from what seemed to its adolescent eyes the night of time. But those champions had very nearly made the fatal mistake of philistinism. In the third five hundred this persistent shadow still haunted them. The challenge to its chill menace spread far beyond the limited sphere of aesthetic activity. At every facet of the strange mosaic of medieval society defiance of the Church's vindictive condemnation of the *corpus vile*, though its religion had far more to offer humanity than such perverse bigotry, led to a riot of eroticism. It will be cursorily surveyed, with certain examples of its absurd or fearful consequences, in the following pages.

III Holidaymakers

i DANCERS

TOWARDS the end of the fourth century St. Asterius, Bishop of Amasia in Cappadocia, censured the males in his diocese for dressing up as women on New Year's Day and roaming the streets 'in long robes, girdles, slippers and enormous wigs'. The contemporary Bishop of Caesarea, Basil the Great, complained that after the Lent feast, in April, the women 'casting aside the yoke of service under Christ and the veil of virtue from their heads, despising God and his angels, shamelessly attract the attention of every man. With unkempt hair they hop about, dancing with lustful eyes and loud laughter. As if seized by frenzy they excite the lasciviousness of the youths ... transforming the holy places into scenes of lewdness. With harlots' songs they pollute the air and sully the degraded earth with their feet in shameful postures'.

The Christian rhetorician Lactantius (260-340) had seen in action the pagan original of these 'incitements to lust', to wit, the April Floralia festival of ancient Rome. It had first been instituted, innocently enough, to mark the exhilarating advent of 'the flowers that bloom in the spring'. But Lactantius notes that in his time the females taking part were obliged by public demand to appear naked. 'The people,' he records sadly, 'shouted for the women to strip and wriggle.'

Later in the fourth century St. Chrysostom, in talking (Sermon 42) of wedding celebrations, suddenly thunders: 'Unbridled sensuality reigns! Those present seem to go out of their minds! Some neigh amorously like horses, others kick like asses! All are dissolute and confused! No sanity, no dignity! All is devils' pomp, cymbals, flutes, indecent songs!'

Bishop Isidor of Seville (560-636) has this to say about the New Year dancers of his day in Spain, then ruled by the Visigoths: 'These miserable creatures,' he growls, 'transform themselves into monsters, womanising their masculine faces and making female gestures, romping, stamping, clapping, both sexes together in the ring dance, a shameful thing, a host with dulled senses intoxicated by wine.'

It was not just the dregs of the population who went on like this, at the great Christian feasts of Christmas, New Year's Day and Easter. Basil of Caesarea's tone in the original Latin is tearful rather than contemptuous. There is evidence from an early period, ninth century at latest, that, at the May festival anyway, even decent women let themselves go.

Some of the clergy, who themselves often took part in these dances, excused them on the ground that they symbolised the trampling of vice underfoot and also the leaping out of hell's clutches into heaven. But the bishops were not so easily refuted. They prohibited such scenes of dissolute jubilation again and again throughout the centuries. But their fulminations had not the slightest effect, even when the formidable Pope Innocent III in 1207 definitely banned all public frolics of this kind.

In the lifetime of Isidor himself even nuns were dressing up, dancing and singing gaily, in the privacy of their convents, whenever the calendar enjoined all Christians to rejoice. But naturally many of these dates coincided with those of the heathen feasts that had preceded them. The popular tradition of lascivious excitement on such occasions could not be suppressed. When the nuns, in their originally pious mirth, elected one of their novices as 'abbess' for the time being and turned all their normal routine upside down, as the ancient Romans had during the *Saturnalia,* it inevitably happened that some of the younger girls behaved improperly and were not always seriously reprimanded by their seniors. That was the thin end of the wedge. It thickened scandalously as time went on.

Satyrs had always figured prominently in the religious revels of Greek and Roman antiquity. Consequently, much of the fancy dress adopted by the Christians for their own festivals took the form of horns, tails and other features of these lecherous monsters. Feminine participants were sometimes facetiously called 'little hinds' (*cervulae*) and were expected to disport themselves accordingly.

As early as the seventh century these public orgies of choreomania, vainly condemned in 635 by the Council of Toledo, had reached epidemic proportions. Mass hysteria and fraud made their appearance. The hard core was generally composed of neurotic psychopaths. But others who were perfectly sane joined the transvestists, both in order to share in the alms then freely distributed to the dancers and also to seize the opportunity of indulging their lusts in something more practical than mere capering and bawling. 'Many girls forgot themselves and many husbands were deceived,' writes a contemporary chronicler, perhaps not without relish. Whether he was one of the masked and travestied priests, daubed with soot as a further precaution against being recognised, who mingled with the frenzied rabble, is not quite clear.

At Liège in 1374 a band of these fanatical balletomanes is said to have actually plotted to murder all the clergy. This plan was apparently concocted by the dancers under the impression that their hysterical fits had been imposed on them by heaven for their supineness in putting up with a concubine-keeping priesthood, which they therefore resolved to destroy. But the scheme got nowhere.

While the higher ecclesiastics struggled against the craze and the lower more or less candidly defended or even joined in it, open-air dancing spread to all the seasons of the year and all conceivable occasions and locations, particularly churchyards, where it had the excuse of cheering up the dead on the one hand and animating the living to defy mortality on the other.

A seventeenth-century antiquary at Trier in the Rhineland vividly describes the antics of the fourteenth-century near-epileptics, basing his account on contemporary records now lost. 'The dancing couples were so placed that one would advance towards the other in an unseemly fashion.... They indulged in disgraceful immodesty. For many women during their shameless dancing and mock-bridal singing bared their breasts. Others of their own accord offered their virtue.'

The obverse of primitive anger and fear, as every anthropologist knows, is primitive hilarity. Civilised people have always followed suit. The austerities of worship, propitiation and sacrifice, the endurance of restraint, were succeeded by more or less organised gaiety, in ancient Egypt as in ancient Greece and Rome. So too the medieval Christian contrasted the intense solemnity of High Mass with the reckless jollifications of carnival. These included, as well as dancing, rudely extravagant parodies of the cathedral services.

The Church, after many useless prohibitions, decided at last to smile benevolently upon these last riotous processions, not only from the tact required in a successful missionary, but also on the sound Christian principle of the exaltation of the humble and meek at the expense of pride and arrogance, enshrined in the Canticle of the Virgin, or *Magnificat,* sung at Vespers ('He hath brought down the mighty from their seat and exalted the humble').

The first clear record of the famous 'Feast of Fools' during which these sonorous lines were thundered out in the streets, dates from the end of the twelfth century. The proceedings took place soon after Christmas. Details varied in different parts of Europe. But lay and clerical participants generally wore the insignia of their social or ecclesiastical superiors, such articles being often actually issued by manorial or Chapter authorities. In addition, a donkey was so regular a feature of the processions that they were frequently referred to as celebrating the 'Feast of the Ass', as well as the 'Feast of Fools'. The choice of this animal is obvious enough to the secular mind. But Christ had entered Jerusalem on an ass and the Virgin, according to legend, had ridden one on her flight into Egypt. So a girl, in some cities, mounted the beast.

The point of a mention of this ceremony in the present connection is that it stood mainly for a revolt against clerical despotism, which in its turn concentrated so heavily upon the sin of lubricity, a mood so liable to raise its head whenever crowds make merry. As soon as the donkey was led into the church, with the singers braying like asses at the end of every verse of a Latin hymn specially written by some humorist for the occasion, horseplay broke out. Females were kissed, smacked and fondled. Obscene gestures and noises were made. Scatological phrases were chanted. Wine was drunk, spilt and evacuated by mouth or urethra. Dogs and falcons were let loose by young nobles, vermin and poultry by merchants and artisans. Everything, in short, was done, and on consecrated ground too, which the priests were always forbidding.

Nothing could have shown the men of God more clearly that the men of this world meant to have their cakes and ale, though the Day of Judgment might be at hand. The hierarchy, for its part, grinned and bore this species of blackmail by the populace, much as modern industry tolerates the occasionally preposterous exactions of its trade unions. For if the 'Feast of Fools' had been suppressed by force and its hobbledehoys dismissed, they would immediately have reinforced the already dangerously turbulent urban proletariat, to the fury of the secular authorities, and the Church would never have been able to attract sufficient recruits to its lower ranks to make up the deficit. For one of the chief allurements of a clerical career, in the case of young men of spirit, was the prospect of going berserk at least twice, if not oftener, in the year.

The learned and gifted Herrad von Landsberg, Abbess of Hohenburg, near Strasbourg, illustrated with her own pious hand, and perfect propriety, a celebrated manuscript of the twelfth century entitled 'The Garden of Delights'. But she had no patience with the 'Feast of Fools'. 'What nowadays happens in many churches?' she laments. 'Not a customary ritual, not an act of reverence, but one of irreligion and extravagance, conducted with all the licence of youth. The priests change their garments and go forth as a troop of warriors.... The church is desecrated by feasting and drinking, buffoonery, unbecoming jokes, dicing, the clash of weapons, the presence of shameless wenches, the vanities of the world and all sorts of disorder. Rarely does such a gathering break up without quarrels.'

This dignified and cultured critic, by no means a bigot, approved of the performance of 'decent' drama, i.e. the so called 'mystery plays', in churches and wrote some such pieces herself. What annoyed her was the element of mocking parody allowed at the periodical festivals. It was maintained by the saying of Mass backwards, by singing hymns out of tune, by burning shoe-leather, frying sausages and boiling puddings instead of using incense and by gormandising, wine-bibbing and gambling on improvised altars.

In such an atmosphere sexual excesses in word and deed naturally accompanied other kinds of impudence. St. Augustine in the early fifth century had already deplored the reckless libertinage of congregations in church. But neither he nor any of his eminent successors down to our own time could prevent more or less open acts of concupiscence in the excited, tightly packed crowds that jammed the squares and main avenues at carnival time, to say nothing of lateral lanes and alleys, both by day and by night. In certain Italian cities on Christmas Eve conduct little short of orgiastic can still be observed, as it is sometimes in Hyde Park on Sunday evenings in the summer or in the East Sussex capital of Lewes on Guy Fawkes night.

Some attempt was made, at the beginning of the twelfth century, to control the grosser abuses of the sex instinct prevalent on these important dates in the calendar. They often led, as Herrad noted, to bloodshed in the churches themselves. In 1198 certain songs, stage farces and obscene caricatures of bishops and cardinals were prohibited by the Chapter of Notre Dame in Paris. But they continued to be presented outside the cathedral. Deacons and the inferior clergy, shameless as the ordinary public, stripped off their vestments and habits, danced about naked and assumed indecent attitudes.

In the thirteenth century, as the idea of centralised monarchy took shape in most European areas, the 'Feast of Fools' was extended to celebrations of such public events as coronations, the State visits of sovereigns, royal marriages, tournaments and national victories. Castruccio Castracani, for instance, the tyrant of Lucca, after defeating the Florentines at the battle of Altopascio in 1325, arranged naked foot-races for both sexes. At a Magdeburg jousting in 1279 the first prize was the local 'beauty queen', i.e. the best looking harlot present. When Queen Isabeau of Bavaria, the eighteen year old wife of Charles VI of France, entered Paris in 1380, she was received by semi-nude girls acting as nymphs at fountains.

Towards the close of the medieval period such 'showladies' often stripped to the buff. When King Louis XI entered Paris in 1461 he was confronted, on reaching a certain public fountain, by 'three handsome girls, entirely naked, representing sirens. Their splendid, upstanding breasts, well separated, round and solid, were most agreeable to see.' Charles the Bold of Burgundy at Lille in 1468 was similarly greeted by a *tableau vivant* of the Judgment of Paris. The three young Flemish women taking the parts of Hera, Athene and Aphrodite stood there without a stitch on them. The same Duke had put on a public show himself in 1453 when one of the attractions comprised a live group consisting of 'a virgin one of whose bare breasts spouted a continuous stream of spiced wine, while a male child beside her supplied a flow of *vin rosé* from his codpiece'. Such exhibitions, always accompanied by riotous dancing, grew even more daring in the following century.

Between 1200 and 1500 the 'Feasts of Fools' could be referred to either religious or secular origins or a mixture of the two. They could also be called by other names, such as the 'Innocents', the 'Sub-deacons' or the 'Cuckolds'. But whatever they were called they were never anything more or less in reality than excuses for public orgy. The idea of sacrilege, an offence which involved severe penalties normally, was forgotten for the time being.

During the torchlight processions, the lascivious dances in the porches of consecrated buildings and the travesty of High Mass that followed, a rabble dressed as Court jesters, monsters or even whores, with priests in lay garments and all sorts of citizens masquerading as bishops and cardinals and sometimes actually popes, thronged the aisles and the streets. They yelled lewd ballads, staggered and jostled, exchanged clothing and enjoyed amorous struggles. Occasionally they paid off old scores. Then the uproar would rise to a crescendo as daggers were drawn and blood flowed over the cobbles or across the sacred pavement. The generally unpopular higher clergy were often beaten up in the confusion. At Tournai in 1498 the citizens seized a group of chaplains who had refused to act as 'bishops', half stripped them and locked them up for three days in a tavern.

In certain French towns notoriously bigoted or debauched ecclesiastics—it didn't seem to matter which—were dragged from their beds in the early morning of one of the twelve days after Christmas and led through the freezing streets, completely nude, to the nearest church, where they were duly 'baptised' with icy water. In 1327 the Bishop of Pamiers felt obliged to issue a decree condemning processions carrying effigies of prelates and flourishing banners embroidered with pictures of the male and female pudenda.

Matthew Paris of the Benedictine Monastery of St. Albans reports on less authorised infringements of respectability, mentioning 'pilgrims who, when they visit holy places, sing lecherous lays whereby they inflame the hearts of such as hear them and kindle the fire of lechery ... also those most sacrilegious persons who tread down the bodies of holy Christians in the churchyards, where they dance on saints' eves and kindle the living temples of God with the fire of lechery, flocking to the churches on saints' days and eves and holding dances....'

In 1445 the Faculty of Theology in the University of Paris made a further solemn attempt to suppress this sort of thing. The homily refers to 'priests who dance in the choir dressed as women, panders or minstrels ... and finally drive about the town in shabby carts, rousing laughter with infamous performances, foul gestures and verses scurrilous and impure'. But in the preceding year, on the 4th December, in good time for the Christmas explosions of impropriety, the Chapter of Sens had used much milder language. It merely begged the revellers to see that the clerics who were douched retained at least their breeches.

In 1212 the Council of Paris forbade 'Fools' Celebrations' in the nunneries. Yet a generation later the Archbishop of Rouen complained that the ladies in coifs were at it again, putting on lay costumes both male and female, squealing filthy ditties and capering with non-clerical visitors. In the monasteries, needless to say, the same 'Christmas games' were played. The 'Fools' Abbot' and the 'Fools' Abbess' might be real ones, disguised for the occasion. The 'abbot', with a numerous retinue, would visit the 'abbess' in her convent on holidays. He would sup and drink with her, put a ring on her finger as a symbol of 'marriage' and not infrequently go to bed with her. Such scandalous proceedings could of course always be represented officially as mere charades. At any rate there was no stopping them. A story is even told that at Evreux two canons who objected to 'Fools' Days' were hanged by their subordinates from the spire of the cathedral.

Other churchmen defended the Carnivals, as already noted, on psychological and even medical grounds. In the early fifteenth century a good-natured theologian proclaimed: 'Barrels of wine would burst if one didn't give them air occasionally. Well, we ourselves would burst too if we allowed the wine of our wisdom to ferment by incessant devotions. Such is the reason why we give up certain days to enjoyment and playing the Fool, in order that we may subsequently resume, with all the greater fervour, our studies in and service of religion.'

It is quite true that not one of even the most frantic participants in these wild relaxations ever tried to prolong them beyond the prescribed periods. The 'Fools' sobered up with remarkable promptitude. Nevertheless, the growing licence on the days and nights of carnival undoubtedly brought religion into contempt. They helped to inaugurate Luther's Reformation. This movement ended for ever the old, characteristically medieval Christianity, with its hearty charity towards the common sensual weakness of humanity, so strangely combined with official thunder against concupiscence. Eventually the medieval Achilles successfully defied this lightning by practically blackmailing his Church into permitting the excesses of the 'Feast of Fools' and coolly continuing his alternate sinning and repenting. Such a situation became intolerable to the more refined society of the sixteenth century. Its puritans grew narrower and its sensualists less in need of charity. It may almost be said to have split in two, for better or worse. Yet it is arguable that but for the dancing holidaymakers of the Middle Ages modern civilisation might never have grown out of the suicidally rigid theocracy of that time.

ii. MUMMERS

As we have seen, the Church had been prejudiced from the start against the heathen practice of 'mumming', i.e. assuming a disguise for either ceremonial, edifying or merely entertaining purposes. Tertullian, towards the end of the second century, tells the story (*De Spectaculis*, c. 23) of a demon who entered the body of a woman at a theatre and excused himself, at exorcism, on the ground that she had trespassed on his property.

No Christian, in those days, might be a *scenicus* (actor or actress, the masculine termination being used for both sexes, a significantly contemptuous convention) or marry one. Nor could any such person be baptised unless he or she renounced the stage. The tradition equating professional comedians with pimps and harlots had come down from the decadence of ancient Rome. Yet the Christians never attempted in medieval times to suppress the theatre altogether, as they often did in northern Europe after the Reformation. It was the Saracens, not the Christians, who killed the theatre in the East during the seventh and eighth centuries. In the West it never died, though it sickened almost to death under the half savage Ostrogoth and Lombard rulers of Rome in the sixth century.

At that period travelling companies expelled from the abolished theatres took to the roads, where they rapidly consolidated their reputation for sexual immorality, if also for wild gaiety. Both as professionals and as amateurs, their ranks being joined by all sorts of people impatient of social restraint, they gave open-air performances, mainly of a hilarious character, in the country districts. They played stringed instruments, sang, danced, juggled and recited. The more accomplished merged in their exhibitions the qualities of the Roman mime and the Teutonic bard. These nomads formed a permanent background, colourful, joyous and reckless, to the ordinary preoccupations of peasants and craftsmen, merchants, knights and scholars, throughout the Middle Ages, and powerfully influenced the rebellion against tabus on love from the pulpit.

Until the eleventh century the wandering minstrels, acrobats, bear-leaders, declaimers and wisecrackers of both sexes seemed to be fighting a losing battle against the relentless persecution of their incorrigible amatory proclivities by the Church. They could sometimes make terms with the bloodthirsty secular raiders of the day, becoming slaves to such hordes until they were wiped out in the next massacre. But the priests were implacable, arresting, imprisoning, excommunicating and executing them on the slightest pretext.

It was the general cultural advance after the year 1000 that saved them. Clerical magnates remained hostile. But the lay knights and barons, the inferior clergy and the farmers and traders who were enjoying more prosperity and leisure after the fearful turbulence of the two centuries that succeeded Charlemagne's death, began to favour men and women who could make them laugh once the day's work was done. Some of the strolling players became famous and pampered. The mime, bard and juggler Taillefer actually led the Norman squadrons up the hill at Hastings, through the Saxon arrows, as he trolled out the Song of Roland, flinging up his drawn sword again and again and catching it in the air.

Humbler persons addicted to art and literature, with or without creative ability, found the 'mummers' congenial company. Young men mostly in minor orders, fairly well educated, but fonder of wine, women and song, not to mention dice, than prayer and sermons, started travelling about in imitation of the troupers, sometimes joining them. Such vagrant scholars made quite a name for themselves. They could often write well in Latin or vernacular rhyme and accentual verse and understood something of music. They also understood quite a bit about adultery which, with the bottle, was the main theme of their compositions.

These were all lyrical, made to be sung, preferably in a tavern or in road-marching. They went to well known hymn tunes, such as the *Stabat Mater* or *Veni, Sancte Spiritus*. Young soldiers have been setting rude words to sacred music ever since. Some of the ditties were sentimental, lovers' laments and so on. Some reached a high literary standard. But most were frankly satirical, riotously celebrating a certain mythical 'Bishop Golias', prototype of the greedy, hypocritical sensualist so often to be found lurking, according to medieval comedians, under the priest's robe. The *scolares vagantes* sarcastically proclaimed him to be their 'master'. So they were also called *Goliardi*, a name applied, in addition, to one of their favourite metres in jogging rhymed quatrains.

Here is a verse from a masterpiece in this strain by the so called Archpoet, a twelfth-century German from the Rhineland, a district even then famous for wine and gaiety.

Res est arduissima vincere naturam,
in aspectu virginis mentem esse puram.

*Juvenes non possumus legem sequi duram
leviumque corporum non habere curam.*

A rough unrhymed translation of this lilting trochaic stanza might run:

'It's a very *hard* thing to conquer human *nature*,
to look upon a *maiden* and still be pure in *spirit*.
Boys like us just *can't* obey so difficult a *ruling*
and take no note what*ever* of pretty girlish *figures*.'

It would be a short step from such singing, with probably musical and/or dance-step accompaniment, to a miming by two or more players of the scenes suggested by the words. Thus the strolling comedians and their friends gradually came to act short farces, closely connected with the age-old rustic games, very often carrying a sexual reference, such as races, ball throwing or kicking, riding the 'hobbyhorse' (originally a punishment for unpopular characters), mock fighting, raiding and capture, in short any expression of physical exuberance.

At Coventry women used to tie up men, as it was said Danish prisoners had been tied up after an English victory. In 1290 'seven ladies of the queen's chamber took King Edward I in bed on the morrow of Easter and made him fine himself'. The household record from which this quotation is taken notes that they were paid for doing this. No doubt the monarch, like the 'Danish prisoners', had a good romp in resisting his fair captors.

Such raiding and seizing games can be traced back to the ritual of human sacrifice in primitive ages. Variations of it were played on the 28th December (Innocents' Day or Childermass) celebrated in memory of Herod's slaughter of Jewish infants born on the same day as the son of Joseph and Mary, reputedly destined to be 'king' of his country. On that morning girls could be the object of a burlesque 'attack' in their beds. At Avignon students had the right to pull up the skirt of any whore they met and smack her. But she, like King Edward, could escape this indignity on payment of a fine. 'Giving the Innocents', both in public and in private, lasted as a custom well into Renaissance times. It is even said to have been inflicted on Queen Elizabeth, when a princess, by Sir Christopher Hatton, afterwards Lord Chancellor, and others.

In the circumstances of the Middle Ages these ceremonial pretexts for lechery were regularly based on Biblical legend. The very popular story, for instance, of the life of Mary Magdalene before her repentance and conversion, was acted out in highly realistic detail. By the fourteenth century a cautiously indulgent Church, with comparatively few dissentient voices, such as that of John Wyclif, was tolerating these rude exhibitions. For at least the masses of the people would thereby be brought to familiarity with the Bible.

Thus, according to a stage direction by William Jordan, who followed medieval tradition in his play called *The Creation of the World* (1611), Adam and Eve are to appear either naked or in fleshings of white leather. It is also likely that the 'Mystery Plays' watched in remote rural regions of England by the literary historian Thomas Warton (1728-90) preserved the old conventions. Warton writes:

> 'In these Mysteries I have sometimes seen open and gross obscenities. In a play of *The Old and New Testament* Adam and Eve are both exhibited on the stage naked and conversing about their nakedness.... This extraordinary spectacle was beheld by a numerous assembly of both sexes with great composure. They had the authority of Scripture for such a representation.... It would have been absolute heresy to have departed from the sacred text in personating the primitive appearance of our first parents, whom the spectators so nearly resembled in simplicity.'

But mere naturalistic nudity was not enough for the fourteenth century dramatists. The Devil, when he made his frequent appearances, was provided with an immense artificial phallus, like the satyrs in the ancient Greek ceremonies in honour of the god Dionysus. Even amateurs such as King Charles VI of France and his courtiers disguised themselves as these ruttish beings. One night when they were all drunk the palace caught fire. Several of the nobles were burnt to death. The young Duchess of Berry, who was in the audience, saved the king's life. But he never wholly recovered his mental balance after this experience.

Towards the end of the century 'Moralities', in which the characters were ethical abstractions, not religious figures, came into fashion. Impersonations of the Seven Deadly Sins, especially

Luxuria or Lust, opened the door to every kind of extravagance. In a morality play called *The Castle of Perseverance*, which inculcated the saintly virtue of constancy in affliction, the fiend Belial, by the contrivance of an alchemist, had smoke and flames issuing from his anus. In *Mind, Will and Understanding* the heroine Anima ('Soul') is attacked by imps who run under her skirts and up her legs like mice. As for the female personifications of chastity, industry, forbearance etc. they had to attract the interest of the spectators by being at least half naked. They were usually in fact, in real life, actresses or concubines noted for the very opposites of these qualities.

Women in assumed labour pains, for example when acting the parts of St. Anne, mother of the Virgin, and even the Virgin herself, writhed on the stage. Bawds were always prominent and behaved in character. Satirical teasing of the clergy, high and low, multiplied in the fifteenth century. A midwife delivers, in full view of the audience, an abbess of a child whose father is the reverend mother's secretary. A priest who can't find a certain woman he is in pursuit of swears he would give God a beating if he could catch him. If he can't catch the woman he'll go and be a Mohammedan. Another sells his concubine to the devil and a third relates that a certain Salome refused to believe the Virgin a virgin and wanted to put the matter to the test with her own hands, which thereupon fell off. Sighs of edification, mingled perhaps with a few guffaws, no doubt greeted this performance.

Such plays were often staged in semi-seclusion by the clergy themselves, with an extraordinary amalgam of naïve piety, half digested classical learning and prurience. Thus in 1361 the Bishop of Meaux dramatised parts of Ovid's *Metamorphoses*, which recount the love affairs of the pagan gods. In this production Danae figured as the Virgin Mary, Christ as both Apollo in the guise of a shepherd chasing Daphne and the swan which raped Leda. The three Gorgons were various kinds of Lust. Andromeda, lightly clad of course, was the soul chained to the rock of sin.

As time went on the mummers, both lay and clerical, persisted in giving their shows not only at holiday times but all the year round. The *soties* ('Follies') of the fifteenth century in France were conducted by the association known as the *Enfants Sans*

HOLIDAYMAKERS

Souci ('Boys Who Don't Care'). They satirised the whole 'Establishment', political and legal as well as ecclesiastical. It goes without saying that these riotous comedies gave rise to just as much violence and lascivious conduct as the regular carnivals. The authorities only intervened when blood began to flow.

iii. FLAGELLANTS

Crowds are of course capable of carrying into immediate effect impulses of all kinds which most of the individuals present would control if they were alone. Consequently, the very frequent medieval processions of every description, even the most solemn, provided an outlet, just as in the heathen centuries, for the most ungovernable instincts of mankind, that of sex more often than any other.

In antiquity the phallus had been openly paraded by both the Egyptians and the Greeks. Cakes in the forms of the male and female generative organs were exchanged by the ancient Romans. This custom was not forgotten when the empire became Christian. Such fertility symbols were then carried in procession at certain seasons of the year, for instance on Palm Sunday and Corpus Christi Day, by women and girls of unimpeachable respectability. The cakes were blessed by the clergy and retained throughout the year by their devout bearers, being regarded as amulets or charms against this or that misfortune.

In medieval times, accordingly, the mere occurrence of a procession of any sort could easily bring to mind the mechanism of human reproduction and all the subsidiary ideas associated with it. It was generally understood, in any case, that conventional conduct was not to be expected on such exciting occasions, especially if they followed periods of ecclesiastically ordained fasting and abstinence from sexual intercourse.

In the pagan world processions had always gone bare-footed. Later on more portions of the body were uncovered. At first the intention had been to promote, by stripping off outer clothing, the notion of humility in petitioning heaven for favourable agricultural or political results. But soon a single garment became the fashion. Finally, in the year 1224, the wife of the French king Louis VIII staged an unprecedented procession to pray for his success in a campaign against the English invaders. Some of the marchers then stripped to the very skin in the zeal of their patriotic fervour. By 1315 processions of naked men, but not women, had grown quite common in Paris.

Nudity could also be observed in public when individuals or groups, either voluntarily or after judicial sentence, bared their bodies for the scourge as penitents. Whipping had been recommended as early as the third century as a punishment for certain confessed sins. The practice was at first confined to monks. But these recluses soon found that the ascetic impulse initiating their action developed with startling rapidity into erotic stimulation of the type technically known to-day as algolagnic (sado-masochism). The spread of this feeling in monasteries must indubitably have played its part in the notorious lechery of their inmates, proverbial almost as soon as such communities were instituted.

It was in the eleventh century that the Italian Benedictine St. Pietro Damiani first organised group flagellation for laymen. He probably did not realise that he was thereby introducing them to a species of enjoyment which might well become, as in fact it did, a dangerous mania.

Two hundred years later the first procession of fanatical flagellants, both priests and laymen, set out under the auspices of no less venerable a figure than St. Anthony of Padua. This saint, a Franciscan theologian and preacher, stood no nonsense from those of his Order who suggested mitigations of its rigour. It is impossible to suspect so austere a personage of deliberately adding to the sexual ferment which, whether he knew it or not, has always been closely associated with extreme religious exaltation. One can only suppose him to have been sure that if you hit hard enough with the right weapons pain would outweigh any conceivable pleasure.

The tools were soon forthcoming. In 1260 unofficial processions of voluntary scourgers, each member heartily belabouring another in front of him, started streaming through Italy and out into northern and central Europe. The participants, all male, were naked to the waist and hooded in linen cloth. They carried banners and candles as well as their businesslike whips. They sang vociferously as they marched.

Beginning as earnest groups, these penitents were soon

organised into a self-conscious sect, then a Brotherhood. The brethren became a familiar sight in the streets of cities, parading two by two in long columns. Clergy accompanied them. By now the flagellants comprised all ages and both sexes. They sported hoods and loincloths only (*solis pudendis honeste velatis*). They also roamed the countryside for weeks on end, in all weathers, using leathern lashes both on themselves and those nearest them, till the blood flowed.

As usual this last effect excited those who saw it to frenzy. Shouts, groans and shrieks resounded. When night fell, the exhausted, semi-nude battalions threw themselves down by hundreds, ostensibly to sleep, in forests or on moors. But undoubtedly the majority then indulged in promiscuous copulation or sodomy during the hours of darkness. For their bodies had been heated to a state of furious eroticism by the beatings they had undergone. At the same time their minds still reeled in the grip of a contagious mania in origin religious but flaring inevitably into a specifically sexual ecstasy.

In the middle of the fourteenth century the terrible metaphorical scourge of the Black Death descended upon all Europe. The disease was generally believed to have been inflicted upon mankind as a punishment for its outrageous sinfulness. Consequently the numbers of the wandering bands of fanatical, self-flagellating penitents multiplied beyond computation. But both they and the rest of the population of the continent fell fast under the most lethal plague it had ever known.

In 1348 Pope Clement VI ordered a solemn intercession to be staged at Avignon, to which city the papal Court had removed in 1309. A long line of priests and laymen, barefooted and barebacked, with ashes scattered on their heads, paced slowly along the packed streets. The deep groaning and wailing of the spectators, as they knelt in prayer or stood with their arms stretched to heaven, drowned the hissing of the whips and the wild cries of *Mea culpa! Mea maxima culpa!* Time after time individuals in the crowd or in the procession dropped to the cobbles, writhing in the mortal throes of infection. The epidemic they had gathered to avert showed no signs of relenting.

By 1349 flagellants in all the Christian countries were wearing short, hooded cloaks, with red crosses embroidered on front and back and grey, pointed hats with upturned brims, also similarly adorned with red crosses. Like pilgrims, they carried staves. A white lower garment fell from hips to feet. Both feet and back were of course bare, the cloak being only wrapped about the neck and shoulders. Scourges were thonged and knotted, sometimes fitted with iron nails. But these were now only used when the procession came to a halt in some market square or meadow, as the light was fading. Before the inevitable nocturnal orgy began certain of the brethren preached to the assembled citizens, informing them that thirty-three and a half days of continuous beating with the blood-drawing appliances now in operation would free anyone of the taint of any sin, however atrocious. The period mentioned corresponded with that of the years of the life of Christ. But this teaching was considered heretical by the orthodox clergy. For it meant that a persevering flagellant would have no need of official confessors and penances.

Meanwhile the erotic aspect of these excursions was increasing. After sunset most of the inhabitants of any medieval town went to bed, unless any duly authorised ecclesiastical or secular festivals were in progress. But as a rule there would be no indoor accommodation, in a small settlement, for any exceptionally large group of visitors, such as the peripatetic Brethren composed. In these circumstances the panting and groaning flagellants would take to the neighbouring woods and fields for their night's rest. Often their ranks included women. But if not, the city strumpets were usually available. Otherwise, and perhaps even so, homosexual relations followed, under the stars.

Later in the century these riotous episodes began to attract the angry attention of both the civil and the clerical authorities. Such huge processions were forbidden to enter the churches, or gather in any open spaces. Flagellation accordingly became a semi-secret vice, even in its group manifestations. Upon these the municipal forces descended with fire and sword, burning their buildings and encampments—and occasionally their bodies —and massacring the survivors. The medieval Brotherhood eventually died out. Its organised marches are last heard of in Thuringia, in 1414.

But a century later the whole craze started all over again in exactly the same way, with exactly the same results. Church and

State united, with identical ruthless ferocity, to stamp it out. They were successful. Mutual beatings on such a massive scale never troubled European moralists again.

In the later Middle Ages such excesses had been the culmination of a process, the unavoidable combination of mystical and erotic impulses, which had been going on for hundreds of years. Before the advent of Christianity the bacchants and the worshippers of Orpheus and Adonis had mingled profane with sacred passion in their rites. Throughout the medieval period traces of a similar amalgamation can be discerned. Flagellants were not organised into a sect—later condemned by the bishops as heretical—until the fourteenth century. But the practice, both by individuals and by groups, was rife at much earlier stages of the Christian dispensation. It augmented notably, even among the upper classes, after the Black Death, all over Europe, from Italy to Flanders, Germany and Bohemia.

The Pope at that time, Clement VI, first encouraged the Brotherhood, making it a chief contributor to his intercession programme, in 1348, at Avignon. But he soon afterwards excommunicated the addicts of flagellation who performed the act in public, whether singly or in bands. Individual displays of this kind were of course very rare, the exhibition of itself challenging others to imitate it.

Clement gave as his reason for this measure the notorious fact that the scourging tended to excite *luxuria* in the crowds which collected to watch it, certain scandalous scenes having frequently occurred in these mixed and uncomfortably compact assemblies. But the only effect of the Pope's Bull was to drive many of the flagellants into the monasteries and nunneries. In the semi-private seclusion of these buildings the results of their activities may be imagined.

Much of the subsequent gossip by Protestants concerning the appalling debaucheries committed in such communities by men and women dedicated in theory to chastity was invented. But there can be no doubt, on ordinary psychological grounds, that sexual temptations were more difficult to resist in such places than elsewhere, as they are in prisons and hospitals today. Confinement of any sort leads even a healthy mind to morbid meditation. This tendency is enormously reinforced when so universal a preoccupation as the procreative instinct is made the subject of anathema by the authority which invites the seclusion in question as an act meritorious in the sight of heaven. For solitude and idleness or the fulfilment of formalities only too liable to grow mechanical in people without any very special ardour for them soon breed an abnormal interest in forbidden fruit. Nor can regular sermons on the dreadful wickedness of concupiscence have done anything but exacerbate desires already so inflamed. It is certain therefore that the introduction of flagellation into the cells of monks and nuns on an increased scale after the Bull of Pope Clement VI swelled the tumult of medieval revolt against the heavy fetters imposed upon carnal love by the powerful clerical hierarchy for nearly a millennium.

IV The Fool Cult

i. THE FOOL PROPER

THE 'Court Fool' was not a medieval invention. In pre-Christian times wealthy Greeks and Romans had always employed professional buffoons to amuse them at banquets. Orientals do the same even today. These obsequious clowns were known to the pagan Europeans as 'parasites', a word of Greek derivation meaning 'meal attendants'. They figure frequently in the comedies of the ancient world. But the parasite, whether stylised for the stage or active in real life, was by no means a fool, normally, in the ordinary sense of the word. On the contrary he usually had sharper wits than most people. He might be cunning and unscrupulous to the last degree. At other times he might give good advice on behalf of oppressed minorities or warn his patron of conspiracies.

Such hangers-on of the rich were also engaged in whole bands, like a personal staff, as by Mark Antony in Asia after the second battle of Philippi. They enlivened triumphal processions and tours of conquered territory by victorious commanders. Plutarch asserts that the Eastern parasites whom Antony recruited for this purpose were much more amusing, as well as bolder, than those born in Italy.

The custom had, in fact, originated in the Middle East. But most of such quite conspicuous personages were in those regions mere brutes, often of defective physique. Their bodily shortcomings, however, by a well known law of psychological compensation, accounted in certain cases, like that of the Homeric Thersites, for a notable incisiveness in retorts to teasing.

Some historians have considered that they were often of the

'temperamental artistic' type, given to fits of melancholy and, in short, fundamentally manic-depressives. Men of this kind would be by nature, as they are today, sympathetically interested in all sorts of people, from the highest in rank to the lowest, just as an outstanding modern novelist might be. In any case it appears that the medieval 'Fools' were used from time to time by social reformers anxious to gain the ear of the prince favouring such entertainers.

It was St. Chrysostom who first described a clown of this sort as 'he who gets slapped'. At Constantinople in the fourth century he had often seen them made butts or laughingstocks by their social superiors or brutally tormented by rival competitors for the empress's favour or by underlings at the Court who envied their privileged position. But some Fools, as we shall see, themselves slapped so hard that they played a definite part in the anti-clerical movement of the Middle Ages, designed to throw off restrictions on the freedom of amorous appetite.

On the other hand there is plenty of evidence that many of the jesters maintained by great men were simply feeble-minded. Their stupidities alone made them popular objects of after-dinner sport in restive assemblies. Others again, there is no doubt, were deliberate frauds. They cynically pretended to be crazy in order to obtain a share of the rich meals and soft beds of nobles and prelates. They had determined to cash in on the indulgence extended to their coarseness and impudence. The idea of the *morbus sacer*, the divinely inspired malady of idiocy, is prevalent in the East to this day. In medieval Christendom it still lingered. As late as the fourteenth century the judicious Arab historian Ibn Khaldun propounded the notion that the madman's spirit is only loosely connected with his body and therefore more closely in touch with the supernatural than that of sane persons, however learned and pious. Fools, therefore, could be respected on occasion as prophets. It followed, among the Christians, that a professional jester, who simulated madness, could be forgiven extravagant demonstrations—of lust, for instance, towards ladies of high degree—which would have resulted in any other culprit being stabbed on the spot or hurried to a gibbet.

The superstition that lunatics might be unconscious bearers of tidings from heaven remained current among the European masses long after official recognition of the Christian religion. But men of wider experience and superior mental ability could not have shared such an illusion. Most of the nobility, higher clergy and rich merchants were more likely to choose as their Fools, not so much maniacs as born comedians, men as ready of tongue as they were impertinent. Such independent, anarchical spirits could then as now be found in every rank of society. In any case the religious awe of the insane had practically died out among all classes in Europe after 1400.

Nevertheless, an ideal Fool would possess, in addition to a bold wit, a definitely repellent aspect. For in the first place ugliness lends extra point to a daring repartee, unexpected from such a quarter. And secondly the employer and his family, especially the ladies, could rejoice, by comparison, in their own superior faces and figures. This requirement for a top-ranking domestic buffoon was the more easily met owing to the frequency with which high intelligence, at all times and in all countries, is associated with a poor or displeasing physique. In such cases the mind in the unhealthy or crippled body tends to develop the very type of sardonic audacity most agreeable to the 'tired business man', the baron or the bishop, weary of the cares of office or worried by the risks of fraud or loss.

The nineteenth-century alienist Paul Moreau suspected that a good proportion of the misshapen clowns of the Middle Ages suffered from rickets. He describes the material symptoms of this disease as a big head coupled to a lean torso, ultra-sharp facial features, bony joints and high blood-pressure. The figures of jesters surviving in medieval woodcuts and other illustrations certainly show individuals with some of these repugnant traits. Even the feverishness can be detected in their often contorted attitudes.

Moreau was informed by a colleague that the appetites of rachitics were generally enormous and that they were malicious and lecherous in the extreme. He added that he knew one, aged thirty-four, who masturbated incessantly, even on his deathbed. Others he had found to be abnormally frigid sexually. Such evidence as exists of the personal characters of medieval Fools also sometimes supports this alternative.

The jesters were certainly all inclined to be eccentric and

gaudy in their dress, even if they did not actually wear the cap and bells and the rest of the fantastic uniform supplied to them in their heyday. They were also usually talkative, conceited, credulous, cowardly, irritable and tearful in company. Or at any rate they would feign to be so in order to amuse or impose on their hosts. Some of these sham neurotics might be performing penances, like the legendary 'Robert the Devil' of Normandy, who was directed by a hermit to pretend to be mad and solicit illtreatment by way of punishment for his atrocious crimes. He became Court Fool, in one version of the story, to 'the emperor at Rome'.

Actual monsters—apart from dwarfs and hunchbacks—were very rare among duly accredited buffoons. But King James IV of Scotland (1488-1513) is said to have had one with two heads, four arms, one waist and two legs. One half of this dual creature is declared to have been intelligent and handsome, a tolerable musician and popular with the ladies of the Court. The other half is described as a drunken imbecile, resembling the Caliban which Shakespeare invented nearly a hundred years later. The two halves quarrelled interminably, struggling for the bottle which the inferior half would never let out of his hand. When the latter's alcoholism finally began to kill him, it was the other who died first.

Like many modern clowns the medieval Fools often had fathers and grandfathers who had exercised the same trade. King Charles V of France, called the Wise, in 1372 ordered the city of Troyes in Champagne to send him another Fool 'as usual', because his had just died. The extant document purporting to be the royal letter on this occasion may be a forgery. But there is no reason to suspect the sentiments expressed. For Thévenin, the Fool in question, was an exception to the general rule, if the noble face and figure shown on the tomb which the King erected to his memory can be trusted as a good likeness. In any case some princes undoubtedly grew very fond of their buffoons. Charles writes:

> 'God rest his soul. For he never failed in his duty to provide mirth and seemly jesting on our behalf. We have therefore commanded a sepulchral monument, with a suitable epitaph, to be erected in memory of the said gentleman (*Sire*).'

THE FOOL CULT

The tomb, eight and a half feet long by four and a half wide, represents the recumbent form of the dead comedian in long robes, carved in marble, with the face and feet of alabaster. The effigy wears a tasselled skull-cap and a cowl. Two purses lie on the chest and in the hand is a 'bauble', i.e. a short staff adorned with bells and terminating in a reproduction of the holder's own countenance.

The King had three other Fools and his Queen a female jester named Artaude du Puy. The letter to the burgesses of Troyes suggests that the office was hereditary, provided that the son displayed eccentricities of mind and body similar to those of his father. It was in the earlier centuries that dwarfs or other cripples, often really insane, were preferred.

These peculiarities naturally gave their victims feelings of inferiority which they generally relieved, as still happens, by developing aggressive sexual interests. But in the social conditions of the Middle Ages this almost automatic counterbalance had less point than it would have today. For a hideous, deformed and more or less crazy creature then stood a very fair chance, on those grounds alone, of being taken into a rich man's household to entertain his family and guests by idiotic behaviour. On the other hand, if such a queer-looking character happened to possess a shrewd as well as an unconventional mentality, his fortune was made. He was quite likely to become an influential personality and do pretty much as he liked in the sexual section of the domestic field.

He would of course be hated by the other male employees at the castle, manor-house or abbey. The German satirical humanist Sebastian Brant published in 1494 a hard-hitting allegory in which he lashed with unsparing vigour the frivolity and vices of fools both with and without the capital letter. His *Narrenschiff* (Ship of Fools) has no one aboard among either passengers or crew, who is not a professional Fool or someone else who deserves the name. They steer for the 'Fools' Paradise', Narragonia. Brant mentions Caillette, the Fool of Louis XII of France. This probably genuine idiot had an adventure typical of the risks such creatures ran from the envy of the rest of the staff.

Some pages caught him and nailed his ear, which heard more gossip than was good for it, to a post. A courtier came along later, pulled out the nail and asked who had committed this outrage. Caillette answered, 'A Fool!' 'Ah, you mean one of those naughty pages?' asked the courtier. 'Yes.' 'Could you recognise him?' 'Certainly.' The courtier sent for all the pages employed in the palace. They all denied having had any part in the attack on Caillette. 'Well, you are the only other Fool here,' said the courtier. 'Was it you yourself who nailed your ear to the post?' 'No.' 'You must be a liar,' retorted the courtier. 'Nail his other ear, boys!'

If, as in this case, a Fool proved too dull, he was either savagely punished or given, like a dog or a monkey, a master to teach him tricks. But since the jester was a human being he would also be taught to sing, dance, tell funny stories and use the latest slang. If, after all this instruction, he still failed amuse people, he was thrashed and sent to wash dishes in the scullery.

But the successful Fool enjoyed privileges which exceeded on occasion those of his masters. He could be as rude as he liked in word and deed, even in a sexual context. What did it matter? He was only the Fool, a 'madman' not responsible for his actions. His conduct in fact began, at a very early period, to prove so shocking that an ecclesiastical decree dated 789 forbade the clergy to maintain 'jesters'. Naturally enough this ordinance was largely disregarded or circumvented. In 1212 the Council of Paris had to limit the prohibition to the presence of Fools in an episcopal residence. Yet even then many of the wealthier bishops continued to defy the Council in this matter. For by the thirteenth century the domestic clown had become what would now be called a 'status symbol'. No self-respecting magnate could expect social recognition if he could not produce his own private buffoon to go with the wine and the music of the entertainments offered to visitors.

The medieval Fool, of course, like his ancestor the parasite, was constantly represented on the stage. He figured in the early farces as one of a crowd of acrobats, jugglers, minstrels and bear-leaders. Later on both amateur and professional actors played the part of a Court jester in more elaborate dramas.

Many typical examples of Fools' witticisms have survived. In 1461 at a Leipzig banquet all the guests politely praised the wonders they had seen in the neighbourhood. The host's Fool, one Claus, was asked in his turn what he most admired. He replied that he had been greatly struck by three extraordinary phenomena. In the first place, the poor monks, who went about barefooted, had the most extravagantly glorious monasteries to live in. Secondly, they possessed enormous quantities of corn, though they didn't grow any themselves. And thirdly, though they were celibate, they had lots of little children, which perhaps they had borne themselves or produced, like vegetables, in their private kitchen-gardens.

Claus seems to have been one of those polished ironists not uncommon among fifteenth-century jesters, when the clergy in general had become one of the chief subjects of bitter sarcasm in lay gatherings. Earlier clowns had been much cruder. In the thirteenth century the Fool of King Henry III of England, who prided himself on his taste and learning but was a weak, ineffectual ruler, said to his affable sovereign: 'You are like Christ, Sire.' The King felt most flattered. 'Oh? Why do you say that?' 'Well, you see, Christ being God, had the same wits at birth as he had at death. And you, Sire, being a man, have the same wits today as you had at birth.' Henry, in a rage, ordered the fellow to be hanged forthwith. But, as the Fool was being hurried away, the monarch, notorious for his indecision, changed his mind again. 'Thrash him and let him go,' he commanded. Henry was never cruel to individuals.

A hundred years earlier still John of Salisbury, the author and diplomatist who became Bishop of Chartres, complains that illustrious persons who should know better allow buffoons to frequent their houses and 'perform before the eyes of all disgraceful actions with the obscene parts of their bodies, so that a veritable cynic would blush to see them. Worse still, these fellows are not ejected when in the turbulence of their hinder parts they cause the air to reek by emitting a series of loud noises which add to their deplorable conduct'.

Wind-breaking seems to have been a regular accompaniment of medieval obstreperousness, laymen and the minor clergy constantly imitating the paid clowns in this respect. In 1349 some clerks in the service of the Bishop of Durham did not hesitate 'to vent several times, most loudly and vilely, disgusting sounds of wind from the rear portions of their backs under the crucifix itself' of York Minster.

Rabelais in Book III, Chapter XLV, of his immortal work recounts an adventure of his hero Panurge with Triboulet, the famous sixteenth-century clown of both Louis XII and Francis I of France. This Fool is not strictly speaking medieval. But his gifts and behaviour were unquestionably traditional.

The great French humorist writes:

> 'When Triboulet had done with his drinking, Panurge laid out before him and exposed the sum of the business wherein he was to require his advice... But, before he had altogether done, Triboulet, with his fist, gave him a bouncing whirret between the shoulders, rendered back into his hand again the empty bottle, flipped and flirted him on the nose with the hog's bladder ... and answered nothing else but this: "By God, God. Mad Fool. Beware the monk. Buzansay hornpipe." These words thus finished, he slipped himself out of the company, went aside and, rattling his bladder, took a huge delight in the melody of the rickling, crackling noise of the peas. After which time it lay not in the power of them all to draw out of his chaps the articulate sound of one syllable. In so much that when Panurge went about to interrogate him further, Triboulet drew his wooden sword and would have struck him therewith.... "He is a great fool," quoth Panurge, "that is not to be denied. Yet is he a greater fool who brought him hither to me. And myself the greatest of all for imparting my thoughts to him."'

Triboulet here behaves very much like an eccentric man of genius pestered by an importunate busybody. Panurge is of course such a type. And the author seems slyly to hint that the Fool was 'great' in more senses than one, not only famous for his 'madness' but also intellectually superior to his tormentors.

The 'hog's bladder' and the 'peas' referred to in the passage above formed part of the Fool's most usual equipment. The characteristic costume and attributes no doubt developed gradually. A Roman pre-Christian relief shows a man wearing the hood with long earpieces. This headgear suggests an animal generally considered comic, or at any rate as stubborn as most unconventional human beings, the donkey. In any case many alienists believe that ears which project like those of a satyr indicate a combination of greed, malice, stupidity and lasciviousness. The medieval pointed bonnet of this type, with its cock's comb (whence 'coxcomb'), as worn by professional jesters, had little bells on the earpieces. Their jingling helped to create the right atmosphere of frivolity as the clown came capering into the hall of a palace, castle or abbey, along a street at festival time or among other actors on a stage.

His jacket was also cut into points or segments of circles, to which bells were attached. The uniform thus presented a symmetrically ragged effect, suggesting simultaneously a beggar and a certain decorative quality appropriate to the presence of persons of rank. Both cap and tunic, made of serge, were generally striped or chequered in yellow and green. The pattern was often quite complex, as with bands half yellow and half green, one of these colours crossing the other alternately. Green and yellow patches of various kinds of silk, known as the 'motley', could also be sewn on the jacket here and there. One leg of the hose would usually be green, the other yellow.

In the Middle Ages these hues were rather unpopular with respectable people, yellow being associated with whores and green with outlaws. Bankrupts also wore green caps in the pillory and so did those sentenced to the galleys. Moreover, criminals convicted of offences against royalty had their houses daubed yellow by the hangman. Yellow, again, was worn by lackeys and lawcourt guards. In 1254 St. Louis (King Louis IX of France) ordered Jews to wear a yellow patch on the front of their gowns.

Anyone, therefore, who saw a Fool in full rig would immediately think of rascals. His ugliness and servility aroused contempt. But on the other hand his caustic tongue, trickeries and generally reckless conduct inspired fear. Occasionally red, the colour of danger and uproar, would be added to or substituted for the green or for both green and yellow. But such variations were uncommon.

Accordingly, the green and yellow garments of the Fool, often of considerable magnificence, symbolised his general character. The saffron obtained from the crocus was supposed to render those who ate it shamelessly exuberant in their appetites and behaviours and to lead, in particular, to sexual promiscuity, being for this reason worn by prostitutes. Green recalled the leaves of the forests where bandits like the fabulous 'Robin Hood', i.e. a robber wearing a hood to mask his features, roamed and held their 'bohemian' revels. So the approach of those who, like the Fools, were clothed in both yellow and green warned women to look to their chastity and men to their property.

Incidentally, the legend of the 'pied', i.e. dressed in multi-coloured clothing, 'piper', i.e. seducer, of Hamelin in Hanover, enshrines the type of the vagabond Fool, in this case ostensibly a ratcatcher who took his revenge for the non-payment of his fee by luring the children of the town, with his flute, to follow him to a precipice or cave where they all perished.

Fools who travelled the roads like the Piper of Hamelin would however normally pay their way by absurd gabble or acrobatics. They thus increased their knowledge of the world and consequently their entertainment value to their fellow-citizens. Like the wandering minstrels of the day they would seek temporary admittance, which often became permanent residence, to the houses of rich men or corporations. Once installed as a species of human pet, their insolence was liable to outdo that of any favourite concubine. In fact they sometimes waged a more or less secret war with such rivals, as an anecdote about a late fifteenth-century Archbishop of Cologne seems to hint.

That dignitary's Fool, it is asserted, was accustomed to sleep at the foot of the prelate's bed. One night the jester noticed that there appeared to be more than a single pair of legs kicking him. Seizing first one foot, then another, he demanded of his reverend patron: 'Whose is this? And this? And this?' 'Mine,' retorted the ecclesiastic calmly, on each occasion. The Fool jumped up, rushed to the door and roared at the top of his voice: 'A miracle! A miracle! Come quickly! Our Archbishop has grown four legs!' The attendants of the venerable Father in God poured into the room. They were just in time to catch a glimpse of a nude female form, afterwards proved to be that of a nun, disappearing behind the arras.

This was not the first time, or the last, in European history when a Fool turned out to have more sense than his employer.

THE FOOL CULT

In fact many of these bold rogues, hideous, witty, solitary, defiant of all authority and generally beyond the reach of any serious chastisement, tended to be the admired focus of any gathering they found themselves in. They often enjoyed the same sort of romantic reputation, during the Middle Ages, as eighteenth-century highwaymen or nineteenth-century poets like Byron, Baudelaire or Poe came to have in later times. The sagacious and successful King Philip Augustus of France, who reigned in great splendour at the turn of the twelfth and thirteenth centuries, kept at one time quite a crowd of Fools at his Court. But after a while their ungovernable debauchery exhausted even his patience. He sent them all packing.

Few women, as already suggested, could resist, in these fellows, their combination of fascinatingly grotesque physique, wickedly amusing chatter and privileged social position. They were also usually too clever for the courtiers and clergy, who hated and feared them. Their inbred cynicism saved them from the unhappy love affairs which were the fate of so many medieval wits, in particular the lyric poets known as the 'troubadours', who set a fashion in the twelfth century for such frustrations. This literary pattern lasted on, in one way and another, until the age of Petrarch and Chaucer. Yet the original troubadours, except for their better education, sometimes bore a distinct resemblance to the gaily libidinous tramps in green and yellow. The main difference was that the latter really cared for nothing but intrigue and the satisfaction of their gross appetites, exasperated as they were by the more or less jovial scorn their deformities, immorality and non-military character aroused in both secular and clerical magnates and, on a first acquaintance at any rate, among aristocratic women.

The jester carried a sceptre (the 'bauble') to indicate his temporary sovereignty over any assembly he entertained. The staff ended in a carved replica of his own head, with its harlequin hood and bells. He would talk to this effigy as a modern ventriloquist does to his doll. Sometimes, like the later harlequin, he also flourished, as did Triboulet in the passage from Rabelais quoted above, a gilded wooden sword. Again like Triboulet, he nearly always waved a pigskin bladder, also known as a 'bauble', containing dried peas or else stuffed in various shapes, which might be obscenely suggestive. It was hung either to his sceptre or on a plain rod.

Other significant appendages might be a fox's brush dangling from the Fool's posterior or a calfskin of the kind which in Shakespeare's *King John* (III. i. 129) Constance, the King's sister-in-law and mother of Prince Arthur, tells the Archduke of Austria he ought to wear instead of a lion's hide. She was accordingly charging him with the fraudulence and cowardice traditionally characteristic of a Court Fool of the day. Nothing, naturally, could be more offensive to a reigning prince. Even an Elizabethan audience would shudder to hear such an insult. That was why the dramatist, having got the spectators where he wanted them, made the pugnacious Bastard, like a true son of King Richard I, repeat Constance's phrase, with appalling insolence, not once but twice.

Shakespeare's plays are of course a mine of information about the medieval clown, who had changed his character very little by the end of the sixteenth century. In *All's Well That Ends Well* (IV. v. 32.) the Fool of the Countess of Roussillon tells the old lord Lafeu, in the Countess's presence, that he would give his 'bauble', which in this case was probably stuffed so as to resemble a penis, to any man's wife 'to do her service'. In *Romeo and Juliet* (II. iv. 97) Mercutio talks of 'a great natural', i.e. Fool, 'that runs lolling up and down to hide his bauble in a hole'. The reputation of jesters for lechery could not be more clearly established. In a previous generation, too, the Scottish poet Sir David Lindsay (d. 1555) had described a professional buffoon who cuts out a courtier, a merchant and a clerk. All three had vainly tried to seduce the wife of an old man. Only the Fool succeeded.

But the obsession of these figures of fun with fornication sometimes enabled them to make a point worthy of a serious historian. In a German play, for instance, a stage Fool tells the audience that the great lords spend so much on women that the said magnates have to sell their lands and start wars to replace the estates lost through concupiscence. Other accredited jesters did in fact occasionally take a hand in high politics. Danderi, for example, employed by the ninth-century Byzantine emperor Theophilus, who objected to images of the saints, told his master that certain statuettes the suspicious bigot had seen in the bedroom of his empress, Theodora, were only dolls for the lady's daughters. It is true that Danderi afterwards gave Theodora a dreadful fright by harping on the subject at dinner. But this leg-pulling only bored the emperor and a row which might have cost the empress her life was averted.

Again, in 1047, one Golet, a domestic clown kept by Duke William of Normandy, the future conqueror of England, broke into the ducal bedchamber to warn William, just in time, that assassins were coming up the stairs. It may be too much to deduce that, as a result of this incident, the whole history of the island took the course that it did and that if Golet had not been so wide-awake, brave and loyal, British civilisation would have assumed an entirely different character. But it certainly seems reasonable to note, once more, that the Fools, as Rabelais probably and Shakespeare unquestionably recognised, were not always such fools as they looked.

Most of the surviving stories about Fools date from the twelfth century, when they suddenly became very fashionable, perhaps owing to oriental influence during the Crusades. A certain king in those days is related to have asked his Court Jester, maliciously enough no doubt, to make out a list of the biggest 'fools' in the country, worthy to be the clown's brothers. The buffoon instantly cited the sovereign himself and his Council. Asked why, he retorted that it was because they had lent money to an alchemist. 'Ah, but,' said the king, 'what if the alchemist pays the sum back?' 'In that case,' rejoined the man in motley coolly, 'I shall substitute his name for yours.'

It was no wonder that such fellows continued until the early seventeenth century to be as welcome in high society as film-stars are today. Royal and episcopal palaces, castles and abbeys, monasteries and manor-houses, competed for their services. War and pestilence, the scarcity of books and other resources for indoor entertainment, the boredom and the quarrels naturally arising within walls beyond which it was often dangerous to venture and where there was so little to do, all put a premium on the professional comedian.

His tantrums and sexual aggressions were considered a light price to pay for the laughter and surprise elicited by his weird antics, his snappish repartees, his lewd songs and tall stories, the games he invented and the practical jokes he played. Ladies and their female attendants in particular, including nuns, delighted in his wild incursions into their apartments, where a great part of the day would normally pass in monotonous sewing, weaving and stale gossip. When he lifted up their skirts or put his hand into their bosoms, they only giggled and pushed him away, whereupon he was quite likely to stand on his head, pretend to copulate with some unseen person or sit up and beg like a dog.

But whatever he did would be accompanied by diverting noises of one kind or another, such as rapid tap-dancing, the thrumming of a lute, a dramatic farce, usually erotic, in which he took all the parts himself, or else mere crazy chatter. The favourite medieval amusement of farting would probably, though not necessarily, be reserved for a male audience.

No one dared to interrupt a Fool. For he might be 'possessed' by either angels or demons. Both these spirits could make things awkward for interfering mortals. Some clowns were so athletic that heaven or hell might well be thought to be in their bodies. Hainselin, one of the buffoons of the mad king Charles VI of France, tore his shirt to pieces while wrestling to amuse his moody patron. The clown was such a strenuous dancer that he is said to have worn out no less than forty-seven pairs of shoes in the single year 1404. But when we read that Guillaume Fouel, the jester of Charles's queen Isabeau, wore out three hundred pairs in six months we begin to suspect a fraud of monstrous proportions at this exceptionally dissolute Court. The pampered Guillaume, having found he could get as many pairs of shoes as he pleased, probably indented for vast numbers, which he sold as fast as he received them.

There were also, as we have already seen, female Fools. Both Charles and Isabeau employed them. They rivalled their masculine colleagues in outrageous dissipation. One kept by Duke Philip the Good of Burgundy in the 1430's lived in such ostentatious splendour that she was nicknamed 'The Golden Lady', in reference also, perhaps, to her long and thick fair hair. She happened to be not only very handsome but also a notable athlete and acrobat. This altogether exceptional female buffoon was of humble birth, originally a peasant named Guillemette

Marighier. She could sit on her abundant tresses and attracted great attention at the ducal entertainments for her gymnastic ability. It goes without saying that the favours of her magnificent physique were at the disposal of anyone who could pay for them. In addition, her amorous caprices were legion.

But this champion amazon, who seems to have resembled in several ways many a great comic actress of later times, possesses an even more surprising title to fame. There is good reason to believe that the curiously named Order of the Golden Fleece, founded by Philip the Good on January 10, 1430, the date of his marriage to Isabella of Portugal at Bruges, owed its appellation to the phenomenally luxuriant locks of the girl tumbler who afterwards became the most conspicuous feminine figure at the Duke's Court. The twenty-four Knights of the new Order were dedicated to the Virgin and St. Andrew, as well as to the already fast waning ideals of feudal chivalry. No one, apparently, saw anything strange in the relation of the fleece they wore over their armour to the crowning glory of one of the most remarkable courtesans—and Fools—of the age. Whatever Guillemette may have pretended to be, she was certainly only mad, like Hamlet, 'north-north-west'.

Rabelais tells another story (III. xxxvii) which seems to prove that he well understood how many jesters were wiser than they seemed. Pantagruel begins by telling Panurge that 'the answers and responses of sage and judicious men have in no way satisfied you. So take advice of some fool and possibly by so doing you may come to get that counsel which will be agreeable to your own heart's desire and contentment. You know how, by the advice and counsel and prediction of Fools, many kings, princes, states and commonwealths have been preserved, several battles gained and divers doubts of a most perplexed intricacy been resolved.'

He then relates how 'Seyny John' (*Le Seigneur Jean*) 'the noted Fool of Paris and great-grandfather to Caillette' settled a dispute between a cook and a porter. The important personage in question belonged to the city guild or fraternity of Fools, constituted on religious lines like an abbey, like the *'abbaye de Thélème'* of Rabelais himself. Such societies were often founded in towns where the 'Feast of Fools' had been dropped from the cathedral celebrations.

The hungry porter, standing in a narrow lane, had been holding the bread he had brought with him in the smoke of a goose being roasted in a neighbouring cookshop. After he had eaten the bread the cook demanded payment for the smoke. A long argument ensued. The parties nearly came to blows. Seyny John, who was in the crowd of onlookers, being asked for his opinion, ordered the porter to hand him a farthing, tested the coin in every conceivable manner, including flipping it with his nail in the palm of his hand, and then 'holding his bauble in his hand, muffling his head with a hood of marten-skins, each side whereof had the resemblance of an ape's face, sprucified up with ears of pasted paper, and having about his neck a bucked ruff, raised, furrowed and ridged with stiffeners of the shape and fashion of small organ-pipes,' he pronounced the following sentence: 'The court declareth that the porter who ate his bread at the smoke of the roast meat hath civilly paid the cook with the sound of his money.'

In the Halles (market-hall) at Ypres in Belgium the wooden support of a girder was carved in the fourteenth century into the shape of a grinning head, probably that of a Fool, with corkscrew curls and a most engaging expression, the eyes being tightly shut in mirth. It might well represent Seyny John after his Solomon-like judgment.

Some of these Town Fools were paid good salaries and marched in procession on ceremonial occasions with other municipal dignitaries. They also staged sophisticated dramatic entertainments, such as are popular at this moment in London and New York—as they have always been popular in Paris—satirising important people and events of the day. Sometimes these groups, in the Middle Ages, got out of hand, scandalising their audiences with drunken blasphemies and obscenities. In 1420 the Bishop of Evreux in Normandy felt obliged to abolish the so called *Cornards* (Cuckolds), a local organisation which went on like this.

In 1381 an Order of Fools was founded at Clèves in the North Rhine Province of Germany. The local Count and thirty-five other landowners met annually at vintage-time, on the first or second Sunday in October, marched to the cathedral and then

THE FOOL CULT

rioted in private for a week. These revels, in addition to the usual features of wine, woman and song, were distinguished by the temporary abandonment of all distinctions of rank, just as in the regular 'Feasts of Fools'. The society of the day was of course highly class-conscious. But it is remarkable how often, on all sorts of occasions, visits to the public baths for instance, the instinctive rebellion against privilege, both clerical and secular, made itself felt with impunity.

A somewhat similar but grander society, that of the 'Mother Fool' (Mère Folle) of Dijon in Burgundy was started in the fifteenth century. There were five hundred members, including high officials and prosperous professional and business men. They joined in all public ceremonies, when they dressed like jesters in green and yellow, not omitting the eared hood, bells and bauble. They spoke only in verse. Their chief, the 'Mother', wore a woman's robes but held court like a king. Their alternative title, L'Infanterie Dijonnaise, indicated their military character, stressed also by their employment of chariots and heralds. But their main function, like that of the other Societies of Fools, was to stage what we should call *revues*, of an intimate and witty rather than broadly facetious character.

The dwarfs kept by medieval noblemen in addition to or in substitution for Fools had as a rule less interesting personalities. They were curiosities to the eye rather than stimulants to the mind, good for laughing at and teasing, but little else. One named Turold appears in the Bayeux Tapestry (eleventh century) in the guise of an otherwise ordinary enough young male attendant. Few of these undersized hunchbacks were as drunken or sexually debauched as the Fools proper. On the whole they were treated more like pet animals than human beings. In any case they were seldom admitted by either men or women to such intimacies as the Fools enjoyed.

There was no limit to the latters' freedom of speech, even to Queens. An old story with many variants probably dates back to medieval times. A certain royal lady, chatting one day with her male Fool, happened to say that she was so fond of two widely separated places in her dominions that she would like to have a foot in each. 'Like this,' she added innocently, stretching her legs as wide apart as they would go. 'And I,' retorted the Fool instantly, 'Would like only to be right between the two,' naming a city equidistant from both those she had mentioned. In some versions he added that he would be 'happy to set up his standard there'.

Another Fool told an Italian nobleman who was suspected of heresy that he ought to go and bugger the Pope in the presence of as many cardinals as possible. For then, said the clown, everyone would realise that he was a good Catholic. 'But be sure,' the jester went on, 'that you afterwards give the anus of His Holiness a thorough syringing, with duly consecrated water, in order to wash away all traces of your sin.'

Such language is nowadays uncommon among educated adults —if we assume that undergraduates have not yet completed their education. Its tolerance in the Middle Ages does not only prove that both gentlemen and ladies then expressed themselves quite regularly with a coarseness that would be regarded as insufferable in polite circles today. It is true that their elaborate circumlocutions and compliments on formal occasions would be regarded as equally insufferable.

But these ingenuous tales also bear witness to a realism and a charity in everyday communication which the modern world has largely lost. Medieval man, often so brutal in speech and action—though no worse in the latter respect than his twentieth-century descendants—nevertheless never forgot, unless carried away by passion of one sort or another, that he shared with others the common frailties and foibles of humanity. That was one of the main contributions of Christianity, so obtuse and cruel in many other ways, to civilisation. For even the Greeks had a hearty contempt for weak-minded people.

The Church had taught from the first that all men were necessarily brothers before the Lord. Accordingly, what we should now consider foul talk and behaviour did not shock the average medieval citizen. If they came within the long categories of sin he would repudiate and punish them both in himself and others and call for repentance in both cases. Otherwise he only laughed at such unconventional words or deeds. The modern squeamishness and complex systems of local tabus, really a form of pharisiacal self-worship, would have been as incomprehensible to the armed or tonsured men and the voluminously garbed women

THE FOOL CULT

of those days as modern insularity and timidity, far more widespread now than then in both the moral and physical spheres.

ii. STUDENTS AS 'FOOLS'

But the mildness in this respect of the medieval Church could turn, officially, to the sternest severity against what even Shakespeare calls 'the deed of darkness', sexual promiscuity. Against actual heretics, to say nothing of atheists and infidels, it could act with the most murderous savagery. The bishops could be as stupid as peasants in blocking scientific progress and even that of common sense. Yet they were not only lenient to professional Fools and real or assumed insanity.

Youth was then to a great extent, as it is today, exempt from serious formal control or even criticism. Young people in all ages have been the fools of love. Their excesses were largely condoned in the earlier Christian centuries. Otherwise there could never have arisen so many hair-raising accounts of the unpunished misdeeds of 'students' and *meretriculae*, courtesans of the baser sort. The rise of the universities, originally spontaneous groups, as in ancient Greece, of teachers and pupils, on the lines of tradesmens' guilds, had by the thirteenth century produced large, cohesive bodies of young men in several European cities. They felt themselves to be a separate element in the community, especially as many of them were at first foreigners. The traditional hostility between 'town' and 'gown' began very early in the history of organised learning in Christian Europe.

Naples and Bologna in Italy, Toulouse and Paris in France, Oxford and Cambridge in England, Seville and Salamanca in Spain, were among the first centres to receive the impact of 'students'. During the fourteenth century many such schools were founded all over Europe, especially in the German-speaking lands. But long before this, in 1218, the civil authority of Paris had already been obliged to forbid the members of its university to carry arms within the confines of the city, under pain of excommunication. In the fifteenth century minor offenders were still being publicly whipped. Throughout these three hundred years, i.e. from about 1200 to about 1500, the 'students' in the big towns formed the unofficial opposition to ecclesiastical, royal and even papal policy, just as they do in many States, not only in Asia, Africa and South America, today.

The medieval 'Establishment' retorted by fulminations to which we owe much of our knowledge of just how far undergraduates then went in their incessant challenges to the existent order of society. As its defender in the sexual field Peter of Blois (c. 1135-c. 1205) showed himself particularly aggressive. This ill-tempered cleric from Brittany occupied the posts, successively, of Archdeacon of Bath, Dean of Wolverhampton and Archdeacon of London. He writes indignantly: 'Some students keep concubines. Some seduce other peoples' wives, each taking his pleasure where he finds it. And the worst of it is that these wicked scoundrels don't make the slightest attempt to hold their tongues about their disgusting exploits, but on the contrary boast of them endlessly at their boozing parties.'

About the same time a Chancellor of Notre Dame delivers himself to much the same effect.

'How shameful it is that our students should live in conditions of disgrace that not one of them, when at home, would even dare to name! They dissipate the glorious treasure of the Crucified Redeemer on courtesans. Their conduct, besides bringing the Church into contempt, covers both teachers and pupils with ignominy, scandalises laymen, dishonours their native land and constitutes an insult to God Himself!'

Another Chancellor, elected at the University of Cremona, describes undergraduates as roaming the streets at night, armed to the teeth and breaking down the doors of honest citizens. They also, he says, bear voluble false witness in the lawcourts, when some poor little whore complains of being beaten within an inch of her life by these learned young louts, who were in the habit of tearing the clothing of the strumpets they engaged to pieces and cutting their hair off.

Cardinal Giacopo de' Vitri (d. 1244) calls the students of his younger days drunken lechers, bullies and sometimes murderers. They would burst into a private house at any hour of the day or night, carry off all the women they found, steal anything portable and smash the rest. 'On the other hand,' he goes on, 'prostitutes used regularly to drag, by main force, into their dens, any clerks—' i.e. obviously literate persons—'whom they saw in the streets. If the men thus assailed repulsed such women, the latter accused them of homosexuality, a vice so rampant in Rome at the time and yet simultaneously so abominated, that the average citizen was glad enough to clear himself of the imputation of it by keeping one or more concubines.'

'Sometimes,' the Cardinal continues, 'a house would have lecture-rooms on the upper floors and harlots at ground level or in the cellars. Both sections were noisy. The higher storeys resounded with the thunders of scholarly debate and the lower with the shrieks and yells of the trollops and their keepers, who quarrelled incessantly.'

Paris seems to have been 'gay Paree' even in the eleventh century. Adalbert Archbishop of Mainz (d. 1072), a German prelate of high intelligence and strong character, had studied in the French capital as a youth. He wrote that the city 'made the poison of carnal delights curdle in the veins of young people'. Evidence of uproarious carousals, abduction of married women, rape of their daughters and other acts 'disagreeable in the sight of God' is recounted generation after generation.

Something must be allowed for the sheer enjoyment by these erudite priests of their own elegant Latinity, a language unsurpassed for invective even by Arabic. And that 'hatred of youth by age' which Shakespeare understood so well also played its part. But all the same the position appears to have been serious even by the relatively lax standards of public order current at the time. Very little, however, was done about it.

A few isolated and private efforts were made to stem the rollicking tide of harlotry in the larger centres. In one case the students themselves were asked to subscribe to a fund for starting a convent in which these women could be taught to live more decently. For it was they, as usual, who were chiefly blamed for the lads' debaucheries. The undergraduate supporters of this scheme, as might have been expected, put up less than a quarter of the meagre subscriptions which came in from members of the public. The situation remained unchanged.

At Cahors in south-western France a fifteenth-century professor of law at the university lamented, quite in the style of a modern 'fuddy-duddy', that young women of all classes paraded the streets 'half naked'. They provoked, he said, their masculine coevals to 'the most detestable actions'. One night, he adds, two young students kidnapped a girl they had noticed in this way. They not only carried her off, by a trick, from her father's house, but actually, by a further ingenious fraud, obtained a written pardon from the royal Chancellery for their crime. But the case was subsequently revived by the Parliament of Toulouse, which duly sentenced the culprits.

In France such abductors could occasionally claim university privilege from pursuit by the civil power. But in Italy the courts were more rigorous. At Bologna in 1321 an undergraduate was beheaded for ravishing the daughter, a noted beauty and bluestocking, of Professor Giovanni Andrea (1275-1348), an expert in canon law, and one of the most prominent personalities in the city. Force must have been used here, for this girl, at any rate, was no fool. She read her father's lectures to the students when he was obliged to be absent. But she did so behind a curtain, lest the young men should be distracted by her exceptional charms. Unfortunately further details of what must have been a most sensational affair are lacking.

But the episode illustrates, like the story of Abélard and Héloïse a century before, both the lawless barbarity of certain well born and well educated men at this period and the high degree of intellectual accomplishment in some of the women. Héloïse, the niece of Canon Fulbert of Paris, was probably even more learned than Novella, Professor Andrea's daughter. Fulbert castrated the brilliant Abélard, himself already a canon of Notre Dame at the age of thirty-six, after breaking into his house with a gang of ruffians in the middle of the night. The perpetrator of this atrocious vengeance on a colleague who, after all, had secretly married the girl, was never punished. Fulbert was a senior dignitary of the Church. But Novella's hotheaded aggressor was merely a member of the student body, though no doubt just as great a scoundrel as the savage canon. So the boy lost his head literally as well as figuratively.

As a rule, however, as already noted, foolish undergraduates, like the clergy and the professional Fools, enjoyed a considerable degree of immunity, especially in France, from indictment by the secular authorities. The kings found their 'students' useful backers in the dangerous quarrels with powerful barons and

THE FOOL CULT

ecclesiastics, in which sovereigns like Henry II of England and Philip the Fair of France were often engaged. Philip told one of his lords, who had protested at the excessive royal favour shown to these turbulent young libertines: 'We believe ourselves bound to recognise with gratitude the labours, both by day and by night, the poverty, the hardships and the perils which students endure for the sake of acquiring the precious jewels of knowledge. We bear in mind that they often leave their friends, their parents and their native lands, sometimes at a remote distance, in order to quench their burning thirst for the living waters of wisdom, with which they then proceed to refresh the entire world.'

This typical piece of unctuous political oratory disguised a real anxiety. Medieval monarchs used every expedient to bolster up their autocracies. For history sufficiently proves that they were constantly threatened and often enough actually overthrown by the most ambitious of the churchmen and nobles under nominal control by the dynasty. In this situation the kings, like modern dictators, did not scruple to cultivate those of their subjects, students for instance, who could be depended upon to be reckless when the time came. For such persons, unlike the property-owning classes, had nothing to lose by unquestioning loyalty to a royal patron, however tyrannical.

Even so righteous a sovereign as the subsequently canonised Louis IX of France (1214-1270), who bears comparison with the best administrators of any age or country, shared the respect felt by his grandson Philip the Fair for undergraduates. Early one morning, while Louis was riding to matins in Paris, one of these lads emptied on his head, from an upper window, the contents of a chamber-pot. The monarch, far from resenting this disagreeable experience, ordered the rude fellow to be richly rewarded. 'For,' said Louis, 'he must be a most industrious scholar to be awake at such an hour.' Such indulgence naturally encouraged the riotous conduct in every respect of the young men in question, prone as they already were, by age and circumstances, to wild living. Their habit, according to Rabelais, of kicking the posteriors of tourists gaping at monuments, seems to have been one of the least of their misdemeanours.

The marked tendency to rhetorical exaggeration of even saints and scholars, in the Middle Ages, is apt to give a modern historian a somewhat heated impression, in general, of medieval sex life. This is especially so when he considers the accounts given of carnivals, ecstatic religious processions, the interest in personal mania and eccentricity and other ways in which Christian Europeans of those centuries boisterously relieved the tedium or oppression of a faith in theory opposed to all amorous behaviour.

Yet, when every allowance has been made for the other side of the picture, a hard core of rebellion, typified by the 'Fool' and the 'student', against these prohibitions does seem to remain. Most citizens were, no doubt, respectable, innocent or even austere in the erotic field. They had been pretty well cowed, as a rule, by the bellowing of their priests against fornication and allied pleasures. An eternity of terrible tortures in the next world, described in the utmost detail, with convincing eloquence, by their preachers, must have had, on the whole, quite a devastating effect. Yet the revolt gathered momentum, for hundreds of years, till it burst into a victory, which at first appeared incredible, in the sixteenth century.

Before then physical love outside marriage had been locked out in law and precept by the ecclesiastical hierarchy. There could be no doubt about the official Christian view of the procreative impulse. It must not be employed except for the specific purpose of 'increasing and multiplying' human souls, to the greater glory of their creator. But since this asceticism, quite novel to Europeans when it first arose, ran counter to the strongest appetite, after hunger, of the human body, for the greater part of its existence, a more or less disguised insurrection began as soon as the at first astonished converts understood for certain what was now expected of them.

The protest took a great variety of forms. For the first few centuries the Church, which had a practical monopoly in the application of intelligence to human problems, wisely tolerated most of these ebullitions, those of 'students' in particular. But it never ceased to express disapproval of them, often in violently censorious language. Many of these diatribes, owing to the eminence of their authors and the unimpeachability of their dogmatic sentiments, have survived to prove that medieval Catholics, for all their admirable virtues, were not uniformly so

THE FOOL CULT

saintly as some modern apologists, particularly in the nineteenth century, have supposed.

The psychological rebellion must be accepted as a fact. But if all Europe in the Middle Ages had been a weltering morass of erotomania, Christianity as a legally established faith would never have outlasted the fury of its enemies. What happened, on the contrary, was the triumphant compromise of the Renaissance and the Reformation.

It had been physically impossible for the Church to do more than denounce, like St. Boniface, the Englishman who evangelised Germany in the eighth century, whole populations. He proclaimed that his own countrymen, who were already ostensibly Christian, 'utterly despise matrimony and live in lechery like horses and donkeys'.

Nor did the bishops presume to reform lay sartorial fashions, always a good index to the attitude of any given period to sexual morality. The tight trunk-hose of males showed clearly the outlines of both buttocks and the generative organs. The buttocks, again, of women, as also their breasts, were encased in equally clinging skirts and bodices.

St. Thomas Aquinas tactfully assured his disciples that prostitutes were 'cesspools necessary to a palace if the whole building is not to smell'. Even prelates like Archembald, who occupied the see of Sens in the tenth century, to say nothing of important clerics in later times, were allowed to keep concubines. The Chapter of this bishopric remained lenient. But there were limits. The canons issued a stern decree in the fifteenth century insisting that 'Fools', i.e. the travestied participants in the revels of New Year's Day, must not copulate within the precincts of the cathedral.

The extraordinary prevalence of anarchical wildness, always predominantly erotic in expression, during the Middle Ages, from the recklessness shown at festivals and in the excursions of *soi-disant* penitents to the freedom allowed to jesters in motley and obstreperous undergraduates, proves the existence of a positive cult of 'folly', which the learned ironist Erasmus was to 'praise' in 1509. A fervent Christian, he was in a position to sum up a whole millennium of the influence of his religion. He must have been aware that it had utterly failed to stamp out 'fornication', which remained as rife in his time as in that of the pagan emperors. So he saw, like Sir Toby Belch in *Twelfth Night*, that virtue without 'cakes and ale' could never defeat vice. He spoke out pretty frankly for an extension of reason to cover the Horatian tag (Odes IV. 12) *Dulce est desipere in loco* ('It's fun to be a fool sometimes').

Erasmus thereby underlines, just as the Middle Ages passed into a recognisable historical category, one expression of their persistent protest against clerical fanaticism, itself so largely responsible for the insolent survival of the more scandalous forms of Venus and Priapus in Christendom.

V   Cowls and Coifs

ST. BENEDICT lived from 480 to 543. He may be regarded as the founder of Western monasticism. It is related that whenever he felt inclined to seek feminine society he went out of doors, stripped and threw himself into a bramble-bush or a bed of nettles. St. Francis (1181-1226) preferred a snowdrift on such 'fervent' occasions.

Long before the advent of Christianity non-European males, though not, needless to say, women, had imagined that the secret of the universe could be discovered by abstaining from all physical pleasure and concentrating upon prayer and meditation. Such communities as the Essenes in Judaea for example, and in Alexandria those known as *Therapeutae*, lived very much as the Christian monks tried to live subsequently. The first of the latter may or may not have consciously imitated these sects. But the nature of the Christian faith, with its emphasis on innate sin and its promise of eternal life through a rejection of the normal attractions of a mortal existence, would of itself suggest the adoption of a monastic system.

It began with the solitary retirement of individuals like the Egyptian St. Anthony in the third century. These hermits were soon joined by voluntary disciples. The innumerable legends of the temptation of St. Anthony in particular by demons disguised as voluptuous courtesans prove that in the popular mind the chief privation endured by the anchorites was the lack of sexual intercourse. It is significant that this saint's most usual emblem was the pig, an animal noted for its ruttishness. The stories about him and his imitators at first aroused general admiration. But very soon they turned to 'blue' anecdotes which persisted in enormous numbers throughout the Middle Ages. Perhaps medieval man laughed more at these tales, which regularly contrasted the outward solemnity of the monk with his secret frivolity, than at anything else. However that may be, the cowled and tonsured men in the long, girdled robes and rope sandals had become, by the sixth century, a conspicuous part of the population in every settled region of Christian Europe.

They had been introduced into Rome by St. Athanasius in the middle of the fourth century. They had been organised by St. Benedict a hundred and fifty years later. His monks, in spite of the nettles, were not compelled to live such hard lives as those of Egypt and the Near East. From their first community on Mount Cassino in Italy they took part in the corporate activities of the lay population which they were supposed to edify. They read a good deal. But of course this relaxation of the early austerity turned out to be the thin end of a wedge. It broadened to admit profligacy.

St. Augustine II, i.e. not the bishop of Hippo (354-430) but the founder (d. 604) of Christianity in southern England, complains of hordes of wandering monks, degraded vagrants who begged, swindled and hawked false relics of the saints wherever they went. They became a nuisance to the civil as well as the ecclesiastical authorities. Worst of all, they preyed on girls and wives as well as on the property of those who conversed with them. All the same, the Benedictines were not exclusively devoted to this sort of commercial travelling. In the tumultuous seventh and eighth centuries they can fairly be regarded as the main stabilising and civilising influence then at work in Europe.

Until the thirteenth century their position in this respect remained unrivalled. Their vows had been made irrevocable by the Pope St. Gregory the Great in 590. But indiscriminate concubinage had even then already started. It was to continue. The celibacy of the priesthood, especially among the minor clergy, was constantly disregarded.

Convents of nuns had been instituted almost as early as monasteries. The former Frankish queen St. Radegunda (d. 587) founded one at Poitiers. Her nuns were of her own pugnacious nationality and pretty tough customers. After Radegunda's death they were excommunicated for rioting. But they defied the bishops who came to enforce this extremely harsh penalty. The holy men were expelled with violence from the basilica and ordered to mind their own business. This situation continued for two years and was not an isolated case. A nunnery at Tours behaved in the same way. At first sight it seems strange that women who took the veil in the sixth century should be fiercer than their male counterparts. But the Franks were the proudest of all the barbarians and nuns at this period, unlike the majority of monks, nearly all belonged to aristocratic families.

The English historian Bede (672-735) mentions lapses at Coldingham. He quotes the report of a visiting Irish monk. 'Dwellings built for praying and reading are now converted into places of revelling, drinking and other forbidden doings. The virgins adorn themselves like brides ... to secure the friendship of men outside.' Aldhelm, Bishop of Sherborne in the seventh century, laments 'the bold impudence and conceit of nuns who wear a vest of fine linen dyed violet and over it a scarlet tunic with a hood, the sleeves striped with silk and trimmed with red fur. Their locks, on forehead and temples, are curled with a crisping-iron. They have white and coloured headgear with bows of ribbon reaching to the ground. Their finger-nails are pared till they resemble the talons of a hawk.'

In the eighth century King Ethelbald of Mercia regularly used the Anglo-Saxon nunneries as if they were brothels and was duly rebuked by St. Boniface for this habit. The Council of Aix-la-Chapelle in 836, however, declared that many abbesses (who had the privileges of barons) were themselves to blame for running their convents as bawdy-houses. It solemnly directed future architects to ensure that no 'dark corners' could be made available for immoral purposes. The truth seems to be that the early nunneries were to a large extent the equivalent of modern 'schools for the daughters of gentlemen' and subject to the same periodical attacks for ostentation and sexual misconduct. The convents would of course be peculiarly exposed, owing to the social conditions of the age, to the depredations of privileged males. But girls were certainly educated there and often left to get married.

It was not until the tenth century that these more or less loose federations of both monks and nuns were closely combined into Orders. The first of these, that of Cluny, some fifty miles north of Lyons in Burgundy, was founded in 910. For two hundred and fifty years the Abbot of Cluny remained the second most important and powerful cleric, after the Pope himself, in Western Christendom. The Cluniac Order stood for a reversion to sterner discipline. It was time. For the last traces of ancient Roman culture had vanished and the continent had been practically turned over to a set of marauding petty chieftains. Many of the prelates themselves did not differ much in character from these robber barons. Pope John XII kept a harem in the Lateran Palace. Archbishops did the same with abbeys, where they installed hawks and hounds as well as their lady friends. Celibacy was openly ignored in diocese after diocese. All Europe seemed to be racing down into what Alcuin of York in the previous century had called a 'flood of fornication, adultery and incest'.

But now the men of Cluny swung the pendulum back. The switchback progress between fanaticism and relative indulgence was to characterise medieval Christianity for the rest of its history. On the one hand it would be felt that moral chaos could only be arrested by measures dependent for their efficacy on reverence for a supernatural source. On the other hand it would be found that men, like other ferocious animals, could only be tamed by a certain degree of tolerance for their wilder instincts. But this policy in its turn could easily be carried too far. Thereupon a further return to coercion became inevitable.

By the eleventh century, following upon the general scare of the year 1000, when it was widely believed that the wrath of heaven over the debauchery of both laymen and 'clerks' would destroy the world, a campaign to eradicate clerical concubinage had been set on foot by orders from Rome. These efforts failed to achieve an objective which human nature itself defended. But the truly 'dark' ages of Europe, outside the monasteries and convents little less than a mere tumult of murder, lust and greed, the scuffling, in short, of beasts of prey, were now drawing to a close. It was sufficiently clear that the abbeys and nunneries were by no means always model prisons of the spirit. But at least most of them were officially conscious of their shortcomings. Reaction to a second medieval period, in a good many respects a decided improvement on the first, could not be long delayed.

The formidable Gregory VII, Pope and Saint—Hildebrand before his election to the pontificate—was determined to impose law and order, education and true piety, upon Christendom. He had succeeded by 1085 in setting the papacy on a permanent throne of supremacy in both secular and ecclesiastical life. He established in principle the custom of a celibate clergy. But he hadn't cared much how he attained these aims. He made a lot of enemies, especially among people who wished to decide their own codes of morality. His friends were occasionally even rougher in their methods than he was himself. While he ruled, some married clergy were castrated by urban or village mobs and exhibited in public in that condition. His devoted follower, Pope Urban II, who acceded to the Chair of St. Peter in 1088, went so far as to offer the wives of priests deposed with or without castration to any noblemen who would accept them as slaves. But clerical celibacy was still not formally enforced, only more or less savagely reprehended.

Another of Gregory's lieutenants, St. Peter Damiani, (d. 1072), a highly controversial, ascetic and peremptory cardinal, had already informed the great Pope's predecessor, Leo IX, of 'the frightful excesses epidemically prevalent among the cloistered crowds of men, attributable to the unnatural restraints imposed upon the passions of those unfitted by nature or training to control themselves'. Damiani and Gregory between them may be held responsible for the start of a theocratic empire. It governed the western world for a long time, even after its disastrous adventures against Islam, disciplining the turbulent European monarchs fairly successfully until the rise of really powerful national sovereignties north of the Alps in the fourteenth century.

Another result of the general tightening up of discipline by these two energetic saints was the democratisation, so to speak, of the nunneries. As already noted, they had hitherto been mainly recruited from the land-owning families. Convents were the only places where girls could be given a decent education to fit them for the running of large households on marriage. Alternatively, if marriage proved impracticable, they could take irrevocable vows and stay on, instead of cluttering up the castles and manor-houses. But now, in the twelfth century, the Church began to encourage the daughters of tradesmen, agriculturalists and artisans to become nuns. For in the first place such young women were less likely to prove obstreperous than the arrogant aristocrats and secondly only too many of them were by this time, in the unstable economic conditions of the day, taking to the streets.

Combined Orders of canons and nuns were instituted, in the proportion of about 300 males to 60 females for each settlement. The innovation turned out a success at first. Scores of penniless and derelict women, even lepers, clamoured for admission. Hardly any were refused it. Even the sarcastic Anglo-Norman scholar and wit Walter Map (d. c. 1210), who hated all monks, especially the Cistercians, whom he called 'pseudo-humble money-grubbers', grudgingly approved the experiment. For the new nuns, he considered, were better mannered and better educated than either their predecessors or their male counterparts.

England had not improved much, in his time, since the days when Earl Godwin (d. 1053) had stormed the nunnery at Berkley-on-Severn and turned it into a 'pantheon of harlotry'. In Map's own lifetime the nuns at Watton castrated a lay brother who had seduced a 'hopelessly frivolous and lazy' girl, one of the new class of novices. In 1126 Cardinal Giovanni of Cremona was sent by the Pope Honorius II to restore discipline among the clergy. He eloquently denounced concubinage to the Synod of London at the first meeting he called. But that same night he was surprised in bed with a prostitute. It is possible that the Italian prelate was tricked into this situation. For the opposition of the English priests to his view had been vociferous. In any case the Cardinal didn't do the slightest good. In 1171 Clarembald, abbot-elect of St. Augustine's foundation at Canterbury, was jovially boasting that he had seventeen bastards in one village alone.

Such men were often deposed—one abbot is reported to have kept no less than seventy concubines—but usually only to be appointed subsequently to some distant benefice. The Church could not afford to lose the services of too many able and experienced men, however immoral they might be, who had attained positions of responsibility. Yet the more the Popes pressed for the principle of celibacy the more scandals were brought to light.

The experiment of double monasteries, with only a wall between monks and nuns—the latter being now in the majority—proved a shocking failure. The women nearly all became pregnant. Some satirical Latin verses written on this subject were translated into English in the late seventeenth or early eighteenth century in the following terms:

'Tho' some are Barren Does yet others
by Fryars' help prove teeming mothers.
When all to such lewdness run
all's covered under Name of Nun.
Th' Abbess in Honour as sh' excells
her Belly too more often swells.
If any She proves Barren still
Age is in fault and not her Will.'

In such circumstances all the endless detailed regulations passed to ensure chastity remained ineffectual. Official celibacy was never abrogated. But it continued to be very largely a farce.

In this same century, the twelfth, the inroads of Islam upon European society, especially its eastern and western outposts in Asia Minor and Spain, necessitated the establishment of Military Orders of monks. The Hospitallers, Templars and Teutonic Knights were encouraged to cultivate male comradeship and contempt for women. As usual in such cases, these bodies were accused of homosexuality. In some instances and periods the charges were by no means unfounded. The closer concentration of the civilian monks upon specifically religious ritual rendered them less open to such attacks, even though they were kept practically imprisoned under the latest fiats from Cluny. But the nunneries which began to be prominent at the end of the eleventh century enjoyed no such relative immunity. For the old pagan tradition of the basic irresponsibility of women, exceeding that of males, had not yet run its course. In fact, it is scarcely exhausted even today.

Early in the thirteenth century a movement arose which was to give a final fillip to the lay sceptics' long-standing distrust of the alleged rejection by the monk of carnal appetites. The four Mendicant orders detached their 'friars' to go out into the world as individuals. These representatives, ostensibly confessors and teachers, were called after their saintly founders. Franciscans began their work in 1210, Dominicans in 1215, Carmelites in 1245 and Augustinians in 1256. The Cistercians or White—sometimes Grey—Monks appeared earlier, in 1098, as a conservative offshoot of the Benedictines. By devoting themselves sedulously to agriculture and cattle-breeding they soon acquired great wealth, especially in England, where they laid the foundation of the lucrative wool trade. It was, accordingly, the Cistercians who introduced the system of 'lay brothers', originally farm labourers employed about the local monastery or abbey. This practice began a relaxation of the former return to severity and led eventually to a commercial spirit, with its inevitably accompanying mundane outlook. Consequently the Cistercian Order, as Walter Map noted, joined those already in far from good odour with the laity.

The friars' duties as confessors involved them, from the first, in circumstances hardly calculated to confirm their chastity. Female penitents, in nine cases out of ten, came to acknowledge the commission of erotic misdemeanours. These had necessarily to be investigated in great detail. For otherwise mistakes might be made in imposing the correct penance. Furthermore, the relatively innocent type of girl had to be warned, in equal detail, against certain acts, language or postures which might excite the young women themselves or others to lasciviousness, even without any such intention. Description of such behaviour required a vivid imagination which often ended by improperly titillating both confessor and penitent.

The nuns who came to confession were even more troublesome to handle than the feminine laity. For many of the former, being mystically inclined, related the most extraordinary hallucinations of a libidinous character. Mechthild of Magdeburg (1202-1277) felt God's hand fondling her bosom. Christine Ebner (1277-1356) believed herself with child by Jesus. The friars had to enquire most precisely into the exact circumstances of such events. In the early days, moreover, they were enjoined, if whipping were prescribed for the sin confessed, to administer this correction themselves upon the nude bodies of their penitents. Worse still, lesbianism and bestiality—with the domestic pets popular in the convents—were pretty often admitted by nuns who had been taught to regard their cowled confidant as a purely spiritual being.

COWLS AND COIFS

These experiences proved altogether too great a temptation for all too many of the friars. In this connection the Chronicle of the Franciscan monk of noble family, Salimbene di Adamo, born at Parma in 1221, is of great interest. The work was composed for the benefit of his niece, an intelligent girl of fifteen, then undergoing a convent education. Salimbene evidently intended to ensure that this promising young lady would never be surprised in later life by any awful stories she heard about men and women in the throes of lust.

He begins by commenting coolly on the widespread vice of homosexuality, 'especially among scholars and clerks,' and touches upon similar practices by nuns. As for blasphemy, one of the worst cases of it occurred when a certain priest, Don Giacopo de Henzola of Mutina, lost his hawk out hunting. Infuriated at this misfortune, he took down his breeches there and then and presented his anus to heaven. Then he galloped home, entered his private chapel and excreted on the altar.

Some of the horrors of senile lechery are then recounted. A bishop named Faventino, for instance, was accustomed in his old age to introduce little girls into his bed, where he contemplated and fondled their naked flesh, by daylight, for hours on end, decorating the features he most appreciated with gold coins, which the children were allowed to keep. This doddering satyr, says Salimbene, was eventually strangled by a burglar, who got away with most of his money.

The chronicler warns his young reader about the common habit of confessors who take their penitents behind the altar—the confessional box was not instituted until 1565, probably to stop this little game—in order to couple with them. He tells the story of a woman who, on one such occasion, remarked, on being seized by the friar: 'There are more convenient times and places than this.' The holy man seemed struck by this suggestion and made an appointment to visit her at her house. He was delighted next day to receive a present from the lady, consisting of a pie and some wine. Wishing to curry favour with his bishop, he passed the gift on to that dignitary, who was nauseated on discovering that the pie was made of human excrement and the wine of urine. He sent for the friar, who said he could not understand why the woman had played him such a silly trick. But the bishop was not satisfied. He demanded an explanation from the vengeful lady. On receiving it, he commended her action and reported the sacrilegious friar to Pope Alexander IV, who duly punished him.

Another woman, Salimbene goes on, confessed to a certain priest that she had been violated by a stranger in a lonely place in the Alps, where she lived. The priest, excited by the particulars she gave him of this affair, dragged his weeping penitent behind the altar and raped her himself. A second and a third priest to whom she confessed perpetrated the same outrages. A fourth gave her absolution. But, catching sight of a knife she was holding, he asked her what that was for. For myself, she answered, sobbing, if you in your turn had so cruelly misused me.

There were monks, Salimbene solemnly tells his niece, who regularly dreamt that they were kissed, embraced and otherwise indecently handled by Jesus Christ and the Holy Virgin. Seminal emissions invariably followed these visions.

He then relates at length the doings of a certain Segarello, who started a disreputable sect of roving evangelists, followed by a horde of harlots and boys who submitted to sodomy. Segarello began his career by telling a widow with whom he was lodging that the Lord had commanded him to test his chastity by lying naked in bed with her daughter. He referred his astonished hostess to the Gospel of St. Matthew XIX. 12. 'There be eunuchs which have made themselves eunuchs for the kingdom of heaven's sake.' He said he was one of them. She was convinced and sacrificed her offspring to this thirteenth-century Mr. Horner. But Wycherley's rake in *The Country Wife* at least refrained from quoting the Bible during his negotiations.

Nor did he imitate Segarello and his disciples in bringing the same sort of pressure to bear on young boys whom they fancied as minions. But all fish came alike to the nets of this gang of tonsured ruffians. Three of them once joined a wedding party and, after delivering some lengthy sermons, proclaimed it to be the Lord's will that a few hours must elapse before carnal intercourse between bride and groom took place. The new wife having been duly installed in bed, the young husband was plied with stoups of ale and hymnology, while the three friars went upstairs one by one to interview the lady. When the last one returned, beaming, he clapped the cuckold on the back and told him he could now go and enjoy his beloved if he could manage the stairs.

Salimbene records, with a relish which no doubt his niece and most of his subsequent readers shared, that these scoundrels were eventually reported to the civil power and hanged. Segarello himself was burned alive for heresy in 1300.

It was no wonder that at the Council of Ravenna in 1261 the presiding archbishop told the parish clergy: 'I cannot with a safe conscience commit the confessions of the laity to you.... For ye lead women behind the altar under pretence of confession and there ye deal as the sons of Eli dealt at the door of the tabernacle, which is horrible to relate and more horrible to do.... Can I commit women's confessions to the priest Gerardo here present, when I know well that he has a whole house full of sons and daughters?'

The Church had been the paramount institution in Europe since the eleventh century. Even now it was building splendid cathedrals and holding magnificent services in them. It was setting shining examples of charity and other labours in the cause of civilisation. But it was losing ground in the hearts of the people. The expeditions to recover possession of the Holy Sepulchre had failed ignominiously. There were many Christians who felt inferior to the heathen not only in arms but also in learning and common sense. There were too many prelates like the Prince Bishop of Liège, who boasted of having had fourteen bastards in twenty-two months, and like those Teutons of whom a Parisian scribe remarked: 'I can believe anything except that any German bishop can be saved.' In that country the word *Pfaffenkind* (priest's child) had already become a common synonym for infants born out of wedlock.

Such sinners often went unpunished, for the reasons already noted. In the last year of the century an honest knight, whose daughter had been ravished by the Bishop of Orléans, tried for months, but in vain, to have this pompous lecher brought to justice. In the end the desperate father drew his sword and hacked the fellow to pieces, mitre and all.

It was, however, especially in Germany, where Christianity had gained a footing comparatively late (in the eighth century) that clerical corruption in the erotic sphere, by the thirteen hundreds, reached its height. The bishops did their best. But they were regularly defied, sometimes with cynical levity. One priest, for example, on being ordered by his diocesan to replace a pretty young housemaid with one of forty, duly dismissed the girl. But he engaged two others both aged twenty, declaring that the tale of years enjoined by episcopal ordinance had thus been fulfilled. Reforming movements were repeatedly set on foot during the next hundred years. But they were always obstructed, until the great Protestant schism finally occurred under the influence of Luther. Then the monasteries, which, apart from an occasional villainous bishop, had been the chief offenders, were destroyed in northern Europe and crippled in the centre of the continent. The era in which the monk had been so often hated or ridiculed by the ordinary citizen came to an end. But he had played his part to the full, whether by personal asceticism or its very opposite, in rendering the Middle Ages the most sexually licentious period, among all classes, of European history.

The nuns, always more separate from the rest of the community, as a rule, than monks, at first worked, in the erotic sense, inwardly upon themselves rather than outwardly upon lay society. In the earlier centuries the pagan or semi-pagan populations had been infuriated by the spectacle of so many Christian women who insisted on remaining virgins. Again and again, like Earl Godwin in England, they stormed the convents and dragged their inmates into slavery. But gradually, for the reasons already mentioned, the educational value of such communities of non-procreative women and their convenience as depositories for unwanted daughters and later on for potential harlots, were recognised as useful to the social structure.

They had in fact begun in Egypt as girls' schools. One of them was attended, according to tradition, by the sister of St. Anthony. It was in the fourth century that they reached Europe as duly organised nunneries, one of which was later controlled by the sister of another saint, Benedict. When the various male Orders arose at the start of the thirteenth century, female branches of them were established. But nuns did not often leave their convents—the restless English were an exception—without being ordered to do so by way of penance, e.g. on pilgrimage to Rome and other holy places. In the later Middle Ages they

COWLS AND COIFS

were seldom seen in the streets. It was only in the early seventeenth century that the modern peripatetic nun became ubiquitous.

The strain upon either sex of living in the absence of the other soon grows hard to bear, whatever conscious fanaticism may be at work. The sexual continence enjoined by dogma or convention tends constantly to break down. The medieval Church, well aware of this situation, took what steps it could to maintain Christian decency. Under King Henry III of England Robert Grosseteste, Bishop of Lincoln, felt obliged to 'test the virtue of nuns' with his own hands. But less brutal measures were commoner. Mortification inflicted by oneself or others, scourging, fasting and many other pains and penalties were zestfully imposed and sometimes willingly borne. The endless jungles of theology and hagiology were thrown open to those who could read, so that they could occupy their spare time more profitably than by dreaming of forbidden delights. The Brothers and Sisters who could write were set to copying wagon-loads of manuscripts explaining Christian ideals. Above all, sermon and prayer were incessantly used to inculcate a fervently pious adoration of the omnipotent Trinity and the Virgin Mother of God, as well as of a great multitude of named saints, martyrs and angels. These exhortations and petitions also forced upon the inmates of the convents an abysmal dread of the damnation, the frightful torments for evermore, in store for those execrable human beings who infringed, without the humblest repentance, the sexual tabus erected, everyone believed, by the archetypal figures of heaven's hierarchy.

The system worked up to a point. Thousands of enclosed monks and nuns managed to survive an existence deprived of physical love. If they did not do the world much good, at least they did it little harm. On the whole they escaped the misery which befell a substantial majority of the laity. The monasteries and nunneries, even by merely subsisting as pacific, non-criminal societies, set a good example to the desperate, the ferocious and the fraudulent. Many unhappy people were sure that the prayers, daily and nightly addressed to the Almighty on their behalf by such unseen communities, might really help to substitute fortune for ruin and joy for sorrow.

But, significantly enough, critics of those who wore the cowl and coif often alluded to the unconquerable devil who persistently haunted these sacred precincts in the guise of Priapus. The ancient Greek garden-god, they sarcastically affirmed, with his invariable insinuating grin and erect phallus, sent a long procession of evil spirits to invade the cells. These demons took the form of either *succubi*, beautiful girls who jumped into the beds of would-be male saints, or *incubi*, handsome young men in a terrifying state of nature, who interrupted the slumbers or meditations of the most respectable nuns, from the Abbess downwards.

In 1491 Jeanne Pothière, a nun of Cambrai, swore she had been forced to copulate four hundred and forty-four times with a demon of this sort. He had demanded introductions to her sisters in Christ and had thereafter chased them round the gardens and fields of the convent till they had to climb trees to get away from him.

Quite a number of those victimised by Satan in this way went off their heads. To all appearance they became as bad as their supernatural visitors. They tore off their habits, assumed the attitudes of copulation, shrieked or gabbled obscenities, blasphemed, seized the persons of their colleagues with evidently libidinous intent and made a lot of extraordinary noises indicative of enjoyment of an act absolutely prohibited by the Fathers once the dress of an Order had been assumed. Exorcism was generally successful for the time being, if accompanied by torrents of ice-cold water, slaps in the face and/or limb-twisting. Oratory alone had little effect.

But just as in the case of other psychopaths there could be no guarantee that the cure would be permanent. Such antics were often repeated later by the same person. There were instances, too, in which the exorcist or his assistant did not resist the temptations of a more or less sadistic sexual assault, despite the strict regulations laid down by the Church to prevent that sort of thing.

In these circumstances no one was really surprised when more and more nuns in particular found that they could let off steam in this way with impunity. For in the official view they were not themselves, but 'possessed' by demons. Some of these women unquestionably feigned madness, like certain Court Fools, in order to indulge their unruly eroticism. Towards the end of the Middle Ages some important laymen grew uneasy on this account, even in the more credulous and fanatical south of Europe. The Doge of Venice, for example, in 1497, roundly declared that many convents were turning into 'houses of assignation', nothing more nor less than common brothels regularly visited by the male lechers of the district. The accusation had been made before, but generally with the exaggeration of malice or because the nuns had repudiated outside interference with their amusements. Now they either innocently or wickedly invited it and more witnesses of their lascivious hysteria were available. This reputation encouraged the revival of raids by boisterous young men even upon establishments that did their best to behave decently.

In 1379 the brutish soldier Sir John Arundel, on his way to the French war, actually carried off from a convent near Southampton no less than sixty women and girls, to amuse his contingent during the campaign. Raping started immediately, aboard the ships. But a storm sprang up in the Channel. In order to lighten the dangerously overloaded and tossing vessels Arundel had all his wretched captives thrown into the sea, where no one dreamed of trying to rescue them. It does not appear that he was ever punished for this pitiless massacre of his fellow-countrywomen. It is unlikely that many of them had been guilty of intentional provocation.

But a certain intellectual degeneration had unquestionably set in among women who took the veil in the fourteenth century, especially after the continental catastrophe of the Black Death. Chaucer's sentimental and too decorative Prioress, whose jaunt to Canterbury, incidentally, was in direct contravention of papal orders, spoke only Norman-French

'after the scole of Stratford atte bowe,
for Frenche of Paris was to hire unknowe.'

Discipline, too, was decaying, as John Wyclif noted, in both England and Germany. Visiting bishops were not always told the truth about the drinking and gossiping, dancing and dressing up, flirting with 'students' and naughty games with pet dogs, monkeys and rabbits that went on, to say nothing of bigger scandals, like that mentioned by William Langland, whose 'Dame Purnell' ... 'a priest's concubine ... will never become Prioress ... for she had a child in cherry time, all our Chapter it wist'. The scribe Wimpherling of Strasbourg agreed with the Doge of Venice quoted above. In 1489 the Archbishop of Canterbury charged the Abbot of St. Albans with appointing a whore named Elena Germyn as his Prioress and sharing her favours with any of his monks who cared to bother about it. Erasmus himself, looking back on this period in his *Colloquies*, considered that chastity was more endangered in the cloister than out of it. A century later the wise and witty English divine Thomas Fuller put the whole trouble with medieval nuns in a permanent nutshell when he struck off the classic phrase: 'Virginity is least kept where it is most constrained.'

It is clear enough, in any case, from the documentary evidence, of which the few examples quoted above are a tiny fraction, that almost from the beginning of the nunnery system the three vows of poverty, chastity and obedience required from dwellers in these settlements were in a rather high percentage of cases quickly abandoned, in that order of progression.

The monasteries, since men are on the whole less prone to uninhibited libidinous frenzy than women, once they are given the chance, at first proved less embarrassing in this way. But scandalous outbreaks of homosexuality did occur. Moreover, abbots and their staffs were in the habit of paying ceremonial or business calls upon abbesses and theirs, or *vice versa*. On such occasions the mixed party sometimes engaged in certain revels after the ostensible object of the visit had been achieved. Those present had even been known to spend the night in intimate communion with their obsequious hostesses or hosts. But until the inauguration of the Mendicant Orders in the thirteenth century there is relatively little evidence of monks who lived permanently in a cloister surrendering to Eros. For in addition to the generally stronger wills and soberer dispositions of males so sequestered, their labours both mental and physical were usually more exhausting and various than the females could be expected to undertake.

All the same, one of the tales collected in the fifteenth century but mostly dating back to a considerably earlier period makes it clear that monks, like modern soldiers in camp or barracks, often obtained leave to visit the nearest town or village. The hero of the following story, one of those included in the volume issued as the *Cent Nouvelles Nouvelles*, is specifically called a monk (*monachus*), not a friar. He fell in love with a virgin who lived close to the abbey. He pursued her so long and ardently that at last she consented to yield to his solicitations. But she insisted that he must take care not to hurt her. So when the great night came he brought to the assignation in the girl's bedroom a thin deal board with a hole in it. He set this board against the *mons veneris* of his innamorata and thrust his penis through the wooden aperture. But, as sometimes happens, this member, owing to the monk's inordinate excitement, had not yet reached a full state of erection. When it did, it stuck fast in the board. The unfortunate lover was obliged to call for cold water, so as to extricate his 'brother Priapus', as the *nouvelle* calls the imprisoned organ, from this painful predicament. The girl fetched a bucket from another room and duly drenched her seducer's captive phallus. But this expedition aroused her family. Their alarmed voices and movements sent the monk leaping from the window in a panic. When he got back to the abbey he was still in such pain from the lesions inflicted on the skin of 'priapus' by the rough wood that he had to send for a doctor. The whole adventure came to the ears of the Prior, who sentenced the culprit to such severe courses of fasting and scourging that the wretched truant wished he had never been born.

Hermits, too, seem occasionally to have got into trouble for incontinence. The fifteenth-century Italian humanist Poggio Bracciolini, one of the boldest anti-clerical rebels of his day, relates that an anchorite with a great reputation for sanctity was once hauled up before the Duke of Padua to face a charge of seducing several ladies of high rank, who had come to the holy recluse to confess their sins. The rascally prisoner, out of sheer vanity, coolly admitted the indictment. 'Let's have their names, then,' said the Duke. 'They deserve to be publicly shamed for their gross libertinage.' The hermit cited half a dozen prominent at the ducal Court. A pompous secretary wrote them all down, much to the malicious amusement of all present, including, very conspicuously, himself. Finally he inquired, between chuckles: 'Is that all?' The prisoner nodded, but in apparent embarrassment. 'Now then, none of your nonsense!' thundered the secretary. 'It's obvious you're concealing someone. Out with it, man, or I send for the torturers!' The hermit sighed deeply, casting down his eyes. 'All right then,' he mumbled. 'If you insist. I've done my best not to enlighten you. But I'm sorry to say that my latest convert to the joys of adultery was your own wife.' The secretary, petrified, dropped his pen. But the Duke roared with laughter and swore he was well served for his bullying of the helpless sinner.

This anecdote, like many more of the same kind, may have been manufactured. Poggio detested the men of religion and never lost an opportunity to discredit them. But such tales, whether true or false, prove clearly enough their general unpopularity, especially among husbands.

For once the friars began to set out on their begging, charitable or confessing errands, they soon found that a traveller enjoying the prestige of a learned intermediary, however suspect as a person, between earth and heaven, could contrive as many if not more opportunities for amorous conquest as any nobleman. The friars' education being often superior to that of the average layman, they were in a position to employ stratagems which a lord could never have dreamed of and which a woman would rarely see through. The intimidation of force, which rank or wealth could apply, need not be exercised by a barefooted Brother. His tricks may almost be said to have constituted the chief items of the gossip of medieval man for a couple of hundred years at least.

One tale of which there are many variants recounts how a farmer's wife asked her confessor if he knew of any remedy for her sterility, which was worrying her husband. The friar answered that certain women had been cured of barrenness by submitting to an incantation which threw them into a trance, during which they had such vivid dreams that they believed they were still awake. Would she agree to that? Oh, yes, cried the poor woman. If only it will stop my husband beating me for not having children! 'Very well then,' the cunning lecher rejoined. 'I will pronounce the necessary formula. But don't forget that anything you may then suppose is happening will be an illusion.' He then mumbled a long Latin prayer, waved his arms about, rolled his eyes upwards, knelt down and then sprang, without further ceremony, upon his dupe and ravished her. On rising he went through the same pseudo-magical ritual as before, then addressed his trembling victim with a reassuring smile. 'Let us hope,' he remarked, with unctuous solemnity, 'That the dream you have just had, whatever it may have been, will have the desired effect. Go with God.' The bewildered woman thanked him profusely and departed quite convinced that no adultery had occurred.

Another enamoured friar, according to one of the *nouvelles,* showed the object of his desires a bandaged forefinger and told her that it was causing him great agony. He added that a doctor had informed him that the finger would have to be amputated unless it could be subjected to a degree of animal heat, for instance that of a female generative organ, which would dissolve the abscess. 'I couldn't, of course, agree to any such impropriety,' he groaned sadly, 'in view of my holy office. Nevertheless, if the operation took place in pitch darkness, in order to spare the modesty of both parties, it would not really be a sin.' The woman was foolish enough to offer her services under these conditions. Not a glimmer of light revealed the exact nature of the subsequent proceedings. But they were characterised, naturally enough, by extreme caution.

Suddenly the friar uttered an exclamation of triumph.

'Ha!' cried he. 'Behold! The abscess has burst and the pus has escaped! I am cured! How right that doctor was!' Whether the lady still believed that she had merely entertained a sore finger and nothing else is not recorded. But it is quite likely that she was never the wiser.

A very old story rehashed by La Fontaine in the seventeenth century tells of a husband who asked a friar to do him the honour of standing godfather to his first child, as yet unborn. But the holy man, who had long had his eye on the peasant's pretty young wife, explained that the work of procreation had been defective and the child would be born a hideous idiot unless some other person were co-opted to improve the structure of the foetus. With pompous condescension he offered his own services.

The appalled couple agreed. During the ensuing act of intercourse the friar had the insolence to urge the wife to play her part with the utmost strenuousness and repeat the performance several times, so as to ensure that a perfect offspring would result. In due time a flawless baby was born. The happy parents could hardly express their gratitude to the friar for thus sacrificing his chastity on their behalf and readily consented not to breathe a word about it.

Many such anecdotes of monks, friars and hermits can be traced back to the jest-books of late Greek and Latin literature, where the characters are of course pagan priests and citizens. One such collection, the so called *Milesian Tales*, was used by the second-century Romano-African author Apuleius, whose *Golden Ass* was read by St. Augustine of Hippo two hundred years later. Book IX of the *Ass* tells a long story about a pair of shoes left in a wife's bedroom by her lover. In the fourteenth-century Christian version the shoes become a holy relic, 'St. Francis's breeches', said to have been brought to the house by a friar as a cure for the lady's alleged sickness, though they were really his own, left behind in a precipitate exit on the husband's unexpected return. The Prior who made this excuse for his guilty subordinate actually persuaded the cuckold to kiss the breeches which had so gloriously restored his wife to health.

It is a measure of the daring of lay sceptics at this period that not only is a common or garden friar here shown up as a hypocritical fornicator but his august master, the Prior, is represented as aiding and abetting him by a gross blasphemy.

But, as already noted, both monks and nuns had declined from their former intellectual and moral standards by this time. Chaucer's Prioress, for example, can speak only Norman French, not Parisian. The English reformer Wyclif and his younger contemporary and countryman, the poet Langland, both wrote contemptuously of the decay of morals and education in these communities. Nuns in particular were going back to the bad old days when they had spent their time largely in drinking, dancing, dressing up, keeping pets, gossiping, quarrelling and defying or deceiving their bishops. In Germany in 1359 the following song was put into the mouth of one of these turbulent girls:

COWLS AND COIFS

'God give him a year of blight
who made me to be a nun,
who bade me take this tunic white
and this coal-black mantle don.

And must I be a nun in truth
and all against my will,
when I could cool a lad's hot youth
and all his passion still?

But he'd better not think to stifle mine!
Such thoughts forthwith he must resign!'

In the early fifteenth century a Lincolnshire Prioress 'wears gold rings, very costly, with divers precious stones and girdles silvered and gilt and silken veils high above the forehead, so that it can be seen of all ... and wears furs of vair and shifts of cloth of Rennes, kirtles faced with silk and tiring pins of silver and silver-gilt ... and a cap of state, furred ... a long silken band on her neck which hangs down below her breast and thereon a golden ring with a diamond.'

'The Land of Cockayne', a satire on monasticism written about 1430, describes the nuns of its imaginary abbey as wearing silk and going in for mixed bathing with the monks, in the river. Trunks and bikinis for outdoor bathing were of course unheard of in those days. The author doesn't even bother to say that these parties were in the nude. The charges of wholesale unchastity grow positively monotonous. They come from every quarter of the continent and from all classes. But reform was steadily resisted by the land-owners, whose unmarried daughters wouldn't go to these places if the regulations were tightened up, and by all sorts of other notabilities, including Popes like John XIII, who found nunneries as amusing to visit as brothels. It was in vain that the Prioress of Appleton in Yorkshire was ordered in 1489 to see 'that none of your sisters use the alehouse nor the watersyde where course of strangers dayly resorte'. She and her colleagues, if they were anything like many named by their accusers, went much further than that. They travelled about all over the place, on one excuse or another, quite contrary to regulations, just like modern female globe-trotters.

It became more and more obvious, throughout this century, that the clerical tabus on carnal appetite had utterly failed to achieve their object and that by no means only among the laity. It is difficult to avoid the impression that the clergy in general and especially the abbeys and priories of women were among the chief offenders. The scandal was none the less for the recognition by the more thoughtful prelates that their temptations were greater than those of the ordinary public. The celibacy of priests had long proved impracticable for a great many. Concubinage was even sometimes forced upon them by their parishioners, notably in Spain and Switzerland, in order to protect the latters' wives and daughters from pursuit by the local vicars and monks.

Yet the absurd principle was obstinately maintained. Pope John XIII, condemned and deposed by the Council of Constance, which he had himself summoned in 1413, for self-confessed incest, adultery, general loose living, homicide and atheism, arrested the Bohemian reformer John Huss in the following year for heresy. Huss was burnt alive at the instance of the Council in 1415. John, after his deposition, was created by his successor Dean of the Sacred College.

Nevertheless, in this extraordinary situation quite a number of worthy ecclesiastics kept their heads and tried to get on with their almost impossible task. Canon Felix Hemmelin of Zürich, in his Dialogue on Nobility, writes:

'I, Felix, travelling through the lands of the Marquess of Baden, at the time of the Hussite terror, rested at an inn full of peasants, as it was a holiday. The whole crowd fell all together, perchance to irritate me and my clerk, to contumelious words against clerics and the clergy, saying that they were worse than any other men in the world for their fornications and concubinage. At length I called for silence, which was granted. Then I told them: "As I came up the Rhine from Mainz I passed by the city of Oppenheim. And there in a field I found twenty-four wheels set up on high in a single group and twenty-four peasants bound on each. All were thieves from one township. There was no clerk among them. Your cruel and reviling words are by reason of but a few clerics. Them you abuse for a natural thing which went on for seven thousand years until Christ's day and for nearly a thousand years thereafter without reproach to our Creator. Since when it has been restricted by man's prohibition and turned into a sin. Yet none the less is it natural and common to you with them."

Then I bitterly proclaimed their thefts as unnatural. They were all disturbed by my words. But I said to my clerk: "Now let us depart." So we did. Else would these men have risen up against us and swallowed us quick, and perhaps in their wrath drowned us in the river.'

The good Canon perhaps allowed himself a smile in the last sentence. But the higher clergy were in a difficult position during this last century of the Middle Ages. Attacked from without for hypocrisy and betrayed from within by the reckless licentiousness of their own superiors and inferiors in the Church hierarchy they still had to maintain the official restrictions on sex expression. The tone of the enlightened Canon Hemmelin's anecdote proves that he understood and did his best to come to terms with the foolish intolerance of erotic appetite so conspicuously displayed by most of the bishops, cardinals and popes. They had condemned to asceticism not only abbots, priors and canons, who had a good deal of freedom, but also the populous monasteries and nunneries which had, apart from their nomadic friars, much less. Christianity could never have survived the paradox inherent in these circumstances if men like Canon Hemmelin had not stuck to the middle of the road.

Cardinal Newman in 1868 (*The Church of the Fathers*) described the orthodox ideal in view as 'the tongue purified from the gossip of the world, the eyes unexcited by fair colour or comely shape, the ear not relaxing the tone of the mind by voluptuous songs nor ... the talk of light men and jesters. Thus the mind ... falls back upon itself and thereby ascends to the contemplation of God.'

It was an impossible aim for a sane being. The pure fanatics achieved it. But they achieved nothing else. The best of the saints, like Francesco of Assisi, knew that they must build, as do men and women who 'fall in love', from physical beauty to spiritual. They knew that only so could Christianity save the world from its constant tendency to selfish barbarity, the only possible result of building on ugliness.

Modern research into medieval history proves clearly enough that it was the majesty of the visible cathedrals, the enchanting tenderness of missal and fresco painting, the nobility of Latin and vernacular poetry and of music in both church and castle and finally in the fifteenth century the dawn of a recognition, through the literature and monuments of pagan antiquity, of true human and natural dignity, that did more for the future achievements of mankind than all the moral axioms coined by no matter how earnest a religion.

VI Witchcraft

THE trade of magic, or the summoning up of presumed supernatural powers to assist mankind in various ways, began as soon as the first religious conceptions entered primitive minds. Ancient sorcery was in fact the mother of religion and for many millennia constituted a faith still known in Italy as *la vecchia religione*. The experts could be either male or female. But the more devious and inconsequential mentalities of women rendered them peculiarly fitted to practise necromancy. The Greeks occasionally burned them, even in the time of Demosthenes. Thrace was held, like Bohemia in later ages, to be a region specially favourable to the birth and training of witches. In republican Rome, according to Livy, magic used against personal enemies could be a capital offence. The emperors started the long-lived fashion of keeping astrologers and wizards at their Courts. But by the fourth century they were passing laws against unofficial practitioners of such arts.

Of these men and women large numbers were Christians. As early as the second century Irenaeus, Bishop of Lyons, complains of one Marcus of Memphis who preyed on rich women in southern Gaul by putting them in touch, for hard cash, with demons prepared to satisfy their cupidity, lust, spite or mere curiosity. The wife of a deacon—clerics often married in those days—is said to have been ruined by the machinations of Marcus. From this time on prosecutions for such offences were regularly undertaken. The Franks and the Visigoths imposed fines. But the Roman emperor Louis I, surnamed the Pious, who was a son of Charlemagne, insisted on the death penalty. He and most of the secular and ecclesiastical rulers throughout the Middle Ages saw in 'the old religion' the most dangerous of heresies, since it set up the powers of hell in opposition to those of heaven.

Witch hunts had been formally inaugurated by Pope Gregory I in the year 600. They were continued by King Kenneth I of Scotland in the ninth century and by the Saxon king Aethelstan in the tenth. In Europe by the thirteenth century they had greatly multiplied. By a Bull of Pope Gregory IV issued in 1233 a German sect of so called 'Stedingers' was accused of communing with demons and committing indiscriminate debaucheries. The Inquisitor Conrad of Marburg was deputed to investigate. He was promptly murdered in mysterious circumstances. In 1258 and 1260 Pope Alexander IV and early in the following century Pope John XII added momentum to the furious tide of persecution, which raced in full flood thereafter until near the end of the seventeenth century. The victims were often merely silly or pretentious old women or hysterical girls. Most of them, however, were clever male swindlers of mature age and cynical morality. A few were serious but easily deceived persons whose scientific itch got them into trouble. For magic was found, to the vexation of the authorities, to possess a strange fascination for the intellectually restless as well as for the foolishly credulous temperaments of humanity.

As late as the mid-sixteenth century, during the high noon itself of the Renaissance, which dissipated so many of the sombre superstitions of former times, one of the most brilliantly intelligent artists who ever lived, the superb Benvenuto Cellini, records his terror of the incantations in which he engaged with a necromancer who was also a priest.

On that occasion they hoped to persuade the Devil to show them how to make gold, a metal required by Cellini not only for fun and games but also for his labours as a goldsmith. 'In the fires of the brazier,' he writes in his famous *Memoirs* (1558), 'fed by stenching chemicals, the Coliseum swarmed with legions of infernal spirits. The child with us yelled with panic, exclaiming that he could see a million terrible and menacing figures, led by four giants armed from head to foot, ready to assault and penetrate the magic circle.'

The god in charge of the medieval ceremonies of this nature was always regarded as incarnate in a man or animal, for example a stag, jackal, goat, bull, dog or cat. The dances, feasts, chants, liturgies and ritual with which this god was worshipped invariably included conspicuous elements of an erotic character, since their aim had originally been to promote fertility. The vicar of Inverkeithing himself, in the Scotland of 1282, led the dance round an idol provided with a huge phallus, which had been set up in the churchyard. This priest was duly hauled up before his bishop to explain these proceedings. But he defended himself so well that, after being severely reprimanded, he was permitted to retain his benefice.

The assemblies of witches were called 'sabbaths' in Christian times. The word means 'days of rest' in Hebrew. Such meetings were held four times a year, at Candlemas on February 2, at Roodmas on April 30, at Lammas on August 1 and on All Hallow Even on October 31. The celebrations started in the evening, lasted all night and ended at daybreak. Their nocturnal character indicates both the mystery with which they were surrounded and the hilarious mood of the participants. Smaller gatherings also took place at other dates, which might be fixed quite arbitrarily. The local experts would then arrive to the number of thirteen, a chief and twelve subordinates. These persons comprised a 'coven' in English, this word being a shortened form of 'covenant', meaning an agreement of two or more individuals to act in a certain way.

The earliest surviving mention of the ceremony as such appears in a manuscript of the early fourteenth century, where the word is spelt 'coueyne'. There it is stated that a priest's daughter, who may or may not have been illegitimate, led a company of twelve 'fools' to dance in a churchyard. In the 1440's the notorious sex maniac Gilles de Rais was declared at his trial to be the chief of a Coven. Gilles, a Marshal of France and loyal companion of Jeanne d'Arc, as well as a generous patron of literature and music, a skilled painter and bookbinder and a learned alchemist, but also a frantically sadistic mass murderer in his later years, was duly hanged after proceedings which will be discussed in a later chapter of the present work. He is only referred to in the context of 'witchcraft' because his career luridly illustrates the close connection always evident between 'black magic', as it afterwards came to be called, and erotic excesses.

In 1484 Pope Innocent VIII addressed a Bull to the Inquisition Fathers Jakob Sprenger and Heinrich Kramer, both German Dominicans, Kramer being also known as Henricus Institoris, requesting these learned authorities to prepare a detailed study and exposure of the whole 'perilous heresy' of witchcraft in order that it might be stamped out for good by the exertions of all true Christians. Central Europe being regarded as the hotbed of these vile practices the Fathers got to work at Innsbruck in 1485 and produced their *magnum opus*, entitled *Malleus Maleficarum* ('Hammer of Female Witches'), in 1487. It remained the ultimate authority on the subject for two hundred years.

The strange mixture of industrious pedantry and morbid interest in appalling sexual crimes is perhaps more often found among the Teutonic peoples than elsewhere. At any rate Bohemia soon began to be and long remained the centre of such preoccupations, as Leopold Sacher-Masoch discovered in the nineteenth century. The *Malleus* is a characteristic product of this sort of mentality.

It aroused the humorous scorn of the stout Protestant gentleman Reginald Scot, who issued his counterblast, *The Discoverie of Witchcraft*, in the same year as the first edition of the German Inquisitors' massive volume appeared. Scot's compilation was edited in 1886 by Dr. Brinsley Nicholson, who found much curious information in it. Witches, it seemed, could 'deprive men of their privities and otherwise of the act and use of venerie'. On the arrest of these women their pubic hair was shaved in order to make certain whether or not the devil had branded his secret countersign on the vulva, or hidden any telltale object in it.

The claim of Sprenger and Kramer that witches 'use incestuous adulterie with spirits' is termed 'a stale ridiculous lie' by Scot. He also calls 'verie ridiculous' the statement that they 'use venerie with a divell named Incubus, even when they lie in bed with their husbands and have children by them which become the best witches'. Similar contempt is meted out to stories of their 'kissing the divell's bare buttocks' by way of sealing their oaths of fealty to him and to the rumour that 'certain magicall heretikes, to wit the Eutychians, assemble every Good Friday night, put out the candles and fornicate, father with daughter, brother with sister and son with mother'. Children born of these

WITCHCRAFT

incestuous unions, says the *Malleus*, are slaughtered and burnt, their blood and ashes being mixed into a potion useful for several nefarious purposes.

At Lyons, we hear, a certain girl got out of bed in the middle of the night, smeared herself all over with a magic ointment and incontinently vanished. Her lover, who had been with her in the chamber, followed her example. He was conveyed to an assembly of witches in Lorraine and in his surprise at their antics invoked the name of God. The witches immediately disappeared, leaving him naked and alone. After returning to Lyons the terrified young man formally indicted his mistress for witchcraft and she was burned alive by the municipality.

The pagan goddess Diana and the infidel princess Herodias, who danced with the severed head of John the Baptist, are said on occasion to lead the covens.* The wizard Merlin, apparently, was born of a succubus (female demon) fertilised by a human male, whereupon the succubus changed to an incubus (male demon) and passed on the sperm within it to a woman.

Witches are also to be seen 'in fields and woods prostituting themselves uncovered and naked up to the navill, wagging and mooving their members in everie part according to the disposition of one being about that act of concupiscence and yet nothing seen of the beholders upon hir'. Afterwards a black vapour rises from the witch's body, indicating the departure of the incubus.

Husbands occasionally catch a glimpse of such a demon in their matrimonial chambers and try to behead it. But the wound inflicted closes at once and the fiend gets to work again on the wife, often to her secret joy, since many women prefer supernatural to natural copulation. On the other hand men who couple with witches often lose their generative organs altogether. One young fellow got his back, but only after half throttling the girl. Another gentleman in this predicament was advised by a second witch to climb a certain tree where he would find a

---

* Herodias, the wife of Herod Antipas, who beheaded John, had previously married Herod Philip. She had a daughter by him named Salome. It is generally assumed in modern literature that this Salome was the unnamed 'damsel' who danced before her mother's second husband. But medieval tradition, supported by the nineteenth century British theologian F. J. A. Hort, supposed the girl to be the daughter by Herodias of Herod Antipas himself, who had named the child Herodias after her mother.

whole 'nest' of male members, twenty or thirty at least, which had been abstracted, like his own, from their former possessors. He seized the biggest he could find, but was at once ordered by the witch, who stood below, to put it back, as it belonged to the parish priest. This obviously manufactured rustic jest seems to have been taken in all seriousness by the reverend Inquisitors.

Another of the same kind relates that a certain lady, believing that she was being assaulted by an incubus in her bed, uttered a loud shriek. The rest of the household rushed into the room. They did not see the incubus. But they found a bishop hidden under the bed. A more credible anecdote reports that a certain saintly nun offered to take the place of one of her colleagues who was being terribly worried by such a demon.

Mr. Scot remarks, very shrewdly, that it is not always easy to discover which cases of alleged 'possession' are genuine and which faked as 'lecheries covered with the cloke of incubus and witchcraft'. He deplores exorcists who find it necessary to couple with hysterical females on an altar in order to drive out the possessing imp from their bodies. He wonders whether lovelorn girls who dish up sections of their faeces to evasive males will really gain their affection in this way, as advised by the local sorceress. He doubts whether angels in fact castrate holy men who are tempted by nuns or other women. He is sceptical of spitting through one's wedding-ring as a cure for impotence. But he believes that if a penis is capable of erection but not ejaculation it must be bewitched. It might then do some good to offer up a waxen image of the offending member in church, at St. Anthony's altar preferably.

For demons 'use great knaverie and unspeakable bawderie in the breech and middle parts of man and woman by tickeling and other lecherous devises'. But stories of terrestrial spirits or 'fairies' swooping down on young agricultural labourers and carrying them off 'a hundred leagues in the air' for an orgy of fornication, after which the lad is found lying senseless in a meadow, miles from anywhere, naked and usually without a penis, are only told, according to Scot, to raise a laugh.

The clergy who were enjoined to study the endless lore of witchcraft in order to disentangle truth from falsehood in all these weird statements, often made on oath, had a difficult task.

WITCHCRAFT

For they were severely handicapped by the belief, then universal, that the sublunary world swarmed with fiends of all descriptions, big and little, capable of anything, from disguises and invisibility to 'possession', rape and murder. But one outstanding fact was clear to the earnest salvationists. Those who 'denied God', of course through the agency of some devil or other, automatically turned into sex maniacs. The evidence appeared overwhelmingly decisive. We can now see that it expressed the more or less conscious rebellion of medieval man against the official tabus on carnal appetite. But to the inquisitors and exorcists it could only be the influence, in particular, of one Asmodeus, the hell-born expert on erotic perversions, from bestiality to lust for the Persons of the Trinity Themselves and even the Virgin Mother of Christ.

Detailed testimony came in profusion. Actual corpses could be animated by Asmodeus and sent to seduce the living, especially on feast-days, when sin would have the most serious consequences. Such festivals were, as noted in a previous chapter of the present survey, the excuse for more than usually riotous conduct by 'Fools' and their cronies. The witches and wizards who submitted to supernatural intercourse on those and other occasions generally complained of the icy coldness of the devil's sperm and of the painful and bloody lesions caused in their flesh by the subsequent withdrawal of the huge, scaly phallus.

The concentration upon such repulsive particulars proves that by the fourteenth century at any rate the revolt had become to a considerable degree hysterical. For this reason Dr. Margaret Murray's ingenious theory that witchcraft was nothing more nor less than the obstinate survival of 'la vecchia religione', with its joyous, irresponsible paganism, can only be half true. There were much more morbid elements than merely jolly and benevolent fertility rites in the flood of obscenities sworn to by prisoners and witnesses alike in the ecclesiastical courts. The famous Bull of Pope Innocent VIII in 1484 charges the covens with the very reverse of life enhancement.

'It has come to our ears that numbers of both sexes do not avoid to have intercourse with demons, incubi and succubi, and that by their sorceries, incantations, charms and conjurations they suffocate, extinguish and cause to perish the births of women, the increase of animals, the corn of the earth, the grapes of the vineyard and the fruit of the trees, as well as causing men, women, flocks and herds and other animals to suffer and be tormented from both within and without, so that men beget not nor women conceive and they thus impede the conjugal action of men and women.'

It is certain, in fact, that many witches brewed poisons and abortifacients, causing sickness and impotence. They could not, of course, initiate bad weather or bad luck. But no doubt they often tried to and were generally believed responsible for such accidents. Witches might indeed promote health and fertility by the use of herbs and concoctions unknown to or despised by professional doctors. But just as often they could and did take vengeance on their enemies or people they disliked by charging them with malevolent witchcraft, discovered by the magical *clairvoyance* of the accuser, herself or himself known to be a witch or wizard.

A second objection to Dr. Murray's theory is the absurdity of the ceremonies, e.g. the kissing of the devil's anus when he appeared in the form of a sheep or goat. Their coarsely orgiastic character also precludes the idea of a serious heathen cult. Witchcraft under Christianity seems much more likely to have been started as a defiant perversion of the official religious worship, a 'Black Mass', with the Devil replacing God, staged by revolutionaries who had sickened of the current convention of sexual austerity.

In any case it is incontrovertible that a mental disturbance or 'black-out', at the very least a clouding of normal consciousness, accompanies both a specific procreative orgasm and religious exaltation. This condition was very generally regarded by primitive peoples and also throughout the civilisations of pagan antiquity as a manifestation of 'possession' by supernatural power. The founder of Christianity himself 'cast seven devils out of' the prostitute Mary Magdalene. His followers in medieval times saw no reason to abandon the belief in question. Both St. Augustine of Hippo and St. Thomas Aquinas admitted its possibility.

WITCHCRAFT

The object of the age-old art of magic, widespread as ever after the conversion of Europe to the new faith, had always been to harness inhuman forces to the service of human wishes. Consequently, any exceptional cases of prolonged and reckless libidinous behaviour, a vice most emphatically condemned by the Church, came to be automatically attributed to 'Demons', the personified subhuman enemies of God.

So if the intermediaries, the 'witches', often superannuated harlots who brewed love-potions and so on, could be found, they were punished by the ecclesiastical authorities. A determined slaughter of them began in the thirteenth century, after the returning crusaders had terrified all Europe with tales of the horrific crimes perpetrated by oriental *djinns*. Satan gradually took shape as the irreclaimable and unforgivable opponent of the omnipotent Creator, who nevertheless allowed the eternally rebellious godling to exist and exercise formidable powers. Theology explained the paradox as part of the divine plan for educating humanity, by way of test and temptation, to be fit for immortal bliss after death.

Once this conception was understood, those persons by nature prone to sexual hysteria, or victimised by it owing to repressions deliberately adopted or forced upon them by others, could safely abjure responsibility for their actions. Women, and especially nuns, found in this expedient a safety-valve for desires they would otherwise have been ashamed to confess. But both sexes would often report that nocturnal visits by demons had aroused their lascivious appetites till they could no longer be controlled.

The Lateran Council of 1215 defined 'demons' as purely spiritual beings without bodies. It therefore contradicted the conclusion of the Second Council of Nicaea (787) which had affirmed their material existence. Not until the seventeenth century were any clearer ideas of the demoniac nature formulated.

The word in Greek (*daimon*) meant etymologically 'full of wisdom'. It was accordingly complimentary, as in the use of the term by Socrates to describe his moral inspiration. But just as the Christians turned the Olympian Apollo, the glorious sungod and patron of music and literature, into the fiend Apollyon so dramatically introduced in John Bunyan's *Pilgrim's Progress*, so the Socratic *daimon* became the 'demon', either Satan himself or one of his minions, of the new theology.

Such creatures, in their aspect of supernatural tempters to sin, especially the sin of sexual excess, had already been imagined in pre-Christian times, notably by Jewish writers such as the author (c. 250 B.C.) of the Book of Tobit in the Apocrypha, a term first applied by St. Jerome to sacred literature of the second rank. The Book of Tobit is essentially a novel. One of its incidents is the pestering of the woman Sara by Asmodeus, the evil spirit subsequently adopted by the Christians as the patron of libidinous divagations. Sara is delivered from him by the archangel Raphael, whose name means 'God heals' in Hebrew. Raphael advises the hero Tobias to put Asmodeus to flight by cooking the liver of a fish. 'For the smoke then arising banishes all kinds of demons for ever.'

St. Augustine of Hippo declared in his *City of God* (XV. 23.) that 'satyrs and fauns, commonly called incubi, have often distressed women by demanding and obtaining intercourse with them'. St. Anthony is said by St. Jerome to have met one of these beings in the form of a dwarfish male with claws, horns and goat's feet. This individual was not in the least perturbed when the saint made the sign of the cross over him. On the contrary he politely offered the holy man some dates. He then informed St. Anthony that he was a mortal inhabitant of the desert, one of those called 'fauns, satyrs or incubi by the Gentiles', and begged the saint to pray for him, since he believed in the Christian religion. On the other hand the Roman philosopher Boethius (480-524) refers in his *History of Scotland* to a young man who was tempted in vain for months on end by such a personage, disguised as a beautiful and highly lascivious young lady.

The traces of classical mythology surviving among the early Christians are clear from these stories. But the various arguments about the real nature of demons were not exhaustively summarised and a definite decision reached until the Italian Franciscan divine Ludovico Maria Sinistrari (1622-1701) of Pavia wrote his *Demonialitas*. This treatise remained, however, in manuscript for nearly two hundred years. No doubt printers feared the censorship of Rome. At last Isidore Lisieux of Paris published it, with an accompanying French translation, in 1875.

Sinistrari was not, of course, a man of the Middle Ages. He was a typical late Renaissance scholar, robust, witty and deeply learned in his subject. The anecdotes he relates in support of his conclusions, if not those conclusions themselves, may fairly be taken, though he is chary of dates, to refer for the most part to the medieval heyday of the 'demon'.

He is careful to divide cases of sexual intercourse between demons and human beings into two classes. In the first place a witch or a wizard might contract to enter the service of Satan in order to obtain a life of power, wealth and inordinate sensuality, as a reward for behaving in a way exactly the opposite of that expected of even a moderately decent Christian. The wizard or witch might guarantee, for example, to commit at least one murder a month and to sin every week to a positively fearful extent of sacrilege and lustful frenzy. The pact would always be sealed by an act of fornication, sodomy or bestiality with a demon, usually the chief sorcerer present at the ceremony of initiation.

Secondly, perfectly innocent men or women might succumb to the lewd approaches of a suitably disguised fiend. If repulsed, he might play various disagreeable tricks on the objects of his desires, such as suddenly causing all their garments to fall off in the middle of a crowded street, leaving them naked to the ridicule or actual sexual aggression of passers-by. A series of such practical jokes might well succeed when more tender expedients, at which demons were universally agreed to be expert, had failed.

But in such cases witchcraft is not of course employed by the human partner. The sin therefore amounts to little more than a practically involuntary 'pollution', as in any ordinary seduction of some otherwise blameless person by the craft or impudence of a libertine.

As for the wholly voluntary human participants in demoniac couplings, they are naturally beyond the pale of forgiveness. During the preliminary rites they were marked on the anus, breasts or sexual organs with a sign representing a toad, spider or other creature detested by most people. In the case of women who actually wished to conceive an offspring from their supernaturally gifted associate in the copulation, he would convey semen for this purpose—since his own would be sterile—from some virile human male, either by submitting to sodomy by such a person or else by manual operation on his penis. The sperm thus obtained would then be transferred by the demon to the woman's matrix.

Sinistrari, a man of versatile erudition, knew enough about biology to discredit this absurd statement by former writers on demonology. He denied that, as some theologians had maintained, Plato, Alexander the Great, Augustus Caesar, Merlin and —of course!—Martin Luther were generated in this way. Nor does he agree with Josephus, Clement of Alexandria and Tertullian that demons are fallen angels. He considers that they are 'reasonable animals with human bodies and souls capable of salvation or damnation'.

He believes, however, that they can sexually possess beings otherwise much resembling themselves, can appear in disguise and vanish when they please. He recommends that women seen to behave in an erotic manner when no one else seems to be present should have their premises searched for evidence of sorcery, for instance bones and skulls, bunched feathers, the wings or feet of bats, live toads or snakes, various sorts of seeds, jars of certain powders and unguents and finally wax figurines for needling so as to torment an absent person, a practice often referred to by pagan writers, as for example in a well known Idyll of Theocritus.

If any such objects are found, the woman should be forced, by torture if necessary, to confess that she is a witch. For only other witches, whose evidence is not legally admissible, could testify to that effect. Sinistrari complacently adds, however, that in Italy, his own country, the death penalty by hanging or burning was seldom pronounced in his day, though it was constantly inflicted abroad.

One of the most amusing of his stories, probably from a medieval source, is of a nun who swore that one of her colleagues, with whom she had quarrelled, was regularly copulating in her cell with some unknown person. She had heard, she said, from her own cell next door, unmistakable sounds of such a performance. They included, to her abbess's horror, the *poppysmata* mentioned in one of Martial's most comic epigrams (I. viii. 18).

WITCHCRAFT

The *Glossarium Eroticum Linguae Latinae* (Paris, 1826) explains *poppysmata* as the kind of hissing emitted by grooms at work on horses.

Martial, in the epigram quoted, addresses a prostitute named Gala. 'Can you wonder if, although you are very good-looking, so few lovers desire you? For your disability is a serious one. You don't speak by word of mouth while the act is in progress. But unfortunately other sounds are then heard over which you seem to have no control. I find these noises most offensive and would much prefer to hear actual speech from you, no matter how silly. Symmachus has suggested that a different form of sexual congress might silence the clamour to which I refer. Such a procedure would certainly be more fun than listening to those dismal *poppysmata*, which take all the heart out of the business both mentally and physically. So please stop them and substitute human speech. If you can't think of anything to say they can easily teach you a couple of dozen phrases.'

Sinistrari's anecdote is designed to prove that sexual possession of a woman by a male demon (incubus) would be mechanistically the same as in purely human copulation. The converse case is illustrated by the great Honoré de Balzac, one of the half dozen foremost novelists in European history. He included a story about a succubus in his *Contes Drolatiques* (1833), which were written throughout in medieval French. Balzac knew what he was talking about. His tale throws a good deal of light on the demonology of the period (thirteenth century) when the events narrated are supposed to have happened. They are allegedly reported by one Hierosme Cornille, an ecclesiastical magistrate of the Chapter of St. Maurice in Tours Cathedral. He had been requested by certain citizens to investigate the behaviour of a demon disguised as a woman. The creature had been arrested and lodged in a dungeon belonging to the Chapter.

This fiend had first been seen, dressed as a Saracen maiden, in the company of a returned crusader, the Lord of Bueil. It was then living at his expense in a cottage rented from a local innkeeper. The crusader looked very ill, the lady full of beans. Nine days after she moved into the cottage the knight died and was buried. His squire told the neighbours that his master had remained 'warmly coupled' to the Moorish girl for seven whole days 'without coming out of her'. She was said to have tied him to her person by her long hair, which was 'charged with hot qualities', being 'the fires of hell in the form of lust' and causing the unfortunate man to continue copulating under this medieval form of electrotherapy until 'his soul was drawn out of his body and transmitted to Satan'.

The innkeeper deposed that after the crusader's death he called on the Saracen to enquire whether she intended to stay on at the cottage. The door was opened by 'a half-naked black man with white eyes', who conducted the visitor to the lady's presence. He found her gorgeously, if scantily, arrayed, glittering with gold and jewels and, shocking to relate, lying on a couch with a second lover. The innkeeper, a thoroughly respectable man, immediately fled, in case he, too, should lose his soul to charms which he described as overwhelmingly seductive.

Other citizens testified to having heard sounds of diabolical revelry in the cottage. It was brightly lit up at night and surrounded, though the season was winter, by tropical flowers and vegetation. The wife of a neighbouring labourer declared that her husband, doubtless owing to the proximity of supernatural lechery, had amazed her at that time by his sexual assiduity.

Another crusader, of unimpeachable morals and credibility, no less than Hardouin V, Lord of Maille, affirmed on oath that he had seen the devilish Saracen maid at Damascus. The deceased knight, he said, had won her in single combat with Geoffroy IV, Lord of Roche-Pozay. Other crusaders who lain with the woman, Hardouin added, told him that they had always found her to be a virgin.

A wealthy Jew then stated that he had sold the girl-demon a great deal of plate, jewellery and textiles imported from the East, together with many rare flowers, spices and wines from the same quarter. In answer to the magistrate he denied that he had provided her with any sorcerers' material. The lady had been perfectly charming to him. He confessed that he had eventually made love to her, for one night only. This affair could not be prolonged, however, for, ever since, he had been absolutely impotent. Nevertheless, he assured the Chapter that if they would release so delightful, if disconcerting, an ornament to society, he would be prepared to foot the bill for completing one of the towers of the cathedral.

After the mother of the dead crusader had sworn that he had refused absolution on his death-bed, the leader of a group of young gentlemen who had tried to rescue the Saracen from her dungeon supported the Jew's opinion of her as most attractive, modest, charitable and now deeply repentant of her sins. The youth, who was only twenty years of age, proclaimed with tears that he had vowed a chaste and eternal love for her. But the magistrate, shrugging his shoulders, dismissed this obviously bewitched witness to the care of his father.

Astonishing evidence was next submitted by a high-ranking abbess. She solemnly revealed that the so-called Saracen had once been a novice in her convent. But the girl had mysteriously escaped and never returned. The abbess, in measured tones, registered her belief that the child had been an emissary of Satan, sent to undermine the faith and morals of her nuns.

The prisoner herself was finally interrogated. She averred that she was born in Mauretania of unknown parents, that her name was Zulma and that she had learnt French in France, where she had lived for twelve years, ever since the age of fifteen. She admitted having entered the abbess's convent and swore she was still a Christian. She had been lured away from the nunnery, she sobbed, by a monk on an official visit to the establishment. He had been the first to initiate her into the pleasures of fornication. Then she fell in love with the Lord of Amboise and ran away with him to his castle. But one day this gentleman had been so imprudent as to allow a visitor, the Lord of Roche-Pozay, to whom he had boasted of her beauty, to see her coming naked out of a bath. The two knights had then fought for her. Roche-Pozay won and carried her off, against her will, on the last crusade. She confirmed the previous evidence that the Lord of Bueil finally took her back with him to France and soon afterwards died, having refused to see a doctor in spite of her fervent entreaties that he should do so.

Taxed with promiscuity, she swore she had never sinned except in true love. She could only regret that so many of her lovers came to a bad end. She had always prayed for the repose of their souls. But she confessed she was hot-blooded and accepted many

valuable presents from gentlemen she could not resist.
She utterly repudiated the suggestion that she had ever been
possessed by the Devil. 'Why then,' demanded the magistrate
patiently, 'do you speak so many languages, as has been here
proved, and why have you never, in spite of so long and incessant
an amorous career, given birth to a child?'

She replied that she only knew two or three words of Latin and
Greek, that French was her mother tongue and Arabic that which
she had learnt in Syria. She put down her childless state to the
will of God and, curiously enough, to the exceptional pleasure
she derived from sexual intercourse.

But her judges were not convinced by this defence. The Court
ordered her to be tortured, so as to expel the demon which had
inspired her story from her body. The Bench also decreed that
her sexual organs should be examined by a doctor in order to
discover any signs of abnormality in that quarter.

The girl thereupon, in a last effort to soften the hearts of her
persecutors, stripped herself. The archbishop presiding threw
down his pen and left his seat in disgust. But Hierosme Cornille,
then aged seventy-nine, was much affected by this exhibition.
Feeling like a young boy again, he adjourned the hearing and
roamed the streets for a long time, wrestling with his temptation.

Then he went to the dungeon. According to his death-bed
confession he found it transformed into a bower of love. He was
feasted and lavishly entertained by the prisoner, who conjured
up all sorts of luxuries for this purpose. At last he was physically
seduced.

He coupled with her for three whole days and nights, his
'loins gripped by the hands, like steel claws, of the succubus'.
She laughed at his shame, excited him further by gross endearments
and teased him by suggesting abominable blasphemies and
caresses. He felt himself being literally lifted up in the air, so
that he flew above the earth with the demon, which continuously
called to him: 'Ride me, ride me, my rider! Hold tight to the
crupper of your mare, to her mane, to her neck! Ride, ride, ride!'

He could see below him cities and chambers in which innumerable
couples fornicated frantically, till the whole sky re-echoed
with their amorous cries. Then he beheld the globe itself copulating
with the sun and emitting a flood of stars, with voices of

storm, lightning and thunder. In a final frenzied effort to imitate the cosmic coition he saw around him, proceeding to the sound of peals of hellish laughter, he fainted.

He awoke in his own bed at home, surrounded by his servants, who were drenching him with holy water and praying with a deafening clamour. Yet he was still vaguely conscious of the succubus. It seemed to be everywhere in the room, tempting him as obscenely as ever. At length the archbishop arrived, bearing the relics of St. Gratien, who had founded the see of Tours in the third century. Thereupon the demon vanished, leaving behind a reek of sulphur so strong that everyone in the room coughed for the rest of the day.

The end of the story is given by Balzac in the form of an epilogue purporting to have been written a century later. Old Cornille, says this new author, had never possessed a woman in his life and knew nothing of their tricks. He believed everything the girl said in court and meant to have her sentence commuted to a fresh novitiate. But one of the cathedral vicars, who coveted Cornille's post, forced the poor old man to confess, on his deathbed, for he had been taken ill soon afterwards, that he had been captivated by her spells and 'performed the deed of darkness with her'. Thereupon the archbishop reopened the trial.

It was found that she had bribed the gaoler, with a diamond hidden in her private parts, to provide her with certain comforts, even luxuries, in her dungeon. This discovery lent colour to Cornille's confession. The gaoler was sacked, the cell restored to its former condition and the prisoner tortured until she, too, confessed to commerce with Satan. A stake and faggots were prepared. A determined attempt at rescue by some young men was quelled by the archbishop's troops. On the way to the place of execution the wretched captive, though now white-haired and nothing but skin and bone, broke away from her guards and took refuge in a church. But she was shot down by an arquebusier and dragged away to the fire, in which she perished most miserably.

It is clear that Balzac in this powerful and appalling tale intended to indicate the tendency to corruption and heartless brutality in a Church which he believed only too often exploited the superstition of the masses to serve a purely mundane ambition. It is perfectly true that the religious fanaticism of the day was determined to stamp out *luxuria* by any means whatever. That sin had of course grown the more rampant the more it was persecuted. But the priests found that the general belief in demons could be made a powerful weapon in their attempts to control excessive carnality in other people.

A prosperous courtesan, for example, like Zulma, set a bad example and had to be eliminated. But one couldn't execute women simply for being whores. So the only way to get rid of her for good would be to persuade laymen that she was not really a human being but a demon, an incarnation of evil to be killed on sight like a poisonous snake. It was always easy to find witnesses, either moral bigots or persons too poor to afford to pay for such a grand harlot's favours. Oaths would then be sworn that things had been seen or heard which proved the woman to be a witch, i.e. a person in league with Satan, the immortal and irreclaimable enemy of God. Her denials and protests could soon be changed, by torture, into confession. Then one could burn her with a clear conscience.

Balzac's story deals in horrifying detail with a case of this sort. But the idea of the succubus or incubus could also be made to work in favour of a notorious fornicator. He or she could say they were helpless in the hands of a wicked fiend they were only too anxious to evade—with the help, of course, of their friends, or in some instances colleagues, the priests.

Such excuses were generally made only after scandalous conduct in ordinary social life by those so 'possessed' had led to exorcism. In this practice, authorised by the Church and often illustrated in plastic art, the clergy performed certain acts and uttered certain formulae for the purpose of expelling evil spirits from the guilty party. The patient could be slapped, kicked and pummelled, stripped and bathed in holy water or searched in the most intimate fashion for hidden evidences of the demon's presence. The priest was also entitled to lay his mouth on that of the subject and blow forcibly down his or her throat, holding the writhing and often nude victim tight in his arms the while. The operator would have been superhuman if improprieties, to say the least of it, had not occasionally occurred. In the case of otherwise alluring females who tore off their garments—a frequent habit of insane or frantically excited persons—and made obscene gestures which might amount to libidinous assault on those who tried to discipline them, temptation was not invariably resisted.

Apart from instances of more or less sincerely imagined 'possession' many people became interested in witchcraft through the belief that the 'black art' would enable them to give freer rein to their lusts by seducing a larger number of persons not otherwise easily accessible. For the mysterious solemnity of magical mumbo-jumbo, the strangeness of the objects employed in its conjurations and the apparent miracles produced by them were well calculated to impress the simple-minded. The object of desire would then submit, as related in many medieval stories, to acts pronounced by the cunning enchanter to be essential for the initiation of the candidate for the devil's aid. He or she would then enter, it would be affirmed, into a kingdom of the spirit replete with unlimited delights and powers far superior to those hitherto envisaged by the neophyte.

This formula for corruption of the innocent by a mixture of religiosity and exotic paraphernalia has of course been followed from that day to this. The amorous conquests of such charlatans as the twentieth-century Aleister Crowley, certain nineteenth-century Mormon leaders and so called theosophists, both male and female, not to speak of the intervening period, prove that a blend of apparently mystical fervour and uninhibited erotomania makes a practically irresistible appeal to the curiosity of youth or inexperience. Both high and low intellectual coefficients tend to respond to it if still relatively untrained or emotionally unstable.

The methods used for libidinous purposes both in the formal Coven and more or less private extensions of it, amounting to sexual orgy when more than two people were present or fetishistic debauchery by a solitary couple, derived mainly from pagan antiquity. The buttocks or generative organs of the chief sorcerer, nearly always disguised as an animal of the kinds already mentioned, but most often a horned beast, would be kissed. Intercourse with him by the females present was obligatory if demanded. The naïve bestiality of both heathen and Christian times lies behind this feature of the ritual. The ubiquitous satyr of classical art originated in the actual known cases of coition between goatherds and their flocks, accounted for both by the loneliness of the human partner and the attractive appearance, obvious to anyone out for a walk in the fields in springtime, of kids and lambs, wide open in their helplessness to sexual enterprise by mankind.

There is some reason to believe, and it is probable on physiological grounds, that an artificial phallus was used from time to time in the copulation of the coven chief with his female acolytes. Only a Hercules could do justice to large numbers of them in a single night. The main object, moreover, of exciting them to orgiastic frenzy could be nearly as well served by a suitably constructed implement. Such aids to feminine sexual enjoyment in the absence of a lover had been brought to a high degree of perfection in the pagan civilisations. The *baubon* mentioned by the Cos islander Herodas (c. 300-250 B.C.) was a leathern reproduction, over a foot in length, of an erect penis. Aristophanes refers to it in the *Lysistrata* (109 sqq.) But he calls it, in his Attic dialect, an *olisbos*. No doubt the leather was dressed in such a way as to imitate closely the texture and consistency of human skin where stretched over the anatomical apparatus at this point of the male body. The secrets of the manufacture of such an article can hardly have been forgotten by the Christian inheritors, in a direct line, of the traditions of heathen magicians.

The confessions of witches tried in the seventeenth century refer again and again to the 'Devil's' sexual organ, variously stated to be half the length of a violin, scaly, resembling a mule's, cold as ice, red-hot and constructed of horn. But such fanciful and certainly repellent descriptions can scarcely be trusted. The prisoners were mostly illiterate old women, on trial for their lives and only concerned to arouse pity in their judges by insisting on the pain of the operations they were compelled to endure. It is likely that, on the contrary, the derivative of the Greek *baubon*, in the Middle Ages at any rate, was much more gratefully assimilable. There is no proof, however, that the medieval mock-phallus, as some authorities have argued on the analogy of modern instruments of this sort, contained a mechanism for the ejaculation of hot milk.

WITCHCRAFT

What did happen, according to the depositions of certain women who accused others, or persons unknown, of casting spells on them and sending demons to them by night, was that the sexual organ of the incubus assumed a bifurcated shape at the instant of contact. One 'prong of the pitchfork', accordingly, penetrated the vulva and the other the anus.

In all these cases the Church had to decide whether the presence of incubus or succubus had been invited by the human partner in fulfilment of an agreement with the Devil or whether the woman or man who underwent these super-erotic experiences could be a victim of sorcery. Those proved to belong to the first category, usually through the admission that they were awake at the time, were handed over to the secular power for execution. The others were more or less violently exorcised by what we should call shock treatment. That this action repeatedly involved the exorcist in sadistic and the patient in masochistic excitation is highly probable.

Medieval witchcraft in general, like that of the East and as a rule unlike that of classical antiquity, was taken seriously by almost everyone, certainly by the laws, the Church and the masses of the people. Among the pagans, sceptics like Aristophanes, Lucian and Apuleius more or less openly ridiculed the practice of sorcery as either fraudulent or insane. Such poets as Euripides (in the *Medea*), Theocritus and Herodas as well as many others in Rome, from Catullus to Juvenal, refer to magic mainly for literary effect. But in Hellenistic times and places, and during the long decadence of the Roman Empire, the steady encroachment of oriental religions, with their strongly contrasting conceptions of abstract good and evil, induced a more severe attitude to witches and wizards.

Fewer and fewer clear heads and mocking dispositions maintained the reputation of the Mediterranean races for common sense. More and more professors of incantation from Africa and the Levant arrived to take charge of Roman citizens who could no longer believe in the gods of Olympus or deified emperors but still felt nostalgia for religious authority. With the advent of Christianity, proclaiming a definite moral dualism, that of the Holy Trinity in heaven and the fallen angel Satan and his imps in hell, the whole picture changed. Magicians were then regarded as either actual demons or deserters from Christ to the Devil. They inspired something like panic as the only incarnate representatives of the formidable underworld to be found on its surface.

The extraordinary detestation of sexual appetites and their concrete expression which the new doctrine imposed officially on its priests originated in extreme reaction from the characteristically chaotic laxity in this respect of a dying culture. The Empire was believed to be perishing from this cause alone, to the exclusion of the vast complex of purely historical, political and economic factors which was in fact responsible. The unworldly early Fathers could not see them as a coherent whole. But they could see the social abuses to which unrestrained concupiscence could lead in so large and still so wealthy and powerful a community. So they came down like a ton of bricks on the naïvely obsessed pursuit of *luxuria* which most differentiates the average sensual human being from a mystical ascetic.

Revolt was naturally inevitable. But it was driven metaphorically and sometimes literally underground, to the private laboratories in cell and tower, in cavern and on hilltop, in thick glades and remote wildernesses, of the devotees of occult science. They advertised, in due secrecy, their nostrums for, in particular, continuing to satisfy the irrepressible urge to promiscuous love-making in despite of all the fulminations of the ecclesiastical hierarchy. Neither its threats nor its promises, they declared, could be implemented in face of the cunning of the demons, so experienced in resistance to divine coercion ever since the serpent tempted Eve in Eden.

Their great advantage consisted, it was alleged, in the fact that they could offer immediate carnal gratifications in this present world without delay, while God Himself could only assure Christions of eternal but rather vaguely defined spiritual bliss after death. In these circumstances it was no wonder that the extravagance of medieval bodily lusts, procreative desire being practically universal, far outpaced that of the equally inordinate austerities and self-mortifications of the relatively few saints and anchorites. Consequently, the reports of sexual frenzy in the Middle Ages seem almost incredible to a modern mind. They generally involved, owing to the hated rigour with which they were persecuted by legal and ecclesiastical decrees, hitherto unheard of blasphemies in the Black Mass and other ceremonies such as those of the covens.

The maniacal fury with which the Christian rituals were befouled reached its height when a slit was cut in the Host itself and used for producing seminal emission in the male. In 1348 the commission of incest on the altar was said to be the only way of avoiding, under Satan's protection, infection by the Black Death. Such grotesque inventions were formalised, with the characteristic medieval love of schematisation, in regular programmes which remind a modern reader of Sade's in *The 120 Days of Sodom* when a quartet of human monsters gathers in a Swiss castle to outdo all their predecessors in atrocities.

According to one chronicler those who sold themselves to the Devil devoted Sundays to the more recondite types of sexual perversion, Mondays and Tuesdays to straightforward fornication, Wednesdays to blasphemies, Thursdays to bestiality and sodomy, Fridays to blasphemy again and Saturdays to further forms of Thursday's debauchery. The classification leaves something to be desired imaginatively. It reeks of the vague horror with which orthodox ecclesiastics regarded the sins grouped under the heading of *luxuria*. Probably the list is an invention based upon an imperfect memory of more logical and detailed information heard with such distaste that it was soon half forgotten. The plan of the *120 Days* is far neater and better thought out.

However that may be, the very idea of the Black Mass, which did take in, on its way to Satan's throne, such perversions as coprophily and necrophily, hardly known in the ancient world, marked a decisive stage in the long history of rebellion against the tyranny, itself perverse, of clerical dictation in the sexual field.

Physical love had been locked out. But it returned, as Horace (Ep. I. x. 24) had long ago warned the fanatics, at a gallop, by the back entrance. Its irruption made a great deal of noise in the Middle Ages. After the fifteenth century its revels, though still formally condemned by bigots, were held much more openly. They proceeded more in the spirit of a classical symposium, with less vindictive repudiation of religious control. For Christianity had grown tolerant under the impact of revised knowledge and appreciation of the civilisations of ancient Greece and Rome. Not until the era of popular revolutions began at the end of the eighteenth century did avowed atheists come back into social favour. By then the excesses of their medieval predecessors were remembered only by a few obscure specialists.

VII Whoredom

THE wits of all ages and all countries have always affirmed prostitution to be the oldest profession in the world. It was certainly organised and regulated at a very early stage in the history of civilisation. Christian Europe inherited from imperial Rome the *lupanaria* ('wolves' dens') or more facetiously *columbaria* ('pigeon-houses'), buildings in which women lived at the disposal of any male citizen who cared to resort to them for the purpose of extra-marital fornication. The systems of establishment and control varied. But payment by the visitor was always essential. A theoretically fixed scale of charges was imposed, graduated according to the supposed attractions of each inmate, assessed by the supervisor of the place, who might or might not be a municipal officer. But of course the whores in question extorted all they could from their clients.

The disciples of Jesus of Nazareth included many harlots, of whom Mary Magdalene and Mary of Alexandria later became famous for their conversion. One of the three saints named Pelagia in the Christian calendar had been a celebrated courtesan in Antioch, where she was converted by the bishop, Nonnus. Other prostitutes who were canonised included St. Afra of Augsburg, where she had kept a brothel. Some clerical clients converted her. But she was caught in the wave of persecution initiated by the emperor Diocletian in the early fourth century and burnt alive. In later times her image could be found in bawdy-houses all over the continent. Other examples of popular female saints who had once led gay lives and whose festivals were famed for their licentious rioting were St. Verena of Zurzach in Switzerland and St. Vreke of Liège in Belgium. The somewhat excessive adoration of these personages by the masses of the people, when much more conventional figures were available for their worship, perhaps signifies a reaction, for which of course there is a great deal of other evidence, against the mania for virgins, as characteristic of the early Fathers as of any oriental despot or Victorian rake, though naturally the learned and austere Christian apologists cultivated chaste young ladies in a purely spiritual sense.

St. Jerome defined prostitution, of which he obviously knew very little, as mere promiscuity. His successors argued solemnly about the numbers of separate lovers of a woman which would be enough for her to deserve the name of harlot. Estimates varied between many thousands and three. By the third century it was being maintained that any woman who copulated for any purpose except procreation automatically became a prostitute, whether she received a financial reward for her complaisance or not.

Medieval gentlemen preferred blondes. All through the Middle Ages the yellow or red haired girl had a better chance of getting on in life, respectably or otherwise, than the brunette. This primitive delight in bright colours extended to representations of the Madonna herself and even Christ, whose divinity was almost always emphasised by a fair beard and light hair.

Some of the early Christian heresies, the Manichean, for example, approved prostitution, partly under Asiatic influence, since in that continent formal religious whoredom was in vogue in the temples, as it had been in ancient Greece. Other ideas were that in the first place amorous ecstasy resembled the exaltation of mystical piety and secondly that the greater the sinner the more joy there would be in heaven over his or her salvation. There was an obvious danger in such notions and the orthodox Church set itself resolutely against them.

Yet the medieval harlot's life was for long permeated through and through with dogmatic Christianity. It was not so much of a joke as might at first be supposed when the bawdy-houses of the Middle Ages were so often called 'abbeys', with their 'abbesses' and 'nuns'. The buildings were full of holy images. In Russia right up to the twentieth century the girls prayed to them before submitting to a client, in the hope that the saints addressed would respond by preventing disagreeable consequences of the act in view, e.g. disease, childbirth or simply sadism on the part of their partners. But after the prayer the image or picture was invariably turned to the wall or covered with a cloth.

Another custom taken over by the Christians from their pagan predecessors was the long-lived opinion that no very great difference subsisted between any public entertainer and a whore or paid sodomite. Brothels actually continued to be called 'musicos' in nineteenth-century Holland. St. Cyprian stated in so many words that the stage was merely a school of fornication. In the fourth century a determined effort was made to get rid of plays and players for good. By the sixth their social prestige had reached a very low ebb, about the level accorded to gipsies everywhere in the eighteen hundreds and under German National Socialism in the nineteen thirties and forties. Musicians and dancers, even the performers of sacred dramas, tramped the roads with conjurers, quack doctors and acrobats. They were patronised only by small rural groups. They were constantly rounded up and imprisoned, or even just slaughtered, by local authorities. At the great Church festivals, however, they remained conspicuous and as a rule immune from interference.

Their irrepressible vitality saved them. After the crusades, when they were reinforced by accomplished Saracen captives and Muslims from Spain and Sicily, they regained popularity under a declining clerical hierarchy which was finding discretion the better part of a discredited valour. All the same, their reputation as exuberant erotomaniacs stuck. It is still not extinct.

Meanwhile the actual professional prostitutes had multiplied in spite of all that the laws, both canon and secular, could do to suppress them. The absence in Syria of so many kings and lords, knights and men-at-arms, who might otherwise have supported these enactments by force, rendered them largely ineffective. Moreover, with so many local males away, young women in the villages and towns grew restless and went to seek their fortunes elsewhere. Unescorted, they almost invariably found harlotry the only resource open to them. By the thirteenth century most of the big cities had flourishing brothels in every street.

In England they were always called 'stews', i.e. vapour baths, the provision of this amenity serving as a transparent veil for their real purpose, in accordance with the obstinate British practice, notable even then, of not looking unpleasant facts in the face. King Henry II had passed strict regulations for their control in 1161. His bishops helped him. The see of Winchester supervised eighteen bawdy-houses in Southwark alone. Their inmates were named 'Winchester geese' by the irreverent. These places, half tavern and half public bath, were registered under such inn-signs as 'The Bell', 'The Swan' and so on.

By 1381 they had become the property of the Lord Mayor of London, Sir William Walworth. He packed them with the Flemish whores, much admired for their full figures and golden hair, who now swarmed in the capital as one result of the prosperous wool trade between Harwich and the Hague. The Kentish rebels under Wat Tyler captured the whole lot for a few days. Perhaps they would have done better politically if they hadn't.

It is rather strange that the Church never seems to have grasped the close connection between drinking and casual fornication. Wine-bibbing, though it so often led to the titillation of sexual appetite, was never attacked with anything like the ferocity that hunted down the concupiscent. It is true that most of the bishops were old and old men find alcohol an agreeable substitute for other carnal pleasures in which they have less capacity. Yet it must have been obvious enough that the tavern existed largely for the stimulation of younger men to erotic exploits, since harlots could always be seen in and about such places, which generally disposed of convenient accommodation for the slaking of quite different desires. The concentration of the ecclesiastical censors upon the persons of prostitutes alone, to the exclusion of those who prepared their victims for the sacrifice to Venus, seems a bit short-sighted.

The early Christian legislators in fact found it difficult to make up their minds what to do about this oldest of professions. Was it really immoral? In 386 St. Augustine of Hippo compared whores with hangmen. 'Remove harlots,' he wrote in a characteristic epigram, 'and you will pollute the whole world with the crime of lust.' He was of the same opinion as modern sociologists who have maintained that in the absence of venal women rape, seduction and adultery, with all the social disorder that they entail, would increase to an insufferable extent.

That there is something in this argument is proved by the prevalence of erotic violence, to say nothing of unconcernedly accepted copulation, in States which outlaw the brothel. It has sometimes been urged that, man being naturally polygamous, monogamy encourages prostitution. But whores have always been as plentiful in polygamous as in monogamous communities. The fact is that the human male, everywhere and at all times, has an appetite for fornication only susceptible of limitation at the primitive stage by force or superstition and in developed cultures by custom, economic circumstance, alternative attractions and moral considerations. The doubts felt by the early Christian Fathers about the degree of guilt in a harlot may be resolved by practical observation of the harm that she can do if allowed to operate in perfect freedom. Where executive administration is powerful, firm and respected, and the population in general educated to self-control, the incidence of breaches of the peace due to lusts of the flesh remains negligible. Elsewhere the retention of this ancient institution in the form of officially recognised and controlled bawdy-houses appears inevitable to realistic sociologists.

Like other institutions it has always needed regulation. In the East it never had much, even after the rise of Islam in the eighth century to the status of a world power. The Muslim white slavers continually raided all the Mediterranean lands of Christendom with great financial success, setting up their brothels, which became something like fashionable clubs for prosperous citizens, all over Asia Minor and North Africa. The turbaned merchants often ruined themselves for the sake of the European girls, whom in the end they had to sell to avoid destitution. Prices might amount at times to thousands of gold sequins. But when there was a slump, as in areas ravaged by war, Spanish, Italian, French or Greek concubines could be picked up for the equivalent of a shilling or two.

The example of the Arabs was soon imitated in western Europe. The first bankers of Lombardy started a chain of brothels supplied from the female captives taken in military expeditions which were often really undertaken only for this purpose, though allegedly to hunt 'heretics' or avenge political 'injustice'.

In Italy, by the eleventh century, the notorious *ruffiani*—a word of dubious derivation—came into existence. They were what we should call 'ponces', men who collected and lived on the earnings of whores, whom they treated just like cattle. Individuals were kidnapped or bought up for a song before puberty, fed, trained, seduced and then hired out regularly or resold outright, whichever seemed most profitable.

In 1260 the Spanish king Alfonso X, called the 'Learned', drew up a code of laws which distinguished five types of ponce. There were those who lived in brothels on the prices obtained for casual copulations by the women they kept. There were those who wandered about like recruiting sergeants to tempt dissatisfied girls and wives to join the great and glorious army of courtesans. There were the wholesale dealers in white slaves, purely business men who resembled stock-breeders. There were husbands who regularly prostituted their own wives. And finally there were landlords who simply leased temporary accommodation for an hour or two to any couple prepared to pay for it in advance. Any such *ruffiani* ran the risk, if caught, of relatively mild punishments, ranging from fines to exile, according to circumstances. But so long as they didn't cause riots and were generous with bribes to the authorities, neither the civil nor the ecclesiastical hierarchy troubled much about them.

The Swiss, then as now, were the most efficient and obsequious of innkeepers. This talent enabled them if they chose, as many did, to acquire big fortunes as exploiters of women. But men did not long possess a monopoly of brothel-running. The experience and shrewdness of the average superannuated harlot gave her certain obvious advantages in managing such places. The 'madam' of later centuries started in business quite early in the Middle Ages of Christendom. Some of these ladies gained such fame as disciplinarians that disobedient girls or wives would be sent to spend a term in establishments so strictly regulated rather than in a nunnery, where life, in popular estimation, was much more enjoyable. In Venice, by the fifteenth century, even nobles and priests were more or less discreetly going in for this lucrative commerce.

François Villon, at the same period, gives a vivid description in his *Grosse Margot* ballad of the daily life of a 'fancy man', i.e. a ponce who was actually the accredited lover of a whore and lived with as well as on her. Some commentators have supposed that the poet himself earned his living in this way. But probably the verses, though written in the first person, are satirical. In the war-torn England of the fourteen hundreds one Laurence Crosbiter gave his name to a system of organised robbery of clients by their temporary mistresses. 'Crossbiting' thereafter became one of the hazards, like venereal disease, of frequenting prostitutes.

The tendency of legislation was always to attempt the concentration of whoredom in the most elaborately governed brothels, keeping the women off the streets and away from the humbler type of tavern. First the Visigoths, then Charlemagne and the Byzantine emperors employed special officers for carrying out this policy. Efforts were made however to prevent married men and priests from patronising brothels. Jews, Turks and Moors were also prohibited in western Europe, at any rate in those areas despotically controlled by the Christian Church, from entering any recognised houses of assignation.

But in spite of all this anxious supervision the European brothel, in Christian as in pagan times, repeatedly formed a centre of disturbance. It is significant that during the late medieval period from the eleventh to the fifteenth century the word in English meant a destructive or at any rate turbulent person. For this reason the rougher whorehouses proliferated in the suburbs of a town or outside the gates, where effective control was less practicable. There the clients and prostitutes habitually assembled at the *puteus*, the well or fountain of the district. The Italian word for a strumpet, *puta*, is to be traced back to this convention.

As a rule the churches and monasteries took care to prevent the erection of brothels anywhere near consecrated ground. But there were whole streets of the grander establishments in the large towns. By the thirteenth century they were mostly owned by the municipality and regarded by it as a valuable source of income. Accordingly, harlots who tried to have a love-life of their own were often prosecuted for wasting the time which, as State employees, they should devote to State business. In 1344, for example, at Augsburg, 'Greta the Shoemaker' ran off with a young apprentice named Bartholomäus, whose mother had just given him the equivalent of about £100. Sentence was passed in Greta's absence that she was to be blinded if she came within five miles of the city.

In the middle of the fifteenth century there was a great row between the Archbishop of Mainz and the town council because the latter disputed the prelate's right to dividends from the local brothels. Often the male manager of such a subsidised house would be a public official, sometimes the municipal hangman. But at this date courtesans were handled with much more consideration, as a rule, than they had received in the early Middle Ages. The best establishments might have a hundred inmates of all ages from twelve to seventy. They lived quite well, getting plenty of good food, baths and fresh air, and were taken to church like so many companies of soldiers.

They got to know all sorts of important people, including even an occasional visiting monarch or bishop, who would patronise the city brothel as an act of courtesy. The ground floors of even the less fashionable resorts of this nature were well provided with amenities for drinking and dicing. The resident women tended, accordingly, to look down on their freelance colleagues, who led a much more precarious and rackety existence, hounded by the Government and the Church, treated like draught animals by their clients, with no redress in law after assault or robbery, the helpless victims of a general mockery and contempt. Sometimes these wretched outcasts banded together to set up an unofficial brothel of their own. But the nearest official one would then generally be given leave, as happened at Nuremberg in the late fifteenth century, to tear it down.

In these circumstances such buildings as served ostensibly for commerce or industry, mills and barbers' shops for instance, would run accommodation for prostitutes as a sideline and allow them to hang about the place. There at least they stood a chance of being protected by the employees from fraud or violence. For such places could not afford riots, fines and the accompanying damage to their commercial reputation. So the girls' patrons would be warned to behave themselves if they valued their skins. But even so the independent street-walker only scraped up a bare living. In 1420 the average price for the use of her body was a quarter of the cost of a single egg.

Homosexual prostitution was more frequent in the tolerant East, since it could be persecuted in the West. In Venice, Paris and Rome, however, parading minions were winked at in the metaphorical as well as the literal sense. The practice so delighted the Venetians that in 1460 a Collegium Sodomitorum was set up to which doctors were obliged to report cases of patients who complained of damage to their posteriors. The formidable harlots of Venice waged relentless war on their male competitors, who could often be seen wearing womens' clothing. But the ladies could only defeat the boys by unveiling their breasts. To this expedient they regularly and vociferously resorted on a bridge still called the Ponte delle Tette.

The reformation of whores on the whole proved a failure throughout the Middle Ages. In 1198 there were mass conversions in Paris, at the height of clerical prestige and influence. All such women became nuns in special 'Magdalen' convents. But most of them soon went back to the old life. Some made of the general religious enthusiasm of the time—that of the last crusades—a new means of support. They begged their way along the roads by calling at nunneries and declaring that they wished to be converted to a more decent way of passing the time. After a few good meals, however, and quiet nights, they usually made their escape.

In England the regulations laid down under King Henry II in 1161 for the management of the 'stews' (see p. 134) provided:

'That no stew-holder or his wife should let or stay any single woman to goe and come freely at all times when they listed:
no stew-holder to keepe any woman to boord but she to boord abroad at her pleasure:
to take no more for the woman's chamber in the weeke than 14 pence:
not to keep open his doores upon the holy dayes:
not to keep any single woman in his house on the holy dayes but the bayliffe to see them voyded out of the lordship:
no single woman to bee kept against her will that would leave her sinne:

no stew-holder to receive any woman of religion or any man's wife:
no single woman to take money to lye with any man except she lye with him all night till the morrow:
no man to be drawne or inticed into any stew-house:
the constables, bayliffe and others every weeke to search every stew-house:
no stew-holder to keep any woman that has the perillous infirmity of burning nor to sell bread, ale, flesh, fish, wood, coale or any victuals.'

In other words every effort was made, with typical British hypocrisy, to keep up the fiction that the stews were simply public baths. The women could go in and out just as they pleased, like ordinary visitors. They must not be served with meals or overcharged if they wished to retire, like other bathers, to lie down while the sweat evaporated. They must not hang about the baths on feast-days or be let into the premises, any more than anyone else, on those joyous occasions of unbounded licence. Nuns and wives are not to be admitted, for such persons, if they came to the baths at all, would probably do so for an immoral purpose. Women are not to demand money from male visitors unless they intend to retire with them all night, for otherwise public indecency would ensue. No man is, of course, to be solicited to enter a place of public resort. The baths are to be inspected weekly to ensure that no criminals are hiding there and that no open improprieties are taking place.

The reference to the 'infirmity of burning' almost certainly implies gonorrhoea, which is of quite ancient origin. The date is much too early for syphilis. Finally, the baths are not to be turned into general stores.

All this regulation really became necessary owing to the growth of large towns. In the earlier Middle Ages western Europe, so often ravaged by invading hordes from every point of the compass, contained very few urban areas which still functioned as they had in the pagan centuries. The most important trading and cultural centres were all in the east, under Byzantine rule. There the brothel as it had been known from time immemorial duly flourished. Elsewhere prostitution, and to a

WHOREDOM

considerable extent life in general, had become largely nomadic.

The travelling markets and fairs attracted thousands of men and women of all types. Knights and men-at-arms acted as protective escorts. The clergy came to look after their flocks, much like actual shepherds in charge of wandering sheep. Pedlars and artisans swarmed, almost overwhelming the merchants and their staffs who formed the nucleus of these roving crowds. They had to be entertained on their long journeys. The gipsy-like musicians and singers, tragedians and comedians, tumblers and conjurers, charlatans and bear-leaders who have already been mentioned, together with their families, the younger women and girls being practically all ready to sell their favours, plus a great host of professional harlots and a few runaway nuns, swelled the multitudes of wayfarers.

Their temporary destination was usually some place famous as the site of a martyrdom. Perfectly serious persons, therefore, often joined these riotous processions of traders, warriors, clowns and whores. Few preserved their virtue for more than twenty miles or so. Such supervision as there was by local authorities encouraged the strumpets to keep the more adventurous males from attacking the women of the district, who had very good reason to fear the wildness of these 'foreign' invaders, ostensibly peaceful but often as dangerous as any barbarians. The ninth century in particular, especially in central Europe after the death of Charlemagne, suffered much from the indiscipline of these outsize mobs.

Prostitutes only gradually came to be distinguished, as a class, from other female citizens. By the eleventh century in Germany and England they were wearing skirts slit up the side in 'Directoire' style, practically to the hip, so as to show the whole of the stockinged leg. The fashion became an easily recognisable uniform, since no respectable woman ever adopted it. Smart ladies were not, in fact, to imitate the dress of whores until the age of social revolution at the end of the eighteenth century. But meanwhile plenty of whores, for obvious reasons, imitated theirs, at the risk of being at best ignominiously or at worst cruelly punished. They were lucky if they were only dragged through the streets naked, sitting on a donkey with their faces to its crupper. For mutilation, branding, burning alive or beheading awaited the more flagrant or unpopular offenders.

They were obliged in most regions to wear conspicuous colours, generally red or yellow or both, and sometimes badges or horned headdresses. Such regimentation was a sign of the hardening attitude of both secular and clerical authority towards venal women. They were beginning to be treated like Jews or infidels, persons supposedly the active enemies of Christian ethical teaching. The eleventh-century French monk Ralph Glaber wrote gloomily: 'We see clearer than daylight that as love waxeth cold and iniquity aboundeth among mankind perilous times are at hand for mens' souls ... Irreligion stalks abroad among the clergy themselves. Incontinent appetite grows among the laity. Lies and deceit, fraud and manslaughter are rife ... draw almost all to perdition ... incest and concubinage rage to an unprecedented extent. ...'

The crusades of the twelfth century offered still further opportunity for young women determined to seek adventure and affluence at any cost to their morals. They crowded to the meetings held to recruit soldiers and stuck grimly to those who rode or tramped off to the mustering places. Camp-followers of this kind being then universal, they had no difficulty in setting off to Syria with the armies. No doubt monks like Glaber and the laymen who agreed with him were glad enough to get rid of these 'eyesores' in the body politic. Yet, numerous as the crusading harlots might be, they represented a mere drop in the bucket of prostitution. Moreover, those who returned from the East had learnt a lot more about their profession and as a rule had discarded the last traces of compunction about it. They were to stimulate as never before the growing revolt of the later Middle Ages against clerical repression of the lusts of the flesh.

In 1180 the French crusaders alone had fifteen hundred whores with them. Many of the older nobles had insisted on their sons taking women of their own along so as not to be exposed to the frauds and diseases of the herds of gipsy trollops. By the beginning of the thirteenth century, with oriental girls pouring into the west with the returning knights, the position had actually worsened from the standpoint of the Church. Severe decrees began to be passed once more and every effort was made to bring

WHOREDOM

prostitutes into contempt with the lay public. It was not only a case of moral indignation. Many theologians believed that if these women got too far out of hand and turned European towns into so many Babylons heaven would smite with terrible retribution both the just and the unjust, wiping out whole communities. The Black Death of 1348 seemed to prove that they were right.

The problem was intensified by the excess of females over males in most centres of population. The men died faster through warfare, dissipation and the perils of the mania for travel which affected not only merchants but persons of all trades and professions, from prelates and diplomats to friars and tinkers. Again, in spite of all the endless tales about the concubinage of priests and the concupiscence of monks, a fair proportion of the clergy did in fact live celibate lives or at least avoided actual procreation if they possibly could. Under the commercial system of the Middle Ages, moreover, apprentices to a guild could not afford to marry anything like so early as they would have wished. On the other hand this enforced chastity did not apply to the huge numbers of maidservants employed. They could always get a job, which generally meant in practice sleeping with their male masters.

The rise of the universities in this century also automatically increased the numbers and opportunities of harlots to serve the students of theology and law who thronged such centres of learning. These young men and their girl friends in the brothels which now began to be as numerous in the west as in the east even shared a common slang. Many undergraduates also joined the freer prostitutes who tramped the roads with the gipsy entertainers. The typical medieval sentence of banishment further increased the numbers of comparatively affluent wanderers who could make it worth an attractive young woman's while to take a chance with them.

In these circumstances the professional whores combined more and more into a rebel force to be seriously reckoned with by the reigning theocracy. They grew so insolent that any man who repulsed or even censured them was liable to be called a sodomite in public. This perversion being already popularly supposed a favourite with scholars and celibates, casual listeners to these disputes were more than likely to back the strumpet against the cleric or grave secular officer.

It was not only in the university towns that the bawdy-houses multiplied at this period. In 1251 Cardinal Hugo, a prelate more jocose than most in those days, spent eight years at Lyons. His farewell address began: 'Friends! When we first came here we found three or four brothels. We leave behind us but one. I must confess, however, that it extends without interruption from the eastern to the western gate.' In Rome itself Bishop Robert Grosseteste of Lincoln, one of the boldest thinkers and practical administrators of the age, whose unceremonious methods of dealing with allegedly wayward nuns have already been noted (see p. 95) was shocked by the swarms of street-walkers he encountered. 'But,' he added with embittered sarcasm, 'just as the whole wealth of the world would not be enough to slake the avarice of Rome, so the total number of the world's prostitutes would not suffice to satisfy its lust.'

In France during the same century it was found necessary to bring the obstreperous harlots who followed the Court under centralised control.

The Frankish monarchs in particular, who held sway prior to the ninth century, had been always on the move, going from one of their big estates to another. Wherever they went swarms of harlots turned up, anxious to profit from the accompanying battalions of wealthy, debauched and half-barbarous courtiers who formed the royal escort. Consequently, the question of disciplining these women must have arisen at an early date. But it is not until the second decade of the thirteenth century that documentary evidence of any such problem is forthcoming.

So far as the French Court whores, later called 'courtesans', are concerned, an important official, directly responsible to the sovereign, governed the proceedings of their keepers, then generally male. He was known as the *Roy des Ribauds*, 'King of the Ribald'. The word meant 'lecherous' in the French vernacular of the age and in its old High German form *hriba* actually a whore. *Ribaude*, in the feminine, was also a synonym for a professionally licentious woman.

The office of the *Roy des Ribauds* is first recorded in 1214 on a list of prisoners taken at the battle of Bouvines, where

WHOREDOM

King Philip Augustus of France (Philip II 1165-1223) defeated the Emperor Otto IV. The *Roy des Ribauds* is noted as having assumed charge of one of the captives.

The functionary in question enjoyed a substantial percentage of the earnings of his subjects, including a weekly tax of about twopence—purchasing power equivalent to a modern shilling or two—paid by each woman under his jurisdiction. An order of the sheriffs of Douai dated 1242 still exists. It lays down in elaborate detail how much and on what occasions both the girls and their keepers are to pay their *Roy*. Any amateurs caught competing are to forfeit their outer garments to him, as lepers also must if they come to reside at Douai without permission. The lumping together of lepers and women, not necessarily prostitutes, who take casual lovers strikingly illustrates the new moral severity of legislation in vogue after the crusades.

A duty also performed by the *Roy des Ribauds*, especially during the earlier history of the office, was to keep ambitious wenches out of the monarch's quarters. As soon as the sovereign retired to bed the whole palace was searched from top to bottom under the *Roy's* supervision, not only for potential robbers and assassins, but also for adventurous young females who might have it in mind to obtain a hold over the almost invariably susceptible King of France by suddenly appearing in dashingly seductive guise at his bedside.

But in the thirteenth century Philip Augustas discovered that his *Ribauds*, male camp followers who brought along with them bands of *Ribaudes* amounting on occasion to some two thousand, rather unexpectedly performed prodigies of valour in his battles. He found it worth while to enrol them as a militia under the command of the *Roy*, who then took, in addition, the title of Royal Sergeant-at-Arms. He soon became one of the wealthiest and most influential officers of the Court. But under the next King he was made subordinate to the Provost of the Crown, whose orders he had to execute. Eventually, in 1422, the office was suppressed. Thereafter a woman of suitable age and rank was appointed (*Dame des filles de joie suivant la Cour*) to take over the *Roy's* responsibilities.

In the almost constant warfare of the Middle Ages he had been what one might almost call an Inspector General of the mobile brothels that accompanied the roving armies. He could certainly inflict, without consulting anyone else, the most savage punishments, including death. In 1396 he was paid sixty-eight Paris *sous*, which would be worth about £4 today, for having a certain female camp-follower, one Pernelle de la Bornette, buried alive at Compiègne for stealing plate belonging to the Court. Philip II had been much more lenient to these girls.

In the earliest regulations for the control of prostitutes the important question of hygiene is scarcely touched upon. According to the *Idylls* of the Christian poet Ausonius (d. 395) no one dreamed, in the fourth century, of cleansing the generative organs. But it seems that during the next hundred years one Moschion wrote a book on the remedies for diseases affecting that part of the body. These of course excluded syphilis, which did not appear in Europe for another millennium.

There is, however, a passage in Ovid's *Amores* (III. 7) which throws some light on the subject. He writes that, to his annoyance, he once spent a night with a courtesan who was unable, despite frantic efforts on both sides, to render his *membrum virile* fit for intercourse. At last she 'jumped out of bed and called to her attendants for water, lest they should suspect, to her disgrace, that no copulation had occurred'. It may be assumed from these lines that pagan women cleaned up after fornication. But many other references to bathing in antiquity prove that such ablutions were more of a symbolical, religious rite than a literally hygienic measure.

A different outlook began with the foundation of the medical school at Salerno in the eleventh century. This institution, which soon acquired great fame, grew up under Norman rule. The little Italian seaport, not far from Naples, had a mixed population, very typical of the cosmopolitan culture of the period. The citizens were familiar with the Latin, Greek, Hebrew and Arabic tongues. They could therefore study in the original languages the best extant medical treatises of these four civilisations, the Greek and Arabic being scientifically of the most value. The Jews, however, were the outstanding interpreters between east and west in those days, to such an extent, in fact, that if their administrative and military talents had been equal to their intellectual qualifications and they had not been generally disliked by the powerful Christian hierarchy as descendants of the crucifiers of Jesus, they might well have succeeded in setting up a composite empire far superior to any which subsequently appeared in global history.

The Salerno graduates, however, had to write in Latin, the *lingua franca* of medieval science. In the sexual field they found that little in the way of authoritative prescription was available for *post coitum* hygiene, except splashing about in a bath occasionally. One Henri de Mandeville had nevertheless already recommended women, whether facetiously or not is hard to make out from his grave Latin phrases, to wash both their inner and outer pudenda, before congress, in order to prevent the more inquisitive male from discovering how old they were.

A certain midwife named Trotula—for women as well as men attended the Salerno school—determined to remedy this deplorable situation. She rattled off the following peremptory advice to her non-professional sisters.

'A woman before coupling should purify the inner pudenda with her fingers wrapped in dry wool. She should then carefully wipe both interior and exterior organs with a perfectly clean cloth. Next, she should part the legs widely to enable all fluid to drain away from the interior parts. After doing so she should insert the cloth and draw the legs tightly together so as to dry them thoroughly. She should then chew the powder I have mentioned and rub her hands and breasts with it, also sprinkling rose-water over the pubic hair, the pubes itself and all adjacent parts, not forgetting her face. She may then, thus well prepared, approach the male.'

No doubt these were counsels of perfection not often followed. But they derive logically enough from the passion for bathing typical of all classes of Christians, as of their heathen ancestors, right down to the sixteenth century. One may perhaps assume that the male organ, if uncircumcised, occasionally underwent similar detergent attentions if the owner were exceptionally fastidious.

But the question of hygiene, except in so far as every effort was made to keep lepers out of the brothels, did not loom very large until the spread of the great epidemics of plague in 1467 and syphilis in 1496. The regular inspections, as in London every week by the magistrates' clerks, and the strict regulations which made many brothels bear a close resemblance to prisons, were directed less against the women than their closest associates, the professional thieves. For men with money to spend were more easily contacted in the bawdy-houses and taverns than elsewhere and would often give their temporary mistresses valuable information about the amounts and locations of their treasures. The brothels were accordingly centres of the criminal underworld. To leave them alone would be to encourage an anarchy already dangerously prevalent. Moreover, important visitors to a city were generally complimented by free entry to these places and had to be protected from assault and robbery if only on political grounds.

Such control was exercised exclusively by the secular authorities who by the thirteenth century owned practically all the whore-houses. The campaign of the Church against harlots as personifying the sin of fornication took more subtle forms. The women were not permitted to receive the rites of Christian marriage, visitation when sick or even burial when dead. They could not, on principle, be refused admission to a sacred edifice or access to the ear of a confessor. But they lived normally in a state of excommunication and ordinary citizens were encouraged to abominate them.

This policy bore fruit to some extent in certain regions. At the village church of Châteauneuf-Calcernier in France in 1387 some of the yokels drove out a group of prostitutes and smashed the bench on which they had been sitting. Students, apprentices and soldiers regularly beat, after due coition, the whores they picked up in the streets, though less often those they hired in the brothels. For there the male staff, the ponces or the thieves, had to be reckoned with. Sometimes the women were ill-treated by casual fornicators in a genuine revulsion of remorse. But usually the blows were a mere expression of the hatred and contempt they had been taught to feel for harlots by the clergy.

Yet by the fifteenth century, as luxury in general increased and gay gatherings in particular multiplied, the age-old profession was fighting back to some purpose. In the big cities they organised guilds and federations of their own and acquired certain civic rights, such as attendance at the regular festivals of the ecclesiastical calendar, by this time much more remarkable for their profane than their sacred character. The trollops' ranks were constantly recruited by poor girls from the country who now had much more opportunity to see how the rich lived. Many acquired wealth, fame and even social and political influence, especially in Italy. In Rome, Florence and Venice their average numbers amounted to anything between twelve and fourteen thousand. They practically swamped the great trade fairs and even the solemn Councils of the Church, such as that of Trent in 1415, where they almost monopolised the prelates' hours of relaxation.

The guilds received royal gifts. King Louis XI of France in 1474 presented the federated Paris courtesans, who numbered four thousand, with a flag and a drum and fife band of their own. They began to be called 'good ladies' (*bonnes dames*) or 'lovely madcaps' (*belles folles*) in France and 'good merchandise' (*bonarobas*) in Italy. The syphilitic might be expelled from their brothels. But they were given alms. And the municipality paid the doctors' bills. For the taxes and receipts obtained by the State from the bawdy-houses constituted a substantial item of its income. Consequently, while the Church—officially—fumed, the civil power saw to it that the girls were kept flourishing and hard at work. For if they slacked or refused clients their keepers could claim exemption from the demands of the revenue officers.

At Nîmes it was already an ancient custom for the town council to hand the chief bawd a modest but sizeable sum, with considerable ceremony, including trumpets and the imposition of garlands, on Ascension Day. In the same city, where fifteenth-century documents happen to be quite plentiful, a formal testament drawn up by a lawyer for a whore in a brothel provides for the cost of a grand funeral—the official prohibition of such processions for a prostitute being got round somehow no doubt —leaves legacies to a brother and—actually—a husband, while another person is named as her chief heir, a girl friend is left a dress and a ring and a sculptor and shoemaker are specified as executors. This complex body of instructions confirms the prosperity and good sense of the *belle folle* who dictated it. She seems to have enjoyed a standard of living well up to that of the wife of a solid burgess. Probably she behaved and dressed, when off duty, exactly like one. For the regulations about special clothing, like all other medieval regulations, could be ignored with impunity if one had enough cash, discretion and good nature to spare. The Nîmes will can only be regarded, in the present context, as one more incontrovertible proof that by the close of the medieval period the Church had lost its long battle of moral principle against the deadly sin of *luxuria* typified by the ubiquitous prostitute.

Wars with physical weapons loom larger even today than accounts of peaceful activities, including the traditional relaxations of the warrior. Throughout the Middle Ages the travelling brothels which formed part of every medieval army are far more frequently, if casually, mentioned than the stable bawdy-houses existing in areas relatively untouched by battle. For these fixed establishments were on the whole less prosperous and conspicuous than the mobile military ones, to which the élite of the body-selling profession mainly resorted. Rewards proved greater in the field than in a back street and everything was so much more exciting in the company of a great expeditionary force in all the panoply of war. As for the comparatively small numbers of independent street-walkers, their lot, as already suggested, remained so wretched that they never represented, as they did in later centuries, any serious competition with the communities of housed or tented women.

Thus the picture of whoredom during the first fifteen hundred years of the Christian era differs notably in its main features from those most evident in the same connection during either previous or subsequent ages. In the first place both the organised and the casual sale of feminine favours existed in far greater bulk throughout medieval society than in ancient or modern times. In the civilisations of pagan Greece and Rome which fell to the northern barbarians, very soon after the Christian emperors assumed control of the administrative machine they inherited, a widespread custom of religious prostitution existed. But there had been no tabus on sexual appetite other than those suggested by common sense. Moreover, so long as the machine held together, both cultural and commercial life, and also to some extent military preoccupations, especially in the outlying regions

WHOREDOM

of the empire, took up a great deal of the time of men who in less developed states of society would have concentrated as naturally upon copulation as upon eating, drinking and fighting.

When the frontier tribesmen broke in from all directions upon the sophisticated but long corrupt and decadent central power, they destroyed, wherever they could find them, the monuments of art and literature, the political, sociological, industrial and commercial systems, which had been growing up all round the shores of the Mediterranean for more than a thousand years. The raiding hosts, though they were not all, as individuals, wholly devoid of civilised traits, brought a squalid misery upon populations formerly used to as high a standard of prosperity and refinement as the European continent has ever seen. In these conditions the underdogs had no resource for survival but to sell their services, including their women, to the conquerors. Prostitution almost at once leaped to unprecedented heights.

From the fifth to the eleventh centuries the adolescent Christian Church alone stood for the reflective as contrasted with the impulsive characteristics of humanity. But the bishops, in their enthusiasm for charity, order and the new paternal monotheism which they felt had been revealed to them in the life, death and resurrection of Jesus of Nazareth, carried too far their resolve to suppress to a minimum the very instinct upon which the continued existence of mankind depended. Their prohibitions of 'fornication' met an immediate and irrepressible revolt. Yet the prelates remained too fanatically convinced of their divine inspiration ever to retreat officially from the moral standpoint they had taken.

Consequently, the concupiscence they vainly forbade and the harlots who ministered to it multiplied as never before. For the fury with which the ecclesiastical establishment pursued even the slightest modifications of their absurdly rigid and narrow dogma initiated as much bloodshed and economic chaos as had marked the breakdown of the dispensations of Plato and Aristotle, Augustus and Hadrian. The Christian wars against 'heretics' proved as ruthless and destructive of cool thinking and feeling as the heathen wars of conquest and defence. Nor has the busy warrior, in the brief respites afforded him from risking his life, ever found a more effective restoring agent of his energy, as a general rule, than the embraces of the opposite sex, whether or not remunerated in cash. Even in the relatively stable societies of modern times both long and short wars have always caused an extraordinary increase in the numbers of venal young ladies. It would have been a miracle, Church or no Church, if in the almost incessant mass violence of the Middle Ages the whores had not positively outnumbered the soldiers, approached the numbers of civilians who imitated the manners of men-at-arms and came to cost in the end, on an average, no more than the price of a frugal meal.

Even after the temporal power of the papacy had reached its apogee in the twelfth and thirteenth centuries the popular reaction against the persistent interdiction of the most attractive enjoyments of the plain man and woman held its ground. For in the midst of so much wretchedness induced by endless warfare, epidemics and famine, by social injustice, enforced celibacy and the menaces of eternal torture after death, the rebels continued to stage, with an obstinacy as fierce as that of their opponents, extraordinary orgies of public and private dissipation, in all of which prostitutes played a conspicuous part.

During the slow decline of priestly despotism after 1300 the rising standard of secular education, the broader views obtained by contact with countries unaffected by Christianity, such as even the China of Marco Polo, not to mention the encircling lands of Islam, accelerated the triumph of the insurgents. As the freedoms and achievements of the antique world gradually came to light, often in the monasteries themselves, and the pagan grace and ease could no longer be seen in the lurid reflections of a supposed hell upon earth, both men and women began to think more highly of themselves. Confronted with so illustrious an ancestry, they grew less amenable than ever to pastoral injunctions of humility and the idea that no human being could be other than a 'miserable sinner'.

The harlots, too, began to assume airs and affected mannerisms, like those whom St. Chrysostom had once anathematised in fourth-century Byzantium. The new type of strumpet foreshadowed the glamorous courtesans of the Renaissance. She was welcomed, perhaps, with even more zest than her relatively drab predecessor in the oppressive days of Gregory VII and Innocent III.

WHOREDOM

Finally, the last two hundred years of the medieval period were ruled and patronised by newly rich national sovereigns determined to outdo their prelates in material glory and the exuberant self-indulgence which many cardinals, bishops and abbots, to say nothing of Popes like John XIII, were already exemplifying in the increasingly tolerant social atmosphere. Mercenary young women naturally led the van of those lesser citizens who profited by the latest splendours introduced in Rome, Venice and Paris. The time was soon to be ripe for the positive enthronement of the *Ribaudes* of the sixteenth century and their decidedly emancipated successors under Louis XIV, at Casanova's parties and in the drawing-rooms of Napoleon's marshals and financiers. Thereafter a certain vulgarity seems to have descended upon this ancient trade. On the whole women were to find themselves, during the next couple of centuries, well able to impose their wills upon society without resorting to a preliminary business transaction involving the more or less prolonged lease of their persons.

VIII   Bathers

TEMPLES, theatres, circuses and baths (*thermae*) had been the most conspicuous public buildings in the pagan Roman Empire. When it became officially Christian only the baths, as a rule, escaped transformation into churches, abbeys, monasteries and convents. The terraced and pillared halls of the *thermae*, the basins, pools and fountains, the corridors, cubicles, recreation rooms and dormitories, lost some of their more frivolous statues and inscriptions. But the various departments were as crammed as ever by people of both sexes and all ages, either stark naked or very nearly so.

During the first thousand years at least of the Christian era no one except nuns hesitated to undress in public if work or play, convenience or circumstance, as in hot weather for instance, seemed to demand it. Nuns had been originally forbidden even to bathe naked. St. Cyprian, the third century bishop of Carthage who issued this edict, does not actually say that between bed and tub they had to dress. But this absurdity can be taken for granted. For both sexes in any case regularly slept in the nude until far into the fourteenth century.

It was not until clothing grew more voluminous in the later Middle Ages that the casual revelations of certain bodily zones caused any particular interest. Subsequent generations only gradually came to regard them as erotogenic. When King Edward I of England sang out: '*Honi soit qui mal y pense!*' on catching sight of the Countess of Salisbury's garter, not on her leg but on the ballroom floor, he was almost certainly rebuking in advance those who might think her a careless supervisor of her maids. He would never have objected to a great Norman lady being libidinously desired by his guests. The proof that she had been ill dressed for the dance was far more shocking. But no gentleman, Edward Plantagenet presumably implied, must refer to the fact. The story really has the same point as that of a later Edward, the seventh to occupy the British throne, drinking the water in his fingerbowl at Buckingham Palace because the Shah did.

Pagan and Christian ideas about nudity, however, did begin to differ right from the start. Clement, bishop of Rome in the third century, ordered Christian women to keep out of the public baths when men were there. This decree seems to indicate that even at that early date separate hours were allotted for the visits of females only. If so, it is nevertheless clear that throughout the Middle Ages the times for mixed bathing were far more extensive.

By the year 500, however, Europeans were being regularly notified by their priests that ecclesiastical sanction would be required for even the slightest approach to sexual emotion. If such feelings occurred outside the bonds of matrimony, eternal torments, in all probability, awaited the transgressor, unless he agreed to the most burdensome penances, from fasting for days to singing psalms, with continual supplicatory movements of the body, for hours on end.

The Athenian invert mentioned by Aristophanes (*Birds*, 137-142), with his wish-dream of a father asking him to feel a son's testicles and even reproaching him for not doing so, had no such threats to worry about. At worst he would be ridiculed by robust heterosexuals like Aristophanes.

Nevertheless, even early Christians were human. And the first of them must have been very like their heathen grandfathers. Consequently, descriptions of the details of torture after damnation for the deadly sin of lust probably spiced dishes formerly commonplace enough. For example, the merely benevolent appreciation of an agreeable physique might be sharpened by the consciousness of conspiracy against or at any rate disobedience of authority. In any case contemporary graphic illustration seems to show that the joy of medieval bathers had much in common with that of robbing an orchard. Neither the Romans nor the Greeks of antiquity would have understood this puerile sentiment.

They would have been much more at home with a Christian attitude to ablutions that in fact antedates all organised civilisation. This was the notion of purification, already given a religious significance in the oldest and crudest communities of mankind and never abandoned down to the present day. The Christians surprised nobody by attaching great importance to both the material and the moral senses of the word. But some of them carried the premiss of pollution rather far.

Clement of Alexandria, Athanasius and Jerome in particular wrote many tedious pages about the 'vile body', that 'sack of excrement', which deserved nothing but neglect. Immersed as they were in the wholly immaterial waters of mystical meditation, they had as little time for personal cleanliness as many an absent-minded scholar of subsequent centuries. But more businesslike prelates, who wished to keep their clergy fit for the most strenuous missionary activities, listened to men of science who had not yet forgotten the sanitary tradition of ancient Rome. As early as 540 Bishop Victor of Ravenna put down the foundations of an elaborate bathing establishment for his clerical staff, as numerous as that of any wholesale manufacturer of today. This complex of buildings, like most of its successors, provided for the monks as much hospital service as accommodation for sweating and washing.

But purification, or consecration by water, preceded all medieval ceremonies, secular as well as religious. The venerable Order of the Bath, for instance, which survives only in Britain, got its name from the font or tank which played an essential part in the bestowal of knightly insignia. The candidate for this Order in the earliest period of its existence had to strip to the skin before plunging into the brimming vessel. Not only his body but also his soul would then, it was supposed, be washed clean. The new garments he assumed on emerging from his Bath typified the new virtues of knighthood, which he may or may not have bothered much about in a less responsible rank of society.

One could start a new life in this way even at home. Pope Gregory I, the 'Great', (d. 604) reports the case of a man named Curialis who committed a peculiarly atrocious murder one Saturday evening and attended mass on the following Sunday morning without a qualm, having indulged in a good hot bath at daybreak. He felt sure this 'purification' had absolved him as effectively as a confessor.

For domestic bathing did not acquire until about 1500 at earliest the entirely private character we now associate with it. All through the medieval period it was regarded as a more or less formal rite at which the presence of other people could not be dispensed with. Even nuns and female saints were closely attended during their ablutions by persons of their own sex, who did not hesitate to report the most intimate details of these scenes. They would be duly edified, for example, by the nicety with which the holy lady, on stepping into the tub, would raise her kirtle, as she sank into the water, so circumspectly as to present, nine times out of ten, only an instantaneous exposure, and that shadowed by her gown or distorted by aquatic refraction, of the pubes.

The occasion was often one of hospitality, as in pagan times. The guests of an abbot as of a Homeric hero or a Roman senator would be made free of the water in their host's bathing receptacles and the ministrations of his dependants. He might even invite specially welcome or honoured visitors to enter his own personal tub. As a rule it would be quite capacious enough for three average-sized individuals at least. At such literally unbuttoned parties solemnity did not always prevail, even in a monastery. Servants or friends, though no doubt more often in lay households, might permit themselves more or less disguised acts of a lascivious nature, either irresistible by the performer or tolerated, encouraged or actually ordered by the recipient.

As in the heathen civilisations, again, young people of both sexes were recruited for the purpose of making guests feel at home in this way. Such boys and girls often enjoyed the same social standing as the chief bather. If the latter were thought to deserve more than ordinary courtesy on account of superior rank, previous or potential beneficence to the family or simply as having come a long way, the host's own children might hover round him as he stripped and wallowed. The pictorial records prove that they were seldom fully dressed and sometimes entirely nude.

Domestic tubs were always portable, so that they could be carried from room to room. They generally formed part of any well-to-do traveller's luggage, like the hip-baths taken along by English 'milords' on their Grand Tours in the eighteenth and nineteenth centuries. In warm weather such medieval accessories to the toilet would be set up in a meadow or forest, not necessarily private property, and shaded from the sun by a canopy. Young or not so young couples, escorted by servants and musicians, would then shed their garments and enter the bath together. There they would caress each other, eat, drink and listen to songs accompanied on the lute or viol, as well as to purely instrumental music. At colder seasons of the year similar scenes took place indoors. Pictures of them are among the most numerous surviving from the Middle Ages. They establish beyond all doubt the specifically naïve, even idyllic, character of medieval sensuality in its everyday aspects. It differed as much from the brutal orgies of a Heliogabalus as from the extravagantly staged perversities of a Renaissance prince or prelate.

Accordingly, the bathers of that period, roughly the millennium from 500 to 1500, in their continuance of the age-old custom of purification by water, faced a dilemma which had not existed before the Christian era. On the one hand the symbolic cleansing of the body on certain occasions was enjoined by the highest ecclesiastical authority. In fact the procedure had then to be certified by witnesses in case it should be scamped or evaded altogether. On the other hand the nudity essential for this purpose could sometimes give rise to that deadly sin most fiercely denounced, in public, by all priests, to wit, concupiscence.

There also had to be taken into consideration the very old tradition that water flowed not only as the emblem of moral regeneration but also as representative, positively, of the clerically abhorred and despised sex act. Aphrodite had been born of sea-foam. Hesiod had affirmed that this substance was originally the sperm of the father of Cronos ('Time'), when that first of deities was castrated by his son with a billhook. 'He hurled the severed scrotum,' writes the poet, 'into the sea, where it drifted away. And all about it poured white foam from the divine organ.'

The Greek word for a water-spirit, when transliterated into English reads 'nymph'. But it also meant in Greek the clitoris. The term accordingly accounts for the derivation of 'nymphomania' or inordinate sexual appetite in the human female. All medieval illustrations of the planet Venus show men and women bathing together. Thus public 'bath' and public 'brothel' came to be practically synonymous in the Middle Ages. The word 'bagnio' was used indifferently for either in the later centuries. But one establishment at least, at Avignon about 1350, had separate departments for prostitutes and family parties or persons not desirous for the moment of instant coition.

As for the above-mentioned dilemma of water in its two opposed aspects St. Augustine of Hippo, on his day one of the most sensible of the Fathers, in the end gave everyone a ruling. Baths, he said, could be taken without sin if the bather were complying with the requirements of ritual or hygiene. But no one should take a bath in the spirit applicable to indulgence in a rich meal or lolling on silken cushions. That would always lead to temptation and transgression. The saint added, however, with characteristic candour, that he himself had once bathed in the hope, which was fulfilled, of alleviating grief at a private calamity, the death of his mother.

It proved a short step from even this mild elasticity of conscience to regarding abstention from the bath as a salutary form of mortification. For many Christians soon came to believe that masochism here and now would atone in some degree for the horrifying self-indulgence and reckless worldly ambition they saw around them. To rush in person to the opposite extreme would, they felt, render both themselves and their fiercer contemporaries more acceptable to heaven. For just as Christ died that men might in future live more decently, so if a few Christians sacrificed themselves today and thus proved that all humanity was not hopelessly tainted with immorality, divine providence might be induced to show more mercy to the race as a whole than might otherwise be reasonably expected.

This tortuous and somewhat dubious argument was derived from pre-Christian ideas, those of Agamemnon for instance, when he agreed to sacrifice his daughter in order to gain a fair wind for Troy from the enraged goddess Artemis. But long before Homeric times the notion that the best must die to save the rest was familiar in civilisations of all degrees of sophistication, to say nothing of savage communities all over the world. The

Christians merely gave the ancient belief a twist to suit their own theology. In any case, so far as bathing is concerned, neglect of personal hygiene, though such indifference had formerly been supposed a virtue, began at an early date to be ordained as a penance by the Christian confessors.

Accordingly medieval man, in this context, soon returned, in a sense, to the point at which he had started. He was bathing for the most part, like his pagan predecessors, because he enjoyed it. Heaven's approval, said the priests, could be taken for granted if the act were one of 'purification'. The ticklish question when and how, exactly, this delight in cleanliness, moral and physical, might assume a carnal tinge could safely be left, the bather himself considered, to the comfortable conscience of a plain citizen who did not pretend to theological learning. Naturally that conscience erred pretty frequently on the benevolent side.

After the domestic bath the normal entertainment of a guest in all households except perhaps the very poorest included massage in bed by the adolescents of the family. A Minnesinger manuscript of the twelfth century—the Minnesingers were the German equivalents of the troubadours of southern Europe—is decorated with a drawing in which both boys and girls perform this service. But well before 1500 the practice had been given up. The growing social luxury and moral scepticism of the age, the fourteenth and fifteenth centuries, immediately preceding the High Renaissance, had corrupted the original innocence and simplicity of these hospitable occasions.

During an era which knew little of any conventions but those decreed by the Apostles it had been natural to leave indoor menial tasks to women and children, both slaves and serfs and the members of the householder's own family. Wives and daughters couldn't play a decent game of chess, sing appropriately, i.e. with due sophistication, to a musical instrument or talk intelligently about war or hunting, theology or politics, architecture or poetry. A generation or two after the crusades ended and the tide turned against the Moors in Spain, European women were being taught by their incoming oriental rivals to do all these things quite well. But that did not happen until the mid-thirteenth century. Less than a hundred years later the clerical tabus on the cultivation of the sex instinct were already losing much of their power over the bolder spirits of Christendom. As wealth accumulated fears of the displeasure of heaven diminished. Accordingly, in those flamboyant centuries successors of the virgins who had attended Odysseus as well as Lancelot would be lucky if they preserved their chastity in the houses of liberally disposed landowners or merchants for more than a month or two.

Communal bathing at home did survive into the early thirteen hundreds. A manuscript dictated by Waltriquet, minstrel to the Count of Blois, tells a story entitled *The Three Canonesses of Cologne*. Women so called belonged to communities vowed to obedience and sexual abstinence but not to poverty. They were by no means so sternly disciplined as nuns and usually of superior social standing. They could read, write and do intricate embroidery. Ever since the eighth century at least they had represented medieval womanhood at its best, gay and uninhibited, well able to hold its own with men in matters of commonsense, insistent upon the courtesies due to the weaker sex and to wellborn members of a religious body, who were formally attentive to their duties as such, but certainly not practitioners of false modesty or mystical exaltation.

One of the illustrations to Waltriquet's narrative depicts his three heroines. They all look quite charming, one being of mature years, one slightly less ripe and one quite young. Seated naked in three small tubs, they are all talking at once, most zestfully, to a normally attired male who sits at a lavishly appointed table. But his position is in front of the tubs. So he can't see the women without turning his head. Evidently, however, he has no desire to do so. For he gazes straight out of the picture with a peculiarly ingenuous, if perhaps slightly smug, expression.

On reading the text of the manuscript one discovers that he is not so much being discreet as ensuring that his importance shall be recognised. For this dining gentleman is none other than the minstrel himself. His reputation as a *raconteur* had induced the three canonesses, who were all of noble birth, to invite him to a meal. But, he goes on, what with the good food and wine, my licentious tales, the heat of the bath-water and the high spirits of the ladies—well! In short, what we should call an orgy wound up the party.

Both words and pictures display in vivid action the transition from early medieval naïveté to late medieval sophistication. Two hundred years before this date perhaps nothing much would have happened at such an entertainment. Perhaps even in the fourteenth century nothing much did happen very often on visits of this kind. Perhaps, again, Waltriquet invented the whole yarn to amuse his master the Count. But if so, he must have had something to go on which would have deeply shocked the early Fathers.

As for more public bathing ceremonies, until late in the ninth century those about to be baptised, whether men or women, adults or children, had to stand absolutely naked at the font in the presence of a considerable concourse of people, mostly strangers. Participants were not always proof against the carnal temptations ensuing. A Flemish manuscript written shortly after the death of Charlemagne in 814 contains a text of the Revelations of St. John. One of the marginal illustrations shows the Evangelist in the act of baptising a nude girl. The artist cannot, of course, be suspected of irony. The physical disclosures involved in the ceremony could not have been intended to offer a sly parallel to the sumptuous apocalyptic visions of the saint's dream.

At the same time the draughtsman shows himself to have been well aware of the incidental improprieties likely to occur on these occasions. Seven men are all trying to look through various doorways and keyholes at the young woman's unclothed figure, probably representative, in its gracefully repentant attitude, of Mary Magdalene. One of the men is tearing his hair because he can't find a good coign of vantage. Another crouches hopefully on a companion's shoulders. Such pictorial details were allowed to enliven sacred texts in much the same spirit as that which impels broad-minded vicars of today to entertain their congregations with rock 'n' roll.

Some of the baptised converts were foreign ladies from Asia or North Africa. From time to time their exotic charms positively electrified the more youthfully inexperienced of the Christian warriors who beheld them. A case in point is the 'fair Saracen' mentioned in a Provençal military epic of the twelfth century. When she stepped into the water one of the knights present became deeply affected. A certain Doon (two syllables), he was attending the rite in the retinue of Godfrey de Bouillon, the future Governor of Jerusalem. The young staff officer's flesh, writes the bard, 'bristled under his ermine cloak'.

> *Pour la biauté de li en frémit tout Doon
> la char li hericha sous l'ermin pelichon.*

It is not quite clear from the poet's phrase whether Doon felt what we call 'gooseflesh' or a still more disturbing physiological effect.

In such circumstances laymen, however eminent, were seldom permitted by the Church to take the chief part in baptising females. By the beginning of the tenth century these ladies, naked at earlier periods, wore a single garment of the lightest possible material. The ministrant had to seize them by the shoulders and plunge them three times under the water. After this act he anointed them on the forehead—in the previous centuries all over—stripped off the wet, flimsy vest and wrapped the shivering neophyte in a long and thick white robe, resembling a priest's alb. John Moschus, a seventh-century abbot, records that one of his monks had applied for exemption from the duty of baptism because 'when he anointed certain women he felt shocked'. (*Quoties quasdam mulieres inungeret scandalisabatur.*)

Baptism could still be regarded as in essence a private function. Public ablutions were quite another matter. They may fairly be said to have strongly influenced the prolonged process that corrupted the relative moral innocence of the early Christian bather. Institutions resembling the pagan Roman *thermae* had been multiplying fast in all the bigger cities of Europe ever since the twelfth century. At that date some were already recognised brothels or 'stews', as they were called in England, from the steam of the 'hot rooms'. In 1435, as noted in the last chapter, one establishment at Avignon had sixteen sleeping cubicles with feather-beds wide enough for double occupation. In these quite elaborate buildings the staff catered not only for bathing, drinking, gambling and fornication but also for all requirements of the toilet, including hair-dressing, and even minor surgical operations and other medical treatment. In addition, the enjoyment of every conceivable perversion, especially that of tribadism or female homosexuality, could be arranged under congenial circumstances. Needless to say, scenes at these 'baths' had grown so riotous by 1500 that sober citizens shunned them altogether and many establishments were closed for good.

It is clear that at their inception they had afforded medieval man, in general, such facilities as modern man expects from café or club, including 'night club'. In twelfth century Paris there was a 'bagnio' in almost every street. Even the villages generally boasted of one or two, naturally of more modest dimensions and attractions, little better than glorified taverns where female customers could be taken upstairs. In Germany a town crier walked round in the early morning proclaiming that the 'baths' were open. People of rank usually then set off for them on horseback. But the lower and middle classes undressed at home, so as not to lose their clothes and valuables, since they could not afford, like the richer citizens, to employ their own servants to guard them. After stripping to a single practically worn out garment or blanket, sometimes just a loincloth, the humbler families and individuals would then race hilariously through the streets to their favourite enjoyment, whatever the weather was like, in an undisciplined mob. Improprieties were occasionally committed and quarrels broke out. But the general atmosphere would be more naïvely light-hearted than at an organised festival, since few could be anything but sober at that hour. There were no separate undressing rooms even for the fashionable contingent and no one dreamed of retaining a single piece of clothing once the water or the vapour chambers were reached.

A remarkably elegant novel in verse, known as the *Flamenca*, recounts the adventures of an ingeniously adulterous young lady in Provence about the year 1234. One passage describes a typical small-town bathing establishment in that part of Europe.

'Here,' the unidentified author states, 'both natives and foreigners could bathe very conveniently. Cripples who attended were all cured if they stayed long enough. No special regulations about time were enforced. Hot as well as cold water was laid on in all departments. The separate sections were roofed over and walled in like little huts. Some rooms were set aside for rest and refreshment.' Such heroines as La Flamenca met their lovers and dodged their husbands in places of this kind, ostensibly for what we call physical culture. But this expression was open, in the hearty medieval manner, to a sexual as well as a therapeutic interpretation. Private cubicles for Flamencas and their friends would always be available for a small additional charge.

A contemporary of the writer just quoted comments on the baths at Alost in Flanders. 'Only one room existed for both sexes to undress in. The great hall, where a high temperature was maintained, contained large circular pools surrounded by terraced benches on which the bathers sat while they perspired. Visibility was everywhere obscured by thick clouds of steam. Massage and the application of unguents proceeded at the hands of lightly clad serving-maids.'

In such somewhat confusing atmospheres, favourable to furtive gesture, one had to behave pretty recklessly to be caught and fined. But even then the authorities took no very serious view of the matter. In the early fifteenth century, for example, a monk of Dijon was seen at the local baths to be taking extreme sexual liberties with two ladies at the same time, though they should have been at home just then, preparing their husbands' suppers. A fine was imposed on the monk by the civil power. But his abbot coolly annulled the sentence.

Others paid up cheerfully, either afterwards or beforehand. It was a regular practice, for instance, to acquire, for a preliminary payment, the right to join any group of women at the baths whether they liked it or not. All protests were silenced by production of the gatekeeper's receipt. Money talked as loudly amid the splashes and the laughter, the twanging and tootling of musical instruments and the squealing or bawling of popular ballads as anywhere else. The songs could only be chanted to hymn tunes, since no others were available in those days. But the melodies were often stirring enough to suit the burlesque obscenity of the words. Lugubriousness sometimes turned out even better, provided one was prepared to risk a charge of blasphemy. But the Church seldom proceeded against uninfluential commoners on such grounds.

Grander persons were by no means averse from the joyous rough and tumble of communal bathing. But, like Haroun-al-Raschid, they preferred to mingle with the proletariat in disguise. Nevertheless, as a rule everyone knew who they were, especially in a small town or one in temporary proximity to a campaigning army or a sovereign's tour. The municipalities then refrained from interfering in any 'orgies' at the baths which might be staged—in the 'rest rooms'—at the request of powerful princes, merchants or bishops. A strong force of disciplined men-at-arms, however, owing feudal service to the visitors, would generally be posted, at the earnest prayer of the town councillors, to keep the rabble at bay.

For more than once in the fourteenth and fifteenth centuries the bulk of the populations of individual settlements or districts had demanded the eradication of the local 'bagnio'. Formerly, they would say, it had been the pride and pleasure of all honest citizens. But now it was a 'plague-spot', a 'sink of iniquity'. The petitioners' livelihood depended upon a steady supply of God-fearing, hard-working labourers. But to these once decent fellows a fatal example had been set by the incursion of a horde of extravagant and shameless 'foreigners', who had not even troubled to conceal their devilish lubricity from amazed native onlookers. In no time at all the once beloved building had been turned into a centre not only of licentious debauchery and extortion but of danger to life and limb. In at least one of such cases the mayor had been forced by public indignation to raze the offending structure to the ground.

But in general the public baths, the most important centres for relaxation in any medieval community, were left to function undisturbed for a thousand years. They began under the first Christian emperors as close copies of the antique Roman institution. They passed into a phase of covert evasion of control by austere fanatics and then into a freedom comparable to some extent with that of the pagan world. Increasing material affluence was accompanied, as usual, by a certain scepticism. Conventions were queried and even ridiculed. Rebellious high spirits became the fashion. It is in this penultimate atmosphere, perhaps, before its inevitable thickening to the fumes of mere brutish rut and riot, that the Gothic Venus of the sweating chamber and the cooling tank seems most attractive to modern eyes.

Attempts were made here and there to separate the sexes at communal bathing establishments. But such measures were never popular and constantly circumvented. Almost the only exceptions were conceded in favour of people who called simply for a vapour bath, without any other diversion or treatment. This sort of patron, being as a rule decrepit, did not expect frolicsome companions. As for the rest, whatever restrictive rules might be promulgated about periods and places could not be enforced. For example, males would pretend to go to sleep and overstay the time limit prescribed. They would be found lying about all over the premises in a state of nature when the women arrived. The latter in their turn, through curiosity or from mercenary motives, would come in too early, alleging they had mistaken the hour or the room reserved for them.

For by this time a passion far exceeding that of the ancients for public bathing had begun to permeate the Christian world. To the natural enjoyment which was all the pagans had cared about there had now been added the insistence of the Church upon spiritual purification by water and the proclamation of its curative properties by the medical profession. Greeks and Romans had enjoyed such amenities in the spirit of epicureans well aware of the physiological results of excess and quite unacquainted with the notion that any carnal appetite, even if satisfied in moderation, could incur the vengeful wrath of heaven. Their calm appreciation could not be compared for a moment with the guilty thrills experienced by populations indoctrinated from birth with the belief that a moment's casual fornication could mean agony in flames for evermore.

In these circumstances medieval citizens, like modern children who grow more and more addicted to the use of lethal weapons whatever stern penalties may be imposed on them for doing so, became almost pathologically attached to the scarcely disguised brothels which the Fathers of the Church themselves had once praised, on perfectly adequate grounds, as essential temples of hygiene. From more than one such institution, however, as the fifteenth century closed, officials who tried to compel discipline were actually ejected, with broken bones, by riotous patrons who wanted the place to themselves. What then happened to the few more or less innocent, and mostly nude, visitors who remained can be imagined.

Yet, until this final lurid period, public baths continued to be approved by doctors and priests as useful and salutary civic foundations, second only to churches. For even on consecrated ground, after all, harlots and pimps could be found in numbers only slightly inferior to those in which they frequented the 'bagnios'. Moreover, the hospital services provided at the baths expanded towards the end of the Middle Ages to include what we should call 'beauty treatment'. It became a feminine mode, for instance, to shave the armpits and pubes. This new habit, perhaps a consequence of the greatly increased displays of nudity during the rise of communal bathing to such unprecedented popularity, could be regarded as a sign of enhanced refinement of manners. But connoisseurs of sexual congress remained divided in their views of the innovation. The up-to-date experts compared neglected tangles at these anatomical recesses with 'a Saracen's moustache'. The old-fashioned sneered at close-clipped surfaces which they likened to 'a priest's chin'. But as usual the advanced guard gained the day. The victorious arguments may have stressed the stimulus to male eroticism provided by the novel tactual elements involved. But more probably the dispute was decided by the firm intention of the ladies to appear younger than they were.

The Church had originally approved, on doctrinal grounds, the 'shedding of vain adornments', i.e. outer clothing, in the public baths. For Christianity taught, strangely enough in the ears of its first converts, that all human beings were equal in the sight of heaven. They were certainly more recognisably so, especially in that feudal age, when they were naked. There really may be something in the opinion of a modern humorist that all formal debates concerned with administration, especially in Parliaments, would be more effective if the participants hadn't a stitch on them. But however much truth may reside in this assertion, during the Middle Ages the democratic character of ablutions in common had the unforeseen result of adding further temptations of a more subtle kind to the obvious suggestions of denuded sexual features.

Elsewhere the splendour or squalor of outward trappings might well inhibit lust in either sex. A cobbler would tend to gaze with awe rather than concupiscence upon a countess. She in her turn, even if he were a handsome and gay young fellow, would only be repelled by the greasy apron and home-spun, unwashed shirt. But if each wore nothing at all, or a mere strip of drapery, the social barriers to intimacy would be as negligible as the physical. The idea of such encounters naturally helped to sharpen the appetites of bathers coming from any rank of society. The wife of a rich merchant could dream of blacksmiths or stable-boys and *vice versa*. For only in buildings devoted to 'purification' could the Lady Chatterleys or Anouilh colonels of the day enjoy the company of gamekeepers or housemaids without the disagreeable ingredient on either side of any trace of compulsion. Only in such places could the poor revel on absolutely equal terms, at any time, with the wealthy.

The democracy of the public bath had been heartily applauded by the bishops for the first few medieval centuries. It symbolised, like the contemporary pictorial representations of equality in death, the ultimate identity of emperor and clown so tirelessly preached, then as now, by the men of religion. The deadly sin of pride, they were convinced, could hardly maintain itself to damnation point in the absence of skirts and breeches. They were largely right in that particular connection. But unfortunately the deadly sin of *luxuria* seemed to rage even more furiously in such conditions than in any others, especially as the Middle Ages drew to a close. For by then the spirit of the times was already waging implacable war against ecclesiastical tyranny. Within two hundred years the movements known as the Renaissance and the Reformation were to demolish the old type of theocracy, which had begun to be absolute under Pope Gregory VII at the end of the eleventh century, for ever.

Meanwhile many Europeans had come to believe bathing to be so healthful in itself—an opinion steadily upheld by most medieval doctors—as to constitute a powerful aphrodisiac, quite apart from any incidental stimulation that promiscuous nudity might afford. A Flemish illustration of the Fountain of Youth, a myth common to several antique civilisations, shows a number of male bathers in the act of displaying unmistakable signs of restored virility. Elderly women, some with crutches, others actually carried on litters, come to join the old men. Earlier visitors have already begun to couple, as a result, evidently, of immersion in the magic waters. Their figures appear in the margins of the scene, the Fountain itself rising in the centre.

In similar pictures of communal bathing found in Germany bundles of birch-twigs or other plants can be discerned. The primary purpose of these *fasces*, which had been used in ancient Rome as emblems of official authority, is the promotion of energy. In the medical field switches of this kind were employed, as they still are in many parts of northern Europe and Asia, to assist perspiration by heating the blood through a mild form of flagellation. No doubt in certain cases these playful beatings at the baths took a severer turn, adding a further species of erotic stimulation to the many others in force at such establishments.

In 1415 the Italian classical scholar Gian Francesco Poggio (1380-1459) who has already been mentioned in these pages as a most notable medieval precursor of the Renaissance—he was a great hater of hypocritical priests and the author of a famous collection of indecent tales in Latin called the *Facetiae* ('Jests')—attended the communal centre at Baden—which itself means 'baths' in German—in Switzerland. He saw there a packed and boisterous crowd of entirely naked bathers, men and women, boys and girls. It is true, he writes, that a so-called screen separated the sexes.

'But it was full of large openings through which the bathers handed one another refreshments and indulged in mutual caresses. This public pool was sunk among galleries that ran at a higher level and were occupied by numbers of lounging visitors, who exchanged more or less polite remarks with the bathers. You could move anywhere you liked from one part of the establishment to another. You could easily take up a position from which you could watch the women going in and out of the water without taking the slightest precaution to hide their most secret charms. They didn't seem afraid of anything. In the narrow passages practically nude men and women continually bumped into one another. The males wore thin trunks, the females a transparent linen robe, open at the side, which concealed nothing. Many bathers used tables floating in the water to take their refreshments. All ages and both sexes mingled at these feasts.'

Poggio didn't himself join the revels, as he couldn't speak German. But a similar ignorance did not deter two of his younger companions. They entered the water and were well received, even to the point of affectionate embraces, by the girls they accosted. No one seemed to mind what anybody did so long as the act was accompanied by plenty of noise, splashings, burlesque greetings and catchwords, guffaws and so on. No husband or lover objected to such jocular and transitory familiarities with the women in their company. Everything short of actual copulation was permitted.

But the girls did expect largesse when they danced or wrestled with one another in the pool. Coins and garlands then flew through the air from the galleries, to be dexterously caught by the sturdy Swiss enchantresses. The Italian visitor played his part generously, to that extent, in a scene which enraptured him by its frankly sensual yet never repulsive gaiety. For in his own native land, by this time, the women participating in such recreations would all have been harlots. At Baden however, he was told, they belonged to perfectly decent middle-class families and were mostly escorted by older relatives.

Elsewhere, as the fifteenth century ended, decadence had finally set in. The public baths scarcely pretended, from York to Palermo and from the Sierra Morena to the Carpathians, to be anything but public brothels. There were quite enough of the latter, it was generally considered by responsible Europeans, in the continent already. The municipalities and the Church at last agreed to forgo their profits from these places and to condemn without qualification the grandiose halls of debauchery which had started as merely business premises devoted to the spiritual and physical health of the community.

The farce of their transformation had often been savagely exposed by medical men. For the doctors had been steadily losing their patients, for centuries, to the barbers, leeches, massage experts and other purveyors of unorthodox remedies for disease practising in the jovial and carefree atmosphere of resorts that catered a good deal less for fleshly ills than for fleshly cravings.

In the fourteen nineties the desperate physicians swore that the public baths were spreading the dreadful new scourge of syphilis. Some of them added, in language better suited to a pulpit than an assembly of men of science, that respectable females were being rendered pregnant, in all innocence, by the sperm ejaculated under water by masturbating libertines. Even in the fifteenth century few conscientious medicos can have believed such nonsense. But any stick decorated with morally censorious rhetoric of this crude description would do to beat competitors who were persistently forcing properly qualified professional healers out of business.

Accordingly, three main attacks, administrative, ecclesiastical and scientific, coupled of course with the general improvement in European intelligence and sensibility after the crusades had failed, combined to bring into disrepute the heyday of the 'bagnio'. The pretentious Venusbergs into which the antique *thermae* had degenerated were to a great extent abolished. They are hardly ever mentioned after 1500. Public bathing, despite its tentative revival at the turn of the eighteenth and nineteenth centuries and also in quite recent times, certainly never again occupied so conspicuous a position in the rites invented by mankind to honour the most obstinately immortal of all goddesses.

IX Danse Macabre

MEDIEVAL Europeans lived on far more familiar terms with plague, famine and violent death than even the populations that have faced the blood-stained, morbid and starvation-ridden twentieth century. Religious fanaticism, not only, of course, in Christian lands, has always exacerbated warfare. At the end of the fourth century B.C. a leader of the Gauls named Brennus invaded Italy and sacked Rome, then merely a city heading a central Italian federation of petty States. According to legend the defenders of the stronghold paid their ransom in falsified weights. Thereupon the foreign chieftain flung his heavy sword into the scales with the ferociously mocking shout of *Vae victis!* ('Woe to the vanquished!').

This brief and terrible motto was adopted by the infant Roman Republic and subsequently ruled every battlefield throughout the Middle Ages. The victors slew without mercy, on commercial principles, the only prisoners taken being those noted as likely to pay ransom. At Agincourt, however, in 1415, the English king, Henry V, had all the French captives, to the number of about a thousand, killed in cold blood. For his little army, though its losses had been negligible—barely a hundred men—was not numerous enough to guard those of the enemy who surrendered. The French chronicler Jean Froissart (1338-c. 1410) records a similar massacre at the battle of Aljubarrota in Portugal in 1385, where five hundred English archers helped the Portuguese to defeat a Castilian army. 'Behold the great evil adventure that befell that Saturday,' writes the Frenchman regretfully. 'For they slew as many good prisoners as would well have been worth, one with another, four hundred thousand francs.' In medieval warfare, accordingly, the common foot-soldier, if he thought his side was getting the worst of it, usually tried to bolt. Few escaped, as a rule, from the pursuing knights.

The Christians of Europe had for long a darker reputation for cruelty, both in the heat of conflict and in their subsequent treatment of conquered enemies, than orientals. In Spain the Moors behaved more decently, on the whole, than the native levies who opposed them. The ferocity of the crusaders scandalised both the Byzantines and the Turks. Crucifixions and mutilations, especially the hacking away of noses and thumbs, were the common lot of Muslim captives. Much of the primitive barbarity that had brought horror and desolation upon Europe between the years 500 and 1000 still survived during the next five centuries. In the West there had been a great gap in civilisation between the break-up of the Roman Empire and the cultural resurrection of the years after the great scare of 1000, when the Day of Judgment was believed imminent. In the East no such abyss had yawned between the days of the Sumerian kings and Saladin.

Yet in medieval Europe, despite the atrocious ruthlessness with which warfare was pursued, the attractions of a military life ensured a plentiful supply of recruits for the eternally quarrelsome lords and princes. The humblest soldier could be enriched for life from the plunder of a sacked city. Defenceless women could be raped with impunity during hostilities. The civilian populations in general deeply admired the bristling man-at-arms in his moments of leisure. To most spirited young men of all classes campaigning of some sort, which could be found going on almost anywhere at almost any time, seemed a natural mode of existence. The probable brevity of that existence and the prospect that its end was likely to be painful and wretched to the limit of endurance did not at first worry the characteristic reckless optimism of youth. Later on the rank and file came to understand clearly enough that deserters would be hanged without ceremony. But in any case they were assured on the soundest ecclesiastical authority that they would go straight to heaven if they perished fighting the 'heretics', who for their part were told exactly the same thing by their own priests.

Sadism in the warrior was encouraged as if it were a virtue.

DANSE MACABRE

The mutilation of the breasts and pudenda of women, the hanging up of male prisoners of war by the testicles, castrations and executions carried out with every circumstance of the most outrageous brutality, were formally displayed in the presence of a victorious host. In the middle of the thirteenth century the struggle for supreme power between the papacy and the so called Holy Roman Empire was at its height. An Italian supporter of the latter near Venice captured twenty-five nobles of the faction opposed to him. After erecting a row of gallows for the hanging of these prisoners as an entertainment for the forces under his command he sent for as many of the wives, mothers, sisters and daughters of the doomed captives as he could find, amounting to a group of thirty in all. He stripped all these women to the skin and lined them up before the gallows in such a way as to be almost directly underneath them. Then he hanged the prisoners, one after the other, so close to the ground that in their death agonies they kicked the faces of their relatives. Then the women were turned loose, still naked, to do what they pleased, if they still retained a trace of human mentality after their appalling experience.

This sort of spectacle, which the Church did nothing to stop, could scarcely be thought to fortify the sexual abstinence which the priests simultaneously recommended. The troops were naturally determined that their lives, if short, must also be gay. Consequently, as soon as they began to wear arms, they automatically turned, almost to a man, into unscrupulously lascivious brutes. In the rural districts their appearance was a signal for the peasants to take to the woods, marshes or mountains. When armies were reported in the neighbourhood of a city its approaches were deserted and ravaged, the walls were manned and messengers despatched in all directions to implore reinforcements at any cost. No one dreamed of negotiation unless the advancing body initiated it.

Yet, while even defending forces were feared on account of their generally ruffianly character, they were also much admired for their professional swagger and joviality and their presumed courage. So the rest of the population, not excluding women, tended to imitate them.

In addition, the hundreds, sometimes thousands, of **female** camp followers who attached themselves to the troops in the hope of sharing in the booty to be expected from a victory and staking their bodies on this off-chance, corrupted the stay-at-homes when the campaign ended. The existence of this purely erotic auxiliary force, available to the other side if fortune favoured it, contributed a further stimulus to the ardours of even a pitched battle in open country. For the conquerors could anticipate as much copulation there and then, with unfamiliar partners, as if they had entered a captured city.

The wars of the European Middle Ages, therefore, developed on lines parallel with the sexual incontinence of that period, amounting at certain times and places to the mere mechanical functioning of haphazard lust. Churchmen could always be found to approve the staging of a massacre of 'heretics' or the organisation of a military expedition in search of them. In fact many bishops galloped with the charging knights, especially in the earlier centuries, and gave as hard knocks as they got. Yet these same clerics were bound officially to deplore the inevitable erotomania which followed the use of weapons on any considerable scale. Each type of fanaticism influenced the other to an incalculable extent.

The phenomenon is of course common to all periods and regions. But the peculiar circumstances of medieval life, the internecine pugnacity of the lords, the religious intolerance, the relative scarcity of mental alternatives to physical violence and the helpless ignorance of the masses of the people, practically captives of their social superiors, rendered the immemorial conjunction of Mars and Venus exceptionally active and incessant.

The clergy were obliged to wink at it. Their power remained enormous in all civil activities. But in camps and battles it could exercise little restraining influence. For no priest could then be enough of a superman, at the same time tactless enough and finally intelligent enough to proclaim, as the essence of Christianity requires, that war is both wicked and useless. The majority of the prelates at least were cleverer and better educated than most laymen. But even the best of these dignitaries could be sincerely convinced that God had enjoined them to smite the Amalekites. Text after text in both the Old Testament and the New justified an uncompromisingly militant policy in the ser-

DANSE MACABRE

vice of Christ. The other side could always be convicted, by theological casuistry, of heretical beliefs. Had not Jesus himself used the strongest language in condemnation of the 'scribes and Pharisees'?

So the strange and melancholy procession began, quite early in the Christian centuries, of men learned in the principles of charity and professing faith in them, yet commanding, often with great eloquence, the organised extermination of their fellow-creatures. It would be accompanied, they knew perfectly well, by the commission of every sin in the confessor's manual, sexual licence at the top of the list. The paradox has continued ever since. Theologians have tied themselves into inextricable knots in order to uphold it. Conform or die is the senseless and hopeless alternative presented to the Communist today as it was presented to Islam in the eighth century and for well over another four hundred years up to the decisive Muslim victory in Palestine.

The merciless annihilation by the medieval papacy of unorthodox Christian sects, especially if they advocated, as they so often did, polygamy or at any rate sexual freedom, would appear ludicrous to modern eyes if it were not so bloodthirsty. The classical world knew better than to crack merely argumentative skulls. According to the comedian Plautus (d. 184 B.C.) there was quite enough of the beast in man without multiplying it by a religious sanction of his depredations on his own kind for the sake of a mere difference of opinion. The Roman's *homo homini lupus* (Trinummus II. iv. 46) 'man is a wolf to his own species', was repeated by the Dutch Roman Catholic humanist of the early Renaissance, Erasmus, nearly seventeen centuries later. Both were indicting that incorrigible, irrational savagery which perpetually negatives not only pacifism but also the sense of proportion in dealing with instinctive feelings. Reason has a hand in each of these conceptual camps. But there is little sign at present of the human intellect coming of age in either respect. As in so much else the medieval mind in war and love was a child which has so far not grown to much more than an adolescent.

The subtlety of that mind was almost wholly expended in the logic-chopping of scholastic philosophy. It was driven by the panic dread of damnation into abstractions of more and more obscurity and even absurdity. As to the nature of angels, for instance, it solemnly asked and long debated how many of these beings could stand on a pin's head. On the purely scientific side the alchemists were impelled by an equally sterile impulse of material greed. It sent them delving into nearly as chaotic a labyrinth, in their fantastic chemical experiments, as that of the schoolmen. The 'doctor' of the Middle Ages, in fact, whether of divinity, sorcery or medicine—these last two studies often coalesced—became so fascinated by the inexplicable oddity of the phenomena he observed and the theories current about them that he sometimes seems to a modern mind to have been ready to believe anything.

The ideas of ancient Greece about bodily ills and their cure remained paramount in Europe until the eighth century, when they began to yield to Muslim research in this field. But as Mohammed had forbidden dissection progress was not notable until Charlemagne in 805 ordered a return to classical studies. The Christian influence showed itself very early, in the anxiety of administrators that doctors should not take advantage of their close examination of female patients to exceed the bounds of sexual decorum. The laws of Theodoric, king of the Ostrogoths (d. 526), forbade any leech to bleed a noblewoman in private. Even as late as the fourteenth century the English surgeon John Ardernn conceived it necessary to give his students the following advice:

'Consider not overboldly the ladies nor the daughters nor other fair women in great mens' houses nor proffer too much to kiss nor touch them ... abstain from harloterie as well in words as deeds in every place, for if he use him to harloterie in privy places, some time in open places there may fall to him the unworship of evil usage.'

As usual in the Middle Ages females below the rank of the prosperous mercantile class were not regarded as entitled to any special respect, whether approached for therapeutic or merely erotic purposes.

By the tenth century medical knowledge had improved to an extent justifying foundation of the School of Salerno already mentioned (See p. 146). Finally, in 1206, the establishment of the University of Paris included a Faculty of Medicine. A College of Surgeons, who had hitherto only been allowed the status of shopkeepers, followed in 1271. An age of famous physicians like Albertus Magnus, Lanfranc and Roger Bacon ensued. Even the feminine touch and pious compassion of nuns, still much appreciated by invalids today, were recognised as peculiarly suitable for medical work. The inmates of convents were encouraged to add the healing art to their other preoccupations.

The hospitals where they ministered were no novelty. The Frankish queen Radegond had built one in the sixth century and laboured in it herself. All through the incessant warfare of medieval times women, whether educated or not, naturally acted as attendants on the sick and wounded men. But if they fell ill themselves they could expect little attention, except in childbirth. Midwives were of course an important body in any community and had their own closely guarded secrets. They were often consulted by lawyers, especially in the very numerous cases of alleged defloration of virgins. No less than fourteen proofs of any such act were admitted by these severe matrons.

The phenomena in question were a certain condition of the breasts (not otherwise specified), bruised lips of the vulva, their circular distension, corrugation of the perineum (between vulva and fundament), a loosened and spongy condition of the vulva itself, its pendent lips, their edges denuded of hair, depression of the clitoris, its fleshy parts in dissolution, inverted condition of the connecting membrane, excoriation of the adjacent skin and the neck of the womb, reddening of this part, collapse of the hymen and internal orifice of the matrix.

This catalogue has a certain scientific accuracy and leaves little room for doubt. But some recipes recommended by the Salerno School, particularly for barrenness, are more dubious. It is hard to see, for instance, how conception could be facilitated by swallowing the roasted dung of a donkey, even on the principles of homoeopathic magic. Such fantasies were the outcome, in medicine as in religion, of the strong influence of oriental occultism.

An age of fervent, uncritical faith in the supernatural only too easily degenerates into one of a cult of fancies for their own sake. It would have been better for medieval man if his theologians had dreamed less and looked harder about them, especially into history and language. It would also have been better for him if his medical advisers had steered clearer of a fondness for miracles caught, like the physical maladies they failed to cure, from a certain atmosphere or certain persons.

For the apocalyptic twilight of these times, livid with alternating clouds of lust and terror, generated an incidence of ill-health positively horrifying in modern eyes. Man, like the other animals, has always been subject to more or less serious outbreaks of epidemic disease. Early phases of urban civilisation increased this tendency by three factors. Overcrowding had a special effect in the cases of infectious illness. Overwork and what may perhaps be called overplay also depreciated physique. For large, confined communities of human beings are inevitably more vulnerable to the pressures of personal ambition than small, scattered and mobile ones. At the same time the forced intimacy involved leads, by way of the competitive and mimetic instincts, to an indulgence of sensual capacities for enjoyment which inclines to become more than the organism can safely bear.

Slavery and debauchery have invariably been conspicuous aspects of life in cities, both in Asia and in Europe, to say nothing of America in the modern period. They are also powerful breeders of sickness and death. For, as Jules Michelet once observed, the epochs of moral depravity coincide with those of high mortality. In the present context, accordingly, the medieval revolt against ecclesiastical tabus on carnal love induced an extraordinary prevalence of sexual irritation which not only afforded an exceptionally favourable climate for the spread of epidemics but was also itself actually augmented by them. Moreover, the idea, not specifically Christian but widely cherished in the Middle Ages, that the natural ills inherited by the flesh ought not to be artificially resisted, practically abolished the hope of any kind of preventive medicine before 1500.

In those centuries of the Christian era the elaborate and exact classifications of identified maladies available to the modern doctor through the technical discoveries of the last two hundred years could not be achieved. All epidemics, for instance, were for long known simply as the 'plague' or the 'pest'. It was not until comparatively recent times that medical men began to

DANSE MACABRÉ

speak confidently of such varieties as bubonic, pneumonic and septicemic 'plague' and of diphtheria, typhoid and typhus, malaria, leprosy, cholera, smallpox, influenza and syphilis.

In the sixth century bubonic plague, probably complicated with smallpox, devastated the whole Christian world for fifty years and undoubtedly hastened the darkening of the moral horizon that ensued. The contemporary Byzantine historian Procopius writes: 'A plague ... spread over the entire earth, afflicting without mercy both sexes and every age. It began in Egypt, passed to Palestine and thence everywhere else, occurring seasonally in each place it affected, however remote ... those persons formerly afflicted not being attacked on the subsequent occasion. It seemed to move inland from the coastal regions.

'In Byzantium phantoms appeared in human form and struck the persons who encountered them, so that these people contracted the disease. Those who locked themselves in their houses beheld the same apparitions in dreams, or heard voices which condemned them to death ... so many died that the corpses had to be piled in public buildings or placed on ships which were then launched out to sea....

'They were taken with a sudden fever ... at first so slight that neither patient nor physician feared danger ... but in many cases, the first or second day or later, a bubo appeared both in the region of the groin and under the armpits, or else behind the ear or at some other point of the body....

'Some went into a deep coma, others into violent delirium ... or else the swelling gangrened and the patient died from excess of pain. The disease was not contagious ... the bodies of some patients broke out in black blisters the size of a lentil. These ... died at once, many vomiting blood ... no remedies availed.'

There were further sporadic outbursts of this pestilence during the next hundred years. St. Gregory of Tours (d. 594) gives an accurate and exhaustive description of symptoms which point to smallpox. Two of his children died of it. It is from this source that the phrase 'God bless you!', still uttered when a person sneezes, is derived. For when a plague-stricken victim sneezed, writes the saint, death was imminent. The Northumbrian historian and theologian Bede (d. 735) refers to similar phenomena in his account of plague in England in his time. It is certain, moreover, from contemporary evidence, that bubonic plague was included among the epidemics of that major calamity compendiously known as the 'Black Death' which raged for a generation in the fourteenth century and is said to have destroyed twenty-five million Europeans in that period. This monstrous figure, which there is no good reason to doubt, represents a quarter of the inhabitants of the continent then living.

The doctors were helpless against this fearful scourge, which was generally supposed an act of God. It was in vain that interceding processions of flagellants stalked the streets and roads, wailing for heaven's mercy as they flogged each other. It was in vain that physicians dressed like divers for their visits and Jews were burnt alive as scapegoats. Civilisation, writes an anonymous observer, virtually stopped. The doomed populations flung themselves into a frenzied orgy of erotomania, determined to secure some concrete pleasure, if only for a few moments, before their lives ended for ever. Boccaccio in his preface to the contemporary *Decameron* asserts that three out of five Italians died in these years of the plague, which he and his friends escaped by fleeing to a remote rural district. 'The best medicine,' he writes grimly, 'was then wine, song and gibe.' He might have added fornication, but probably did not wish to offend the Church by such a suggestion.

The symptoms were mainly rigor or convulsions, fever, vomiting, headache, giddiness, pains in the chest, back and limbs, insomnia and apathy or delirium. The buboes or inflamed glands appeared usually on the second day of such signs, generally at the groin. They were very painful. Death often occurred on the third or fourth day.

Leprosy, the other great and much more permanent curse of the Middle Ages, had long been known in pre-Christian Europe. But it was not until about the middle of the fifth century that 'lazar-houses', named after the leprous beggar in the New Testament parable of Dives, began to be erected, like concentration camps, in open country. They were hospitals for the reception of poor persons suffering from the disease of Lazarus, or from plague, or from other contagious or infectious maladies. The patients were, however, considered incurable, being popularly regarded as smitten by God to bear the sins of the community.

DANSE MACABRE

By the year 1000, when the end of the world was expected, these hospitals were being greatly improved, richly endowed and elaborately organised. The loathing expressed in former centuries for their inmates had been much modified by familiarity and the idea that attentions to these scapegoats might improve one's relations with the Almighty, though undoubtedly many benefactors were impelled by nothing more self-interested than true charity. In any case, by the end of the eleventh century, with the malady at its height of prevalence, leper visiting, like slumming in Victorian and Edwardian England, had become quite fashionable, despite the horrible stench, not only of the disease, but also of the mercury with which it was by this time being treated. There was even, it seems, some competition to join the hospital staffs.

In France the lazar-houses were called *bordes*, a word with the same root as *bordel* (brothel), meaning a small building outside a city wall. There is no reason, however, to suppose that lepers were particularly given to fornication. The coincidence of names is due merely to the resemblance in size and location of lazar-house and brothel.

The patients were dressed in a grey cloak and hat. They carried a begging bowl or wallet and a bell to warn people of their approach, since the disease was easily caught. The appearance of these unfortunate people was so revolting and their energy so depleted that the laws which were passed forbidding them to copulate with the healthy can seldom have been infringed. But the disfigurement in its early stages might escape notice if the sufferer chose to dress in such a way as to conceal it. A famous story is told of the Catalan mystic and missionary Raimon Lull (d. 1315) in his dissipated youth pursuing with libidinous intent a certain lady who took refuge in a church. There she faced him and, opening her robe, showed a breast half eaten away by the disease. This experience is said to have turned the young man from evil courses for the rest of his life. The tale is no doubt apocryphal. It is also related of other well known theologians. The fable, however, may have had its origin in some real incident, when a young woman hard pressed by a detested but importunate lover may have conceived the notion of repelling him by a faked revelation of this kind.

Although leprosy was much feared in the Middle Ages and those infected by it were alternately persecuted, isolated and charitably attended, this endemic but not immediately lethal malady did not have anything like the same drastic social effects as the great epidemics of smallpox, typhus or buboes. It is not certain to which of these three varieties of plague the Athenian pestilence of 430 B.C. belongs. But its description by Thucydides still remains the briefest and most striking general account of the physical symptoms of such scourges and the moral and psychological rotting of society which accompanied them. They were the same in medieval times as in his day, except that under Christianity, with its more oppressive religious climate and consequently more hysterical populations, still more frantic extremes of despair and debauchery must have been witnessed.

The great historian writes:

'The disease began in Ethiopia and then descended into Egypt and Libya. Next, it suddenly fell upon the Piraeus and the city of Athens, so that the people at first said that the Spartans had poisoned the cisterns.' Athens was then at war with Sparta. During the medieval outbreaks Jews, Saracens and other heretics, including of course 'sorcerers', were accused of originating the epidemic in this way. 'I have had the disease myself and seen others sick of it. Suddenly men were seized, at first, with an intense heat of the head and redness and inflammation of the eyes and the parts inside the mouth became bloodshot and exhaled an unnatural and fetid breath. In the next stage sneezing and hoarseness came on and in a short time the disorder descended to the chest, attended by severe coughing and sneezing. There was violent vomiting of every kind, accompanied by great distress. In most cases ineffectual retching produced acute convulsions which sometimes abated directly, sometimes not very long, afterwards. The body was not very hot to the touch. It was not pale, but reddish, livid and eruptive into small blisters and ulcers. Patients could not bear to have on them the slightest covering ... they wished to remain naked and desired more than anything to throw themselves into cold water. Many who were not prevented did so. Most of them died on the seventh or ninth day from internal heat ... after the crisis the disease sometimes attacked the genitals, fingers and toes, so that many patients lost these members. Others lost their eyes also. Immediately after recovery there was often a failure of memory. Many did not recognise either themselves or their friends. The most dreadful thing was the despondency of the victims.'

He goes on to describe the instant increase in crime of every sort and the mad orgies staged by those who plundered the property of the dead and dying. Yet the medieval epidemics at their worst were transitory. They were terrible dictators while they lasted. But they were not always on the throne. An even more fearful, because far longer-lived, tyrant of European society was on the way. This invader broke in upon the continent in the very last decade of the period regarded as medieval in these pages. From 1495 to 1910 syphilis proved, as leprosy had proved up to the early seventeenth century, continuously and obstinately endemic, with infinitely more destructive results than the older malady had ever imposed upon the Christian world. The reason was that this dictator, like others from Haroun al Raschid to Stalin, assumed an almost endless series of disguises.

Not the least effective of these was the moral opprobrium with which syphilis came to be regarded after it had been proved to be transmitted mainly by sexual intercourse. In the Middle Ages, however, this factor, though it was present, did much less to maintain the disease in being than the relentless puritanism of later epochs. For in the last years of the fifteenth century common sense about carnal love was everywhere gaining a footing in the strongholds of religious fanaticism. The bigots were still powerful, especially in the Church. But many scholarly and able prelates had long recognised the difference between an intolerably harsh repression of the sex instinct and a reasonable control of it. As for the lay citizens, particularly if they were widely travelled men of action or business, as so many were at this time, few could then be found to censure the syphilitic as their barbarous ancestors had censured the leper or as top-hatted nineteenth-century doctors scorned or even refused to treat their venereal patients.

Before the advent of syphilis the word 'venereal' had been used, even when applied to unpleasant occurrences, in at least a semi-jocular sense. Usually the Venus-adjective implied a compliment. The mistake made by the twentieth-century cockney in alluding to a 'venereal' old gentleman would not have seemed particularly ludicrous to Europeans before 1495. But after that date the epithet suddenly assumed a distinctly sinister significance, which it has borne ever since.

Medieval writers occasionally mention venereal plague (*lues venerea*). But they certainly often—some authorities say always —meant by this term maladies which we ourselves should not consider venereal. It was only in 1527 that the Rouen physician Jacques de Béthencourt called what was undoubtedly as a rule syphilis a 'venereal' disease. Its usual name at that time was simply the *morbus gallicus*, the French sickness.

The maladies known by the name of the ancient Greek goddess of beauty can hardly be said to have assumed either endemic or epidemic proportions prior to the advent of syphilis. Pope Ubertinus VIII in 1345, just before the 'Black Death', is related to have perished in consequence of a disease of the genitals caused by 'libertinage with women'. In a manuscript preserved by Lincoln College, Oxford, a doctor of theology named Thomas Gascoigne declares that John of Gaunt died in 1399 of 'putrefaction of the genital member due to the performance of carnal congress with women'.

Moses, Hippocrates and Galen, the Roman doctor Cornelius Celsus, a contemporary of Jesus Christ, and the Arab physicians of later times were all familiar with gonorrhoea, which they regarded as an ordinary skin affection and treated accordingly, if we except Moses, who austerely recommended slaughter of the victims, though not, it seems, on moral grounds. A famous mural inscription, moreover, found in the ruins of an antique brothel at Pompeii complains of a girl who, though extremely good-looking, was discovered by her lessee, too late, to be 'a dunghill within'. In view of the enthusiasm of Romans generally for both hot and cold water it is unlikely that this versified lament simply means that the prostitute had not washed. The most probable explanation of her 'dunghill' is that she had gonorrhoea.

Medieval regulations of the tenth, eleventh and twelfth centuries in France, England and Austria forbid citizens to consort with harlots suffering from 'the burning'. An English item of 1430 refers in Latin to 'keepers of women having the infamous disease' (*nefandam infirmitatem*). In the thirteenth century Venetians suffered from *lues inguinaria*, 'groin plague'. In the *Gargantua* of Rabelais (I. xiv.) Master Tubal Holofernes dies of 'the pox' (*vérole*) in 1420. A Dijon police-court report of 1463 mentions that a certain Jacote de Chateauvillain, confronted with a would-be ravisher, a priest, told the fellow she had 'the great evil' (*le gros mal*), whereupon he let her alone.

From such vague and casual testimony only one inference can be drawn. If Europeans knew syphilis before 1492 at earliest they troubled themselves very little about it. So it could never have been recognised as a serious menace to society. But this indifference changed very rapidly to horror in 1494, the momentous year after Columbus's discovery of 'certain Asian islands' and that of the crossing of the Alps, in August, by King Charles VIII of France. He had a cosmopolitan army of thirty-six thousand men. About eight hundred prostitutes of various nationalities dogged the footsteps of the soldiers.

A force of Neapolitans and Spaniards, sent by King Ferdinand II of Naples to stop this polyglot horde, was beaten at Rapallo on the 8th September. Florence, Siena and Rome opened their gates during the autumn and early winter. There was a Spanish Pope, Alexander VI, who was a *bon viveur*, to say the least of him. Rome was packed with Spanish harlots. Charles's army revelled in the Eternal City all through January 1495. But on the 22nd February the all-conquering invaders entered Naples and a resistance movement started.

The greatest soldier of the day, Gonzalo de Cordova, arrived in Sicily from the Spanish Court to rescue Ferdinand II. On the 20th May Charles retreated northwards. His army defeated an Italian confederacy at Pontremoli, between Florence and Milan, a month later. But on the 5th July at Fornovo, a few miles farther north, the Italians took their revenge. Charles fled to Turin, then to Lyons. By April 1498 he was dead, though not apparently, as might have been expected, of syphilis.

Such was the soil, during the pregnant years 1492-5, into

which the seed of *spirocheta pallida*, the causative agent of syphilis, ripened like the dragon's teeth of the old Theban myth to bear an immediate and monstrous harvest. The turbulence and debauchery of the foreign invaders and the panic of their militarily weak victims were obvious invitations to all the horrors of war. Famine, exposure and sickness in overcrowded, insanitary and lawless living conditions were imposed upon a nation at that time not very conspicuous in any case for the sterner virtues. The Italians descended at once to the most abject venality and cynicism. Not for either the first or the last time in history their men grew reckless and unscrupulous, their women morally corrupt, under the disastrous impact of the northern mercenaries.

Naples in the spring of 1495 reaped an appalling crop of acute fevers, racking headaches, intense pains in the joints, stinking ulcers, hideous lesions, delirium, paralysis and death. The most experienced military surgeons of that age of endless warfare, the most learned students of the natural ills of humanity in that erudite generation, could make very little of the awful phenomena with which they were confronted. The only point in which most of them were agreed was that 'the stars' were to blame. The planets Jupiter, Mars and Saturn were observed to have been in a rare conjunction, in the constellation of Scorpio, just before the outbreak.

The dreadful symptoms and the ferociously rapid spread of the malady seem to have exceeded anything since recorded of syphilis, even allowing for the usual exaggerations of hearsay, though the first commentators were generally sober-sided men of science. Epidemics, especially unfamiliar ones, are of course always terribly severe at first, before they are understood. In the fifteenth century, when still only a small minority of persons were literate or capable of taking logical action, the onset of the new disease of syphilis, destined to be endemic, looked almost like the end of the world.

The ungovernable terror of the nations, the powerlessness of the doctors, the abandonment of all moral restraint, the wild accusations of poisoning, the selfishness, cowardice and stupidity of general panic, the hysterical dancing in the shadows of torture and annihilation, all combined to shake society to its very roots.

For it was soon found that a grave abbot, an innocent, secluded virgin or even a eunuch were scarcely less likely to be affected than a pikeman and his punk. None was immune. No one could undertake business of any kind, from shopkeeping to high diplomacy, without having to allow for these frightful accidents.

As during the 'Black Death' of 1348 and the following years the terror inspired increased the range and comprehensive incidence of the epidemic, for such it can fairly be called at this first stage of its grip on Christendom. Patients, like lepers, were left untreated or taken in charge by quacks and cranks, who made them the subjects of grotesque, disgusting and lethal experiments. The sufferers were at first excluded from participation in any kind of public work or assembly. They were persecuted by the majority of priests, who as in later centuries, even the twentieth, found it more convenient to denounce the sin of concupiscence, for which they considered the disease an obvious penalty, than to comfort the victims. For the latter, again like lepers, were all believed to be highly contagious, at whatever point in the progress of the malady they might have arrived.

It was soon being estimated that one in every representative group of twenty ordinary citizens of all ages, either sex and any occupation, anywhere from Cadiz to Moscow, was infected. The seaports, especially in the north of the continent, where low temperatures and consequent high consumption of alcohol ruled, had the highest percentage of syphilitics. For the moral deterioration that generally occurs in hard drinkers causes them to take risks they would not dream of running in their sober senses. It also renders them highly susceptible to physical and particularly nervous disorders, in the latter of which syphilis so often plays a radical part. The mixture of races in such coastal towns, moreover, favoured the dissemination of maladies communicated by sexual intercourse, both because of the exceptional excitement promoted in seafaring visitors from the south by a foreign environment and owing to the exasperation of their lubricity, often exceeding that of northerners in any case, by the prolonged confinement of voyages far more protracted in the fifteenth century than today.

The same principles held good, in part, at the seaport of Naples in 1495. Here the venal, and to a northern eye exotically alluring, south Italian women and boys stirred the rabble of French and other levies from beyond the Alps, though they could hardly be said to have endured a difficult campaign, to a frenzy of eroticism. They had of course, in accordance with the universal custom of the time, their own whores with them. But this fact rather heightened than lowered the fertility of the soil in which the fatal seed so horribly flowered. For the soldiers' doxies were impelled, either by feelings of jealousy and revenge on their faithless protectors, or simply for economic or purely personal or instinctively professional reasons, to offer their services to the inhabitants of the country.

The scientific innocence, the utter lack of any idea of hygiene, the gross superstitions and the lax sexual habits in general of Europeans at the end of the fifteenth century rendered syphilis for thirty years as potent a promoter of the very sin which many people supposed to have originated it, as bubonic plague itself. The Spanish physician Ruy Diaz de Isla (b. c. 1463) called the new pestilence the 'Serpentine Evil'. For, he wrote, 'the hideousness of the disease is such that no better object of comparison than the serpent can be found. For just as that animal is hideous, formidable and terrible, so also is this malady. It eats away and corrupts the flesh, breaks and destroys the bones, cuts and shortens the sinews.'

Diaz, however, tells a ridiculous story about children who frightened their elders by masquerading as syphilitics, with imitation pustules on their faces. Reckless jesting of this sort must have helped to propagate the epidemic. The robust gaiety of that age, of Mediterranean man in particular, was prone to make light of maladies that would have a devastating effect on our own peace of mind. We know, or think we know, so much about bacteria that a cut finger sends us flying to the iodine bottle. But the average fifteenth-century citizen, in his relative ignorance, cared little for his aches and pains until they became unbearable. Even then his instinct was rather to lie and groan till he felt better or died than to seek relief from the not unreasonably dreaded physicians, or those who pretended to be expert healers.

Diaz was writing in the 1530's. But he had first encountered syphilis at Barcelona in 1493. Two years later the Venetian army surgeon Marcellus Cumanus described his experiences at the battle of Fornovo, where the retreating troops of Charles VIII were routed by an Italian confederacy. 'I depose to having seen,' he writes, 'several men-at-arms or footsoldiers with pustules due to boils on their faces and all over their bodies. The pustules resembled millet-seeds and generally first appeared under the foreskin, upon it or on the glans penis. The pustules itched slightly. Sometimes the earliest symptom took the form of a single pustule, like a small vesicle. But the rubbing occasioned by its itching soon gave rise to corrosive ulceration. A few days later acute pains were felt in the arms, legs and feet, with the formation of large pustules. The latter, if not treated, lasted for a year or more.'

A colleague of Marcellus named Alessandro Benedetto added in 1497: 'So repulsive is the aspect of the entire body, so acute are the pains, especially at night, that this disease exceeds in horror even leprosy ... the patient's life is imperilled.' In the corpse of a woman who died of syphilis he found certain bones which had swollen suppurated to the very marrow. 'I have seen elsewhere,' he continues, 'patients who had lost their eyes, hands, nose, feet and other parts of the body.'

In the same year the Paduan professor of medicine Niccolo Leoncino published at Venice a short account of the 'French or Neapolitan Evil'. He observed, like Marcellus, that the pustules began on the genitals but soon spread to the whole body, especially the face. In addition to their disgusting aspect, they caused, almost continuously, great pain. Gaspare Torrella, bishop and physician, called the new disease *pudendagra*. One of his patients 'at first had an ulcer on the penis, accompanied by a long, hard tumour extending radially towards the groin and discharging a thick and virulent pus. After six days the ulcer had half healed. But he was then seized by the most intense pains in the head, neck, shoulders, arms, legs and ribs. Ten days later numerous pustules appeared on the head, face and neck.' Infants, he adds, were often infected by their nurses through a kiss and passed syphilis on in the same way to other women by kissing or being kissed by them.

Josef Grünbeck, a shrewd man of affairs in contact with the most refined society of his time, contracted syphilis in 1496 and published a treatise on it five years later. He saw a company of German soldiers covered from head to knee with wrinkled scabs, bristling with rugged excrescences. 'Their hideous black shapes could be seen anywhere on the face ... and disfigured the neck, chest and pubic parts. They were harder than bark. The face, ears and nostrils produced thick and rugged pustules shaped like the spigots of casks or else diminutive horns, resembling prominent teeth and exuding a stinking liquid.'

Such observations, which could be quoted at far greater length, included all the major symptoms of the primary and secondary stages of the disease as it is known today, though in later centuries they were much more widely spaced. But it was one thing to observe symptoms and another to account for them. The medieval doctors did not guess the existence of bacteria. Without microscopes they could only conjecture the causes of syphilis. These were listed alternatively as the anger of heaven, changes in the sky or the organisation of the stars, the behaviour of the soil, or of the waters of the earth, the operations of magic or the machinations of the devil.

The priests, unlike the doctors, did not hesitate for a moment. The incorrigible sexual immorality of Christians, they averred, had brought this terrible curse upon them from their outraged Creator. Were not the majority of persons infected the most dissipated? What if little children and churchmen of known blameless lives had also been victimised? They had obviously taken the sins of others upon themselves or others were being punished through them.

Some laymen, however, pointed out that quite a few ruffians who committed every sin under the sun three times a day had nothing the matter with them and even looked abominably healthy. What about them? They didn't seem to care when told that hell and all eternity would chastise them after death. The theologians retorted learnedly. But their arguments met with less and less appreciation.

The astrologers stepped into the breach of faith. They explained that God, for reasons unintelligible to the feeble brains of men, had allowed a disastrous grouping of planets to occur. Bishop Torrella's *De Pudendagra* of 1497 supported this hypothesis on the ground that in certain signs of the zodiac 'stars exist which have the property of producing monsters'. Until well on in the sixteenth century the astrologers on the whole outpointed in these debates the theologians and even those who tried to identify syphilis with previous epidemics and endemics, especially leprosy.

Meanwhile the question of prescription appeared even more urgent than the problems of observation and explanation. The bewildered doctors did little, to begin with, but advise sexual continence. But this was a counsel of despair. Accordingly, prospective fornicators were next recommended to consult the position of the planets before consummating their desires. Others received detailed instructions on what to look for and where on their partners' bodies. Although this procedure might have been thought to tone down ardour in the most excitable, the disease nevertheless continued to spread like wildfire. The doctors started treating the question of its control more practically and scientifically.

Bishop Torrella, now official physician to Pope Alexander VI and Cesare Borgia, advised that the primary sore, as soon as it is noticed, had better be sucked 'by some person of low condition', whose subsequent fate would be a matter of indifference, in order to remove the poison. Then the scab should be washed and brought repeatedly into contact with a live bisected chicken or a live bisected frog. Later the good bishop is said, though on dubious authority, to have again proved his interest in zoology by plunging Cesare Borgia, who had shown him a primary sore, into the disembowelled but living belly of a mule.

But doctors as closely in touch as Torrella with distinguished patients did not always find it easy to quote their case histories for the benefit of colleagues and the general public. It was not because cardinals and princes were ashamed of being reported as syphilitic. No one at the end of the fifteenth century would think any the worse of them for that, apart from the diminishing band of those who still believed that the 'French Evil' must be a sign of the displeasure of heaven. The reason why eminent men did not want their disease made public was that a busy public figure rumoured to be contagious might be avoided for purely hygienic reasons by the very persons he most wished to cultivate, even in a private capacity. It would not be his erotic exploits but the state of his health that would make him unpopular.

The ravages of the 'pox', as it came afterwards to be called, and the terror it inspired, entitle it to a place in the long procession of morbid scourges which had so much to do with the furious medieval mania for sexual indulgence. It had been sweeping Europe ever since Christian priests began to censure the amorous so severely. It rose to a barely credible climax in the Holy City itself when the amazing Pope Alexander VI, who seemed to some of his contemporaries an incarnation of Satan himself in his suave cunning and unscrupulous greed and lechery, led the way to every kind of erotic frenzy, normal and abnormal. Such excesses may have been reduced slightly by the mortality of the first fearful onset of syphilis (1493-1503) which is said to have killed a third of the European population. But large-scale outbreaks of lethal disease have been proved over and over again to turn even respectable persons into a herd of 'Gadarene swine'.

The 'herd instinct', in fact, regularly takes charge in periods so afflicted. Just as in war, the excitement of fear reverses the sliding staircase of evolution. Men and women tend to become what Swift termed 'yahoos'. Tennyson described the process as 'reeling back into the beast'. All dispassionate observers throughout history have noted the phenomenon in more or less striking phrases. When plague, smallpox and syphilis struck in the Middle Ages the European populations were already in revolt, clandestine in some places, turbulent in others, against clerical persecution of their sex instincts. Since the enormously enhanced risk of a painful death then shadowed not only the battlefield, the dungeon, the law-court and the torture-chamber, but also the altar, the market, the farmyard and the factory, even the lover at his tryst and the knight at his investiture, the business of everyday life went rotten with concupiscence.

Even pre-Christian as well as Christian tabus were recklessly defied. The statistics of incest and sacrilege mounted. The traditions of hospitality and charity, the innocence of children and the helplessness of the imbecile and the senile were corrupted and violated. Individuals committed atrocities which they would have abhorred if they had not dreaded the onset of a fatal agony at any moment. Even naturally refined minds like Boccaccio's drowned their panic in wild wine-parties and amorous intrigue.

DANSE MACABRE

For all had some beloved friend or relative to mourn, who had died in misery and the 'hideous storm of terror' the Jacobean dramatist John Webster was actually to put on the stage a hundred years after the last medieval pestilence.

In the fourteenth century the Paris Faculty of Medicine itself had declared, during the Black Death, that medical science could do nothing against the wills of either God or Satan. For if the plagues were not the avenging swords of heaven they were the grip of demons let loose upon the earth. In these terrifying circumstances, writes an Italian chronicler, 'Modesty ceased to exist. Nuns hurried from their cloisters to dens of debauchery. The very invalids in the hospitals called for prostitutes, who did not hesitate to expose themselves to certain death in coupling with the sick.'

Such ferocious waves of sensuality are clearly one of the reasons why the number of births invariably increased after the infection of a whole region had run its course. Meanwhile the doctors tried to purify the air of streets and houses by burning therein branches of the juniper, ash and aloe, or amber and musk if these expensive substances could be afforded by the patient or the municipality. Sick-rooms were also drenched with rose-water and vinegar, the latter liquid being also taken internally with bread, cinnamon or thick soup. Plenty of garlic was also advised, in addition to the wearing, carrying or sucking of emeralds, garnets, turquoises and amethysts. Breathing, the physicians recommended, should be kept to a minimum, the mouth and nose being covered. So called antidotes were prescribed by dozens. But not one of them was any use. The average man or woman preferred to try to forget the malady by giving every carnal appetite rein to the point of utter exhaustion.

In the history of epidemics it was only towards the end of the fifteenth century, just before syphilis gained its stranglehold upon the continent, that Europeans made any effort to disinfect clothing and other objects which might be contaminated. It is true that before that date streets had occasionally been cleared of human faeces and other filth and laws had sometimes been passed to prohibit the entry to a city of strangers who might have come from areas ravaged by the pest. But special health officers were rarely appointed before the sixteenth century.

In such conditions epidemics, like wars, devastated Europe almost unimpeded in the Middle Ages. Each type of infliction encouraged lubricity for the same reason as sometimes impels persons sentenced to death by either doctors or lawyers to 'have a good time while they can'—if they can. It is true that, as the medieval physicians pointed out, this sort of excess, i.e. carnal dissipation, generally hastens demise in the case of disease. But few persons living under a rapidly thickening thunder-cloud of imminent dissolution so ardently desired to prolong their lives that they were prepared to spend the brief interval remaining to them in mere meditation, as recommended by the Church. For as a rule they found that thinking simply intensified their wretchedness.

Distraction proved much more popular, and the more exciting the better. The pleasures of *luxuria*, that deadliest of sins, were voted the best of all. It has already been noted in these pages that the masses of medieval people were stimulated to fervent eroticism by a relatively narrow and barbarous psychology. We have also seen how this tendency was fortified, in particular, by reaction against the steady persecution of the lusts of the flesh by the priesthood and in general by religious hysteria and superstition. Further enhancements of sexual mania were provided by the feudal constitution of society itself, by contact with Asian and North African sensual refinement and by the still surviving tradition of pagan lasciviousness under the whip and spur of Venus and Cupid. Both incessant warfare and the actual recurrent catastrophes of nature in the shape of epidemic maladies, on the whole far more frequent and larger in scale than at later epochs, also deepened the preoccupation of the continent in those days with the mechanism of reproduction.

Children are always inordinately interested in their sexual organs. From puberty to middle age most men and women, even in temperate climates and when hard pressed to earn a living, sublimate this interest in love affairs of various kinds, through teenage sentimentalities to the heady romanticism of young adults and the argumentative relationships of maturity. If the classical civilisations are left out of account as a world in which common sense remained comparatively untouched by specifically religious anxiety, it may not be too fanciful to regard the first officially Christian millennium as the childhood of our own more familiar humanity, the Renaissance as its exuberant youth and the long decline of modern times, when first politics and then science ousted art, religion and love from the forefront of the average mind, as corresponding with the last four or five decades in the lives of individuals. However that may be, it is certain that the Middle Ages, for reasons which may now be fairly obvious, but to which it is necessary to add a few more, outdid the epochs of Raphael and Rembrandt, Voltaire and Napoleon, Queen Victoria and Hollywood, in uncompromising devotion to the sexual orgasm *per se*.

X   Privilege

i. LORDS OF MISRULE

THE feudal organisation of medieval society arose naturally from the confused circumstances of a vast imperial civilisation in ruins at the feet of barbarous tribesmen. The primary social need was protection against further large-scale violence, either in the form of foreign invasion, revolution by oppressed minorities or tyranny by such administrative bodies as could be set up. Ordinary people could not secure such a defensive apparatus from anyone but themselves.

Before Christianity the Romans had evolved the relation of patron and client. It suited well enough the clan system of the German hordes, whose chieftains gave shelter and support to freemen who could not maintain themselves in any other way. Land leased by the chief in return for the services of such a vassal was an important feature of this bargain. The Franks of Gaul added a further note to it. Their main characteristic being a boisterous pride in their own personalities, they added to the German scheme a formal oath of fealty, representing ideas of faith and loyalty on both sides. The chiefs who received this oath became nobles when their savagery adopted more civilised trappings. They passed on the mutually protective relationship to their kings or to one another, and finally, on their conversion, to the Christian Church. For the new bishops held huge estates in perpetuity through the testamentary dispositions of pious or speculative benefactors. Such properties, for instance those owned by the sixth-century Pope Gregory I, surnamed the Great and canonised as a saint, had to be worked by thousands of serfs, successors of the pagan slaves. They could be useful in war, the

PRIVILEGE

main business of the secular nobles who swore allegiance to the prelates, and expected the latter to provide them, among other supplies, with soldiers. In due course more serfs were collected by the monasteries than by the palaces or castles.

Of the two depressed classes, serfs and women, it was the latter who made the most progress against privilege in the Middle Ages, though at first there was not much to choose between them. The attitude of the Church was originally equivocal, though inclining on the whole to severity. On the one hand females in the sixth century were forbidden to receive the Eucharist in their bare fingers, which were stigmatised as 'impure'. On the other hand the dogmatic insistence on monogamy, though it was long defied by secular magnates, and the cult of virgins in the earlier medieval period, improved the prospect of feminine emancipation. In the twelfth century the rise of 'chivalry' gave married women the important status in European society which they can fairly be said to have occupied ever since. The clerical side worked hard for the whole millennium to neutralise masculine tendencies to idealise the other sex for qualities other than a rigid chastity. But all this effort never even looked like succeeding. By 1500, though the technical conventions of chivalry had long been abrogated, the rule of the glorified courtesan was at hand. It was to remain potent in lay society until the twentieth century and to constitute one of the most effective weapons in use against ecclesiastical obscurantism throughout that momentous epoch of four hundred years.

The serf differed from the slave only in so far as there were legal limits to the lord's power over him. He could not be killed or sold as an individual, but only exploited as an economically better proposition than a slave for the working of an estate. This condition, that of a tributary peasant attached irrevocably to the soil, obtained in some parts of the classical world, as in the case of the helots of Sparta. Under the pagan Roman emperors such serfs gained further legal protection. The German barbarians who took over as Christians also had their semi-free slaves. Complex laws regulated the degrees of the master's power all through the Middle Ages. It was never absolute for the simple reason that serfs who have some benefit from the produce of their labour will work harder than slaves who have none.

At the same time slaves continued to exist alongside the serfs. It never occurred to the medieval mind, whether secular or religious, that the immemorial and, as it were, automatic institution of slavery could be morally objectionable. Serfs, however, were always in the majority, steadily increasing from about half the population of the continent in the earlier centuries to four-fifths of it in the later, when material prosperity all over Europe had greatly improved. The younger female members of the serf or villein class, i.e. of the most heavily worked and taxed tenant families, were a natural source of supply for the whoremasters. These women, dissatisfied at home with the dull toil to which marriage made no difference, flowed regularly to the highways and brothels, where they led a gayer life for a while, with the prospect of becoming well-to-do bawds themselves in their later years. Such is one of the reasons for the extraordinarily large number of medieval harlots, against whom it was hopeless for the Church to thunder.

As for the out-and-out slaves, they were bought and sold all over Europe, just as in the East. The inter-continental slave-traffic also flourished. White girls were purchased by black or brown dealers and *vice versa*. Venice and Byzantium were the main clearing-houses. Neither popes nor emperors could stop the trade, though they passed law after law against it, less for moral than for economic, administrative or doctrinal reasons. The loss of Christian labour and the importation of heathens, the violence and fraud accompanying the slave-raids and bargains, were major vexations to the governments of Europe.

But after the death of Charlemagne, and even after the rise of strong separate nations on the continent, the evils of serfdom continued. The Church progressively took over the estates ruined and terrorised by the robber barons. But the latter then had to be enlisted to defend the new lands. The system of a local defensive militia independent of the lord's retainers, more disciplined in war and acting as a police in the intervals of peace, never took root on the European mainland. If it had, the old-fashioned French knights would never have been defeated as often as they were, during the Hundred Years' War, by the compact ranks of English archers and men-at-arms. The latter were in demand as far away as Portugal and won many a battle in which their own dynasties were not directly concerned.

There were, of course, many medieval women of the lower classes who never became whores, though they played their full part in the revolt against clerical austerity. Even certain learned nuns read so much that they began to be tolerant of the excesses of their more high-spirited sisters. With such large numbers of young men falling daily in battle or abjuring marriage on taking up an ecclesiastical career, females often outnumbered males in certain regions. As time went on they turned less and less to the nunneries and more and more to the relative freedom enjoyed by spinsters and widows in labour, commerce and industry. There they had far better opportunities for amorous intrigue and the practical work of brewing and baking, weaving and light manufacturing, which they instinctively preferred to study and meditation.

Marriage normally took place at puberty, fourteen or earlier, and was always arranged by parents, relatives or guardians. The girl's own inclinations had nothing to do with it. Whether or not the husband soon afterwards perished or disappeared, his function in nine cases out of ten, biologically speaking, was merely to introduce his wife to the pleasures of fornication. Her appetite for these thus once aroused, she soon fell in love with someone else, and usually pretty often. In these circumstances the Middle Ages were remarkable for the numbers of energetic young women who had little to learn about life and were determined to get the most out of it. The twelfth and thirteenth-century queens of France and England, the 'eagle' Eleanor of Aquitaine, wife of Henry II, the masterful Blanche of Castile, wife of Louis VIII, and Berengaria of Navarre, wife of Richard I, are only the royal representatives of a temper just as enterprising among the wives of merchants and even labourers. History and literature prove again and again that women of all classes were formidable allies of men in the long struggle against medieval theocracy.

It was in vain that as late as the thirteenth century one Philippe de Novaire had written that women need not be educated, since all they had to do was to be chaste and nothing else was expected of them. Unworldly and sour-tempered pedants of this description had really little or no influence on the development of medieval society. It proceeded from the first to an almost masochistic cultivation of femininity, beginning with the adoration of virgins, continuing with besotted knights who begged for their mistress's pubic hair and ending with the apotheosis of expensive trollops at the papal Court. Even rape, in the age of chivalry, had to be conducted by rote. Damsels must not be ravished, runs this rule, unless their escorts are prepared to defend them.

For early in the thirteenth century chivalry, like feudalism, itself, had been codified by the hair-splitting lawyers of the day. The social order was fixed into a system which involved great wealth, prestige, privilege and legal exemptions for certain princes, lords and prelates. This arrangement only began to break down when the ideas of kingship and separate nations replaced it at the end of the fifteenth century.

Accordingly, to be born fairly far up in the feudal hierarchy generally meant throughout the Middle Ages the possession of unquestionable power over large numbers of less fortunate people. The latter were bound by law and custom to submit to almost any caprice of their social superiors. There could be no appeal from one's immediate chief unless he himself fell out with his own. As in the Services and the Church to-day no one would normally be such a fool as to quarrel with the man next above him in rank, unless the fellow really treated him with atrocious injustice. The only difference was that in medieval times, if this happened, one had to put up with it or, if the lord in question had no powerful enemies, be hunted down like a criminal.

Human nature being what it is, unscrupulous abuse of this practically unlimited authority, secular or religious, became common. Women and girls, in particular, had no defence against it. They could be ordered to surrender to any outrage, from the beatings which the otherwise kindly and cultured Knight of La Tour-Landry regularly gave his wife and daughters to the most brutal violation of their persons. It was no wonder that the thirteenth-century satirist Guyot de Provins declared his age to be 'stinking and horrible'. But it is certainly a wonder that in this same century women could be more frivolous, in their dress as well in their behaviour, than ever before in Christian Europe, if we except Byzantium.

PRIVILEGE

Their horned headgear was compared by people like Philippe de Novaire with the Devil's antlers, their extravagantly pointed shoes with his claws, their trains with his tail. Their wigs and bare bosoms, their frolics and wild talk with pages and jesters in the castles and male servants and apprentices in the merchants' villas, scandalised the clergy, or so at least the men of God protested. Chastity belts came into fashion. But duplicate keys could be manufactured. The ladies would endure any hardship or impropriety to get rid of this early form of bikini.

A manuscript of this century called *La Geste des Dames* gives a most vivid impression of feminine high society of the period. 'What shall we say,' writes the keenly observant author, 'of the ladies when they come to feasts? Each marks well the other's head. They wear bosses like horned beasts and if any have no horns she is a laughing-stock for the rest. Their arms go merrily when they come into the room. They display their kerchiefs of silk and cambric, set on their buttons of coral and amber and cease not their babble so long as they are in the bower. There they send for brewes and sit down to dine. They put aside their wimples to open their mouths. If a wanton squire would enter at that moment he could not well fail of privy mockery. Two nimble valets have their hands full with serving all these ladies, each to their own fancy. The one is busy fetching their meats from the kitchen and the other drawing good wine from the buttery. When therefore they have dined at their good leisure, then they herd together to babble in secret. One tickles the other's heart if by chance she may entice some secret from thence. Then when dinner hour is come they descend the steps and trip daintily into the hall, hand in hand. Then doth a man see so many of the fair creatures together that he may not pass the day without sighing for them. But when they are set down to meat they touch no morsel of all that is spread before them. Right coyly they sit there and show their faces. She whom men most gaze upon is she who bears away the prize. When therefore they have shown all that is in front, then they find some occasion to sweep the bench-backs, that men may see the costly workmanship on their backs which was hidden in front. When they arise from table, I say not from meat, for they have eaten but little and yet have well dined, then go they to their bower to entertain each other with subtleties of needlework whereof they love to talk. Then up comes the frilled work and the open work, the German and the Saracen work, the scalloped and the woollen work ... the diaper work and the rod work ... nor is the double samite forgotten, nor do they fail to handle again and again the redener work. She who knows most of these things shall be their lecturess to whom the rest hearken without sluggardy. None sleeps here as they do at mass, for all are cheerful companions in these lists of vanity. Then go they homewards back from the feast. And forthwith they put away their sleek and comely heads.... Then they play the folly that costs so dear. For when they are bidden again to some feast, then for a long time before they are busy unravelling their wreaths and plaited tresses to make all new again. Thus all their heraldry is changed, both field and device. Here they put beads where spangles were before. They cut up a lion and make thereof a soaring eagle or pare a swan into the form of a hare couching. But however well their attire be fashioned, when the feast is come it pleases them nought. So great is their envy now and so high grows their pride that the bailiff's daughter counterfeits the lady.'

One of the reasons why life in a thirteenth-century castle or manor-house tended to erotic romping at informal moments was the absence of armchairs. At table benches were in use. They were placed along the walls after the meal. But in the ladies' workrooms or 'bowers' only beds were to be found to sit on. A male visitor could not be otherwise accommodated. The custom certainly made for agreeable familiarity and flirtations of mounting intimacy. The presence of persons inferior in rank to the hostess and her caller did not worry either of the chief conversationalists. As in classical times and in the East, servants, until near the close of the Middle Ages, were regarded as little more than mobile furniture.

They would be expected to attend their social superiors while the latter dressed and undressed, fondled each other and satisfied every physical need from micturition and evacuation to fornication itself. Like the ancient Romans of the Pompeian frescoes and the pashas of the Levant, the knight and his lady would give orders for refreshments and other services while actually coupled in the closest possible embrace. The effects of such dis-

PRIVILEGE

plays on the sexual susceptibilities of the staff were of course considerable, though probably less so than they would be today. But the valets ('varlets') and maids knew that any improper behaviour on their part, as a result of such stimulation, would be savagely punished. Consequently, they would have to reserve the culmination of their excitement, as a rule, until they went off duty. They may on occasion have imitated the Phrygian slaves mentioned by the pagan Roman epigrammatist Martial, who asserts, without giving his authority, that they masturbated while surreptitiously observing the amorous antics of Hector and Andromache. But no medieval account of any such proceeding is recorded. All the same, these domestic habits of the Middle Ages scarcely made for the continence of libidinous desire so tirelessly advocated by the Christian clergy.

As the general luxury of the ruling classes grew more and more ostentatious in the fourteenth and fifteenth centuries the serfs revolted in arms, again and again, all over Europe, always ultimately in vain. The horrors of the so called 'Jacquerie' in France in 1357—Jacques being the commonest name for a male French peasant—exceeded, though not by much, those of Wat Tyler, Jack Straw and John Ball in relatively pacific and victorious England. In defeated and ravaged France, after the disgrace of the aristocracy at the battle of Poitiers, when King Jean himself was captured by the English under the 'Black Prince' Edward, castles were stormed by the starving rustics and their exquisite inmates slaughtered with every circumstance of cruelty and outrage. In England the sacrosanct archbishop of Canterbury, the second most important man in the realm, was beheaded by the desperate rebels.

But retaliation proved as ferocious as rebellion. Cardinals, bishops and abbots joined the enraged barons in merciless vengeance. The leaders of the serfs were buried and burned alive, disembowelled and ploughed into their own fields by oxen. It was not until more liberal ideas began to prevail in the sixteenth century, due less to the efforts of Christian charity than to the revival of classical philosophies, more humane than their medieval successors, that the masses of mankind could discern some hope of being treated better than cattle.

The notorious custom of the *jus primae noctis* which entitled a landowner to enjoy any bride before her husband was allowed to do so aroused a great deal of indignation in later centuries. It began to be exercised quite early in the medieval period, as much by clerical as by secular magnates. But naturally most of them hadn't got the time to stick to the letter of the law. The bridegroom, unless the girl was a famous beauty, could generally avoid the indignity of official cuckoldry by the payment of a fine. Or again the act could be merely symbolised by the owner of the estate ceremonially stepping over the matrimonial bed in which the woman lay. Even if he definitely claimed the right and duly took advantage of it by actual copulation, many peasants believed that the bride's inevitable resentment of defloration would be better directed against a comparative stranger than the man with whom she expected to spend the rest of her life. Moreover, the prestige of rank was so great that the mingling of the blood of some social superior with that of a labourer's family might be thought to improve the latter's status among their colleagues. It was often in fact noted that in cases where the right was exercised to the full the first child born would be handsomer and stronger, bolder and cleverer, than the subsequent offspring. Probably this did happen sometimes, since the father would at least be better nourished and better educated, at any rate, than the yokel he anticipated.

In general, throughout the Middle Ages, bastards of noble blood, well known to everyone as such and even surnamed accordingly, often reached high positions in society and boasted, like Philip Faulconbridge, son of King Richard I, in Shakespeare's *King John*, that they were all the better for being illegitimate. The degree of heat in sexual congress was generally supposed to influence the mental and physical characteristics of any child born of it. Thus a clandestine and ultra-passionate relationship, for instance, would cause the woman to conceive a more desirable infant than one drowsily begotten, 'twixt asleep and awake', by formally married partners well used to each other.

In such social conditions, so far as girls not yet betrothed and women already wedded were concerned, the local lord could help himself to them whenever he felt inclined without either the prize herself or anyone else daring to object openly. Accordingly the sanctity of marriage, one of the most important pillars of the

Christian faith, often became in practice a mere farce, in the highest and lowest income groups particularly. Only the substantial traders took it very seriously, with the natural consequence that the seduction of a burgess's wife carried more prestige among rich and reckless young men than the cuckolding of one of their own kind or, of course, a simple manual worker.

During the thirteenth century, which may be regarded as covering in many respects the climax of the specifically medieval way of life, since the earlier period so often seems to look back to the pagan decadence and the later forward to the Renaissance, the mercantile class joined the Church and the lay landowners as a decisive social influence. The prose fiction of the time reflects this change. Merchants' wives, daughters and their lovers are very often the central figures. The tone is on the whole more hostile to women than that of the monkish chroniclers and much more definitely so than that of the aristocratic or fashionable poets, who tended to idealise femininity. The business men, naturally, were more realistic. They suspected female morals, resented being henpecked and bemoaned the opposite sex's incorrigible frivolity and extravagance. For the 'bailiff's daughter', by this time, was really forever trying to ape the grotesquely showy garb and hilarious chatter of the castle 'bowers'.

By the end of the century silk was common even in England. The overskirts, long and wide over a short and narrow 'shift', rustled over the floor or ground on all sides. The gaping burgesses compared these 'tails' with those of peacocks and magpies. Prostitutes slit these voluminous garments up the side almost to the waist, revealing legs in closely fitting stockings, generally red, with blue garters. The breasts were accentuated, as in modern times, by well stuffed leathern pouches.

Males did not catch up for nearly a hundred years. But Sir John Arundel in the last half of the fourteenth century—he was famous, as already noted, for the peculiarly callous sacking of a convent—had fifty-two new suits embroidered with gold thread. Prelates like Wolsey also dazzled everyone, even kings and courtiers, by their sartorial magnificence. Chaucer, in his usual ironical style, notes the obscene elements of masculine costume at this time. The trunk-hose were so 'scant' that they showed the outlines of genitals and anus quite clearly. From the back a solidly built man might easily be taken for a masquerading woman. The effeminacy was increased by the general lack of beards and the mania for 'motley'.

In the time of King Edward IV of England the Commons petitioned their dandified and exceedingly lecherous sovereign, proposing that 'no knight under the estate of a lord shall use any gowne, jaket or cloke but it be of such a length that he, being upright, shall cover his privy members and buttokke'. The King and his barons, evidently, might do as they pleased.

A couple of generations earlier, at the Court of the imbecile French king Charles VI, wild orgies took place on feast days, in imitation of the masked revels held in Italian cities. The monarch and his nobles, disguised as satyrs and savages, rushed about with torches, manhandling everyone they met and deliberately trying to convey the impression of 'demons'. As already noted (p. 49) one night they set the palace on fire. Several of the courtiers were burnt to death. Charles nearly shared their fate but was rescued just in time by the young Duchesse de Berry.

His wife Isabeau of Bavaria, as robust mentally and physically as he was weak in both respects, set a fashion for big bosoms, men's boots, loads of jewels and clothing cut so as to show glimpses of flesh through slits and slashes, which the Paris preachers called 'windows of hell'. Agnes Sorel, mistress of Charles VII, carried the denuding process still further. She showed her breasts almost to the midriff. The Middle Ages closed in a blaze of parti-coloured and fantastically cut clothing for both sexes.

Meanwhile, in the countryside outside the capital of the decadent French sovereigns, as the fifteenth century opened, famine and slaughter reigned. The peasants took to the woods like wild animals. Wolves roamed the outskirts of Paris. The English and the Burgundians marched and countermarched all over the country, burning and plundering. It was time for Joan of Arc, who was sexless, to save the sex-mad Court of France from utter ruin.

The almost tropical scenes at gatherings of the privileged classes were not confined to the secular Courts, castles and manor-houses imitated in the burgess's villa. Extraordinary luxury and sexual debauchery accompanied the four-year session of the purely ecclesiastical Council of Constance called in 1414 by a notoriously loose-living pope, John XIII, actually to reform, among other things, abuses within the Church. The chronicler Gebhard Dacher gives the number of priests in attendance as eighteen thousand. They far outnumbered their lay companions, who nevertheless included eighty-three wine merchants, three hundred and forty-six 'clowns, dancers and jugglers' and seven hundred undisguised whores. Even the latter, however, were only those whose addresses the industrious Dacher was able to ascertain. A list drawn up in Vienna comprises fifteen hundred 'common harlots' (*meretrices vagabundae*). Others who for one reason or another kept quiet about the real point of their presence in Constance must have considerably increased this figure. They made a lot of money. One at least is recorded to have retired for life on her profits, amounting to eight hundred florins.

Nor was this assembly an exceptional occasion for clerical fun and games. Gian Francesco Poggio, the precocious humanist already mentioned more than once in these pages, calmly told the Cardinal di San Angelo, who had reproached him for keeping concubines, that Christian priests had been doing so 'since the beginning of the (Christian) world'. Pope Clement VI himself, it was alleged, had received a letter from Beelzebub congratulating him on his wickedness in the erotic line.

The fact is that the peculiar conditions of medieval society had given rise to many more reasons for the prevalence of unbridled lubricity than had existed in the pagan Roman Empire. During the first Christian millennium Europe became far more coherent in its manners and customs than it had ever been before or ever was to be again until the Americanisation of the mid-twentieth century. Even at the height of the heathen Roman power the multiplicity of religious cults and the still strongly marked differences between the many races enjoying Roman citizenship kept the Empire fragmentary. But Christianity and intermarriage had given the continent an almost uniform character since about the year 1000. This circumstance, allowing the medieval passion for travel full play, spread such habits as feudalism and the sexual licence it involved wide and fast.

Secondly, the two great privileged classes, the nobles and the

Church, relatively immune from interference by the laws, were exposed to much greater temptations to erotic indulgence than the rich men who came after them. Thirdly, the impoverished masses of the people, helpless under the tyranny of their social superiors, tended to concentrate their scanty leisure on the only amusement which didn't cost them anything, namely the exercise of their amorous proclivities. Fourthly, and most important of all, the existence for the first time in history of a religious tabu on the most ungovernable of all carnal appetites aroused instinctive resistance.

In a busy, well-ordered community people have so much to do, so many mental alternatives to a primitive preoccupation with their sexual organs, that they have little time left in which to be concupiscent. The indulgence of fleshly lusts then becomes a sort of hobby or sport rather than a permanent refuge from misery for the oppressed, an inexhaustible method of killing hours for the idle or a defiance of censorious authority for natural rebels. The dangers of commercial, political and even intellectual activities in the Middle Ages did not as a rule encourage that sedulous attention to them which would otherwise have kept noses to grindstones. Even the philosopher, as Rabelais remarked, sometimes muffled his venerable head in an ample hood and slunk off to the ubiquitous brothel. The labourer, the merchant, the priest and the knight had still more incentives to practise their kissing.

The *luxuria* of the two former classes is not, in the nature of things, well documented. Manual workers couldn't write and burgesses seldom wrote anything but accounts. If they did, they preferred, like the English Paston family, to prove their sobriety and reliability rather than their erotic prowess or satirical acumen. But there is a very great deal of evidence, on the other hand, as to the libertinage of the powerful clergy and nobility. So far as the ecclesiastics are concerned, much of the testimony is obviously malicious and exaggerated. At worst it is the reckless calumny of underdogs. At best it is the vindictive rhetoric of interested persons, including certain prelates themselves as well as lay scholars like Poggio, mainly impelled by a desire to display their facility in learned invective. But in one famous instance of secular abuse of privilege we have all the documentation we

ii. THE CASE OF GILLES DE RAIS

This altogether exceptional personage was born in 1404 at Machecoul, some thirty miles south-west of Nantes in north-western France. He inherited the immensely wealthy barony of Rais in Brittany and was granted further great estates and cash payments for war services by the Duke, Jean V, his feudal overlord. At the age of sixteen Gilles married a very rich heiress. By 1426 he was fighting against the English, side by side with Joan of Arc. After the coronation of Charles VII at Reims the young king made his most successful male commander a Marshal of France.

Apart from these claims to social, political and military eminence, Gilles was well known as a generous patron of literature and music, a skilled illuminator and binder of manuscript books and a producer of 'mysteries' and 'moralities', as the more or less edifying stage performances of the day were called.

About 1436, long after Joan had been captured and burned by the English, the Marshal became interested in alchemy. For even his huge financial resources were being depleted by the almost regal style in which he lived. He wished, therefore, to 'make gold'. For this purpose he began dabbling in the 'black art' of contemporary necromancers. Some years before this date his wife had left him. Her reasons for doing so only became clear to outsiders in 1440.

In that year he was rash enough to commit an act of sacrilege from the consequences of which even a Marshal of France could not hope to escape, especially since the necromancers had already much reduced funds which might otherwise have been used for bribery. Duly arrested and charged, he secured absolution by confession. But during the proceedings it appeared that he had also frequently committed murder. The ecclesiastical court not being competent to deal with this accusation the prisoner was handed over to the Parliament of Brittany, which found him guilty and hanged him.

The records of these two trials, preserved in Paris, Nantes and elsewhere, cast a sinister light upon the results in the sexual field of the feudal organisation of late medieval society.

At the Court of the Dauphin of France, later Charles VII, in Chinon, Gilles is stated to have been a pattern of virile beauty and elegance, indispensable through his wealth to the poverty-stricken prince, heir to a kingdom in the last stages of devastation by the English. The desperate little Court had given itself up to debauchery of every description. But the Baron de Rais did not join in these orgies. He went off almost at once to try to hold Anjou against the invaders from across the Channel. They were literally too many for him. He returned defeated, but not disgraced, to Chinon.

Joan of Arc had just reached the Court. Charles passed her on to Gilles for instruction in military matters. He took the field with her and shared in her triumphs. But there is not the slightest evidence, oddly enough, that she was ever his mistress, any more than anyone else's. The Baron was at that time, it seems, the kind of man to be impressed by her saintliness. In any case it is clear that he was highly inquisitive by nature. He must therefore have studied her behaviour with intense curiosity, unlike the coarse veteran generals of her staff, who merely regarded her as a prodigy, probably supernatural, and let it go at that.

Yet neither they nor he could save her from the English and their French collaborators. The Marshal was near Rouen, perhaps on the watch for some chance of rescue, when they tried and burned her. It is conceivable that the disappointment, perhaps the despair, of this dashing man of action at these events changed him from a superb soldier with more than a touch of the reflective artist in his make-up to a sour recluse. However that may be, he retired at once to his castle of Tiffauges in Brittany and, at the age of only twenty-six, took no further part in public life.

At Tiffauges, after beginning to live like an aesthete, he turned gradually to demonology and ended as a horrifying monster of lust and cruelty. The satanism can be accounted for as in equal parts dictated by his pressing need of money and his intellectual curiosity. But just as the purest and most resolute spirit he had ever met, Jéhane of Domrémy, whom the English called the witch Joan, could neither show him a France restored to glory and prosperity nor explain her own soul to him, so the foulest devils conjured up by his necromancers could neither give him gold nor satisfy his exorbitant desire to understand the superhuman, the inhuman and the subhuman.

As for the atrocities he then proceeded to commit, Gilles had never previously shown, like so many other medieval barons, the least taste for such abominations. During his military career he had been fond of stringing up French traitors who joined the English. But he never tortured them. Few fifteenth-century commanders showed such restraint. The Marshal's one serious vice, before Joan's execution, had been a pride so ingrained that even at his trial he could say, in confessing heresy: 'I was born under so mighty a star that no one has ever done or ever will do such deeds as I.'

Perhaps he had wanted to be a saint like that marvellous girl, a worker of miracles. Perhaps when this grandeur was denied him he decided to become a devil. The concrete means to this end were available. They were known to him through the frequent trials of witches and wizards in his time. Such prisoners had confessed to masturbating on Communion bread. They had mixed the blood of children, whose throats they cut, with the ashes of other infants whom they burned. They had then diluted the brew to make sacramental wine for their mock Eucharist. They had admitted using a naked woman's rump as an altar for its administration. Cases had even been reported of renegade priests cutting the Host in half, perforating it and using it as a sodomite would use the anal canal of his accomplice.

Gilles sent for people of this sort. One of them, named du Mesnil, demanded the Marshal's signature in his own blood to a document in which he contracted to give Satan anything required except the signatory's life and soul. He signed, thus committing himself to the perpetration of any atrocity. The Black Mass was celebrated in his private chapel. But the Adversary did not turn up as anticipated. Other experiments, complex, tedious, fantastic and disgusting, were tried in vain.

Then Francesco Prelati, a Florentine ex-priest, reputed to be the greatest master of black magic in the world, arrived at Tiffauges in the unexpected form of an apparently charming young man of twenty-three. He told de Rais that the Evil One could only be attracted by the crimes most abominated by the Church, such as rape, sodomy and murder. The Marshal, like any other soldier of his time, had copulated freely with the hordes of female camp-followers in his armies. At the frantically dissipated Court of Charles VII he must occasionally, in the intervals of campaigns, have attended the promiscuous orgies staged by that somewhat melancholy and cynical young man. But by this time Gilles was sick of women. He had begun to detest their figures, their characteristic odours and the very smoothness and softness of the feminine epidermis which so allures the normal male.

He felt, on the contrary, that sodomy, in his present state of mind, would be a crime infinitely preferable to the brutal forcing of innocent young women to serve his now dulled appetite for fornication. Accordingly, he began by seducing the choir-boys of the Tiffauges chapel. They gave him little or no trouble. In the social conditions of the age their submissiveness was natural enough. Some of the lads were already prematurely sex-obsessed. Others lost their fears and nausea in the awe they experienced at so intimate a relation with their almighty master. He seems to have treated them, at first, with some delicacy and real affection.

But soon these almost sentimental transports wearied him as much as had his dealings with common harlots in former days. Prelati pointed out that Satan would hardly condescend to inhabit a soul merely stained with such trifling peccadillos. Lodgings fit for the Enemy of God must be rotted through and through with horrors much more appalling than the mere corruption of a few sordid young ragamuffins, however angelic in appearance.

Gilles had no particular aversion from homicide. He had often enough killed with his own hand helpless antagonists on the battlefield. But under Prelati's instructions he now went much further. His first victim was a little boy whom he obtained, probably by kidnapping, from outside his own household. He cut this child's throat, severed his wrists and extracted the heart and eyes from the corpse. He and Prelati then offered these relics, with due incantation, to the Devil.

But nothing supernatural occurred after this atrocious sacrifice. The Marshal left the room in a rage. Prelati buried the remains that night, secretly, in consecrated ground. But the experiment was repeated again and again. For eight years between 1432 and 1440 the Baron's servants ransacked the countryside. They carried off youthful shepherds from the lonely pastures. They seized schoolchildren on their way home or at play in the streets, fields or woods. None of these captives was ever seen again.

Their grief-stricken families roamed the roads in a vain search for the missing, whose numbers rose week by week. At first evil spirits were supposed responsible. But gradually the terrified peasants began to suspect the truth. The legend of a monster with a blue beard who murdered his wives and hid their bodies in a locked room of his castle still subsists in Brittany. It was used in the late seventeenth century by Charles Perrault in a tale which soon became famous. Somehow or other this piece of folklore, which is probably of very early date, going back as far, perhaps, as the sixth century, got confused with the conjectures of the parents of the children made away with by Gilles de Rais. Even today some Breton rustics identify 'Bluebeard' with the fifteenth-century lord of the Machecoul district. It is possible that Gilles, who was very extravagant, even eccentric, in his dress and toilet, dyed his beard blue. It was a fad not unknown at the time. But there is no definite evidence of any such thing.

The Duke of Brittany ordered an enquiry into the constant complaints of vanished children in the neighbourhood of the Tiffauges castle. A long list of their names and addresses, amounting to several hundred, was drawn up. They turned out to be mostly boys between seven and eight years old, the sons of artisans, labourers, shopkeepers and small tradesmen. Then it was found that when the Marshal changed his quarters, going to other properties he owned in the region, children again disappeared along his route. Some witnesses spoke of a veiled old woman who, when she accosted children, raised her veil to show a youthfully handsome male countenance. It was alleged that the boys and girls who were attracted by the seductive talk of this personage and followed him to the nearest copse or wood were seized by undisguised men and bundled into sacks. The peasants called this pseudo-ogress La Meffraye, the name of a local bird of prey.

It also appeared that Gilles was in the habit of watching for young beggars from the windows of his castles. His reputation for munificence caused quite a number of such youthful vagrants to apply for interviews. The lads would be at first well received. Then they would be relegated to a cellar to await sodomy, death and mutilation.

In 1440, at the Marshal's trial before the Breton Parliament, witnesses estimated the numbers of violated and murdered children at between seven and eight hundred. They swore that none at all were left in the village of Tiffauges. In another of the Baron's castles a whole heap of the corpses of young boys was discovered in the basement of a tower. In a second a huge cask was found, packed to the brim with similar pitiful remains. Even in much later times piles of bones and skulls were unearthed in ruined or abandoned dungeons of the district.

The prisoner gave details of his usual procedure, once the boys had been made ready for him. First they were stripped and gagged, then caressed and finally outraged. Next, he drew his dagger and deliberately dismembered them. He cut open their chests and buried his face in their lungs. He dissected the abdomen of his victim and seated himself, wriggling blissfully, amid the exposed entrails, meanwhile contemplating the last agonised convulsions of the dying child. He added to this soul-sickening catalogue of obscene sadisms the calm statement: 'Nothing pleased me so much as the spectacle afforded by torments, tears, terror and blood.'

Yet even these horrors bored him after a while. He turned to necrophily, fondling and committing fornication or sodomy on the corpses of girls and boys he had just cut to pieces. One day he actually disembowelled a pregnant woman and attempted intercourse with the foetus.

He could go no further with purely physical perversions. The next stage was cerebral. He ceased to play with his victims, dead or alive, like a cat with a mouse. He entered the last and darkest cavern of sexual infamy by enjoying the psychological misery inflicted by the duping of innocent gratitude and affection.

He would order his associates, Prelati and the rest, to hang a child from a bracket in the wall of the luxurious apartment devoted to his orgies. When the boy or girl began to suffocate, he commanded the executioners to release the twitching body. Then he took it, with every sign of care and compassion, on his knee. He caressed the reviving flesh, uttered consoling endearments as the child's consciousness returned and dried its tears. He pointed to his accomplices and whispered: 'Look at those wicked men. They are evil. But, as you see, they obey me. Don't be afraid. I've saved your life and I'm going to take you back to your mother.'

The child would be delighted, hugging him in a loving access of thankful relief. Thereupon he would begin gradually to saw off its head, with his dagger, from the nape of the neck. In the process of detachment the head would droop forward with what seemed, in his own words, 'a gesture of acquiescent languor'. Then, as the blood streamed down shoulders and arms, he would bend the body double and violate it, bellowing like a beast in rut.

Eventually he would turn to the stunned group of spectators with the triumphant scream of a megalomaniac. 'No one on this earth but I would dare to do such a thing as that!'

Yet still Satan, the 'supreme deceiver', as the priests truly called him, refused to manifest himself to this most appalling of all his disciples. For a while the Marshal seems to have really lost his reason. He was seen and heard roaming the empty stone corridors of his castles, uttering wolfish howls that echoed like the wailing of the damned. Similar performances are related of Cesare Borgia at a later date.

Gilles de Rais, however, soon recovered his senses, quietened down and proclaimed penitence, though not yet in public. He wept, fell on his knees and mumbled long prayers. He instituted at Machecoul a collegiate church dedicated to the Holy Innocents massacred, according to the Bible, by Herod Antipas, tetrarch of Galilee, on being informed of the birth of Christ. The Baron also talked of entering a monastery or going on foot, begging his bread by the way, to Jerusalem.

Then suddenly, with the typical instability of hysteria, he plunged once more into sadism. This time he simply rushed at his victims in a sort of delirious frenzy, gouging out their eyes and beating out their brains with a blackthorn cudgel. Thereupon, covered with their blood, he would dart out of the room, with grinding teeth, alternately glaring like a fiend and roaring with demoniac laughter. He would make straight for the woods, leaving his parasites to clean up the mess and bury the dead. In the forest his maddened imagination, like that of the old judge in Balzac's story, presented the trunks and interlacing boughs of the trees as engaged in furious copulation or assuming the indecent attitudes familiar to him from his own lecherous frenzies.

He saw the erect phallus everywhere, either stuck motionless as a central branch between two others resembling parted thighs, or else rising to penetrate beneath a skirt of foliage or alternatively emerging obliquely downwards from a greenish mass of twigs to stab the velvety, moss-grown abdomen of the passive earth. The bark of the tall beeches reminded him of youthful flesh. The oaks recalled the rougher skins of the tramps who visited him, expecting charity and meeting instead with pitiless outrage and an agonising death. Where boughs forked he perceived in their creases, in their gaping orifices and slashed, bulging pads simulations of the human or animal vulva.

When he looked up at the glimpses of sky, the same obscene suggestions excited him. Clouds took the shapes of breasts, buttocks or even male organs, from which a milky flow of sperm drifted. There, too, the forest images were repeated. Giant thighs swelled. The triangle of the female pubes shimmered, beside it a splayed anus cavity and the ridged scars of ulcers, pustules and chancres. The reddened autumn leaves fluttered down upon him like drops of blood. Dryads awaited rape and slaughter within hollow trunks. He longed to wield the axe like a woodman. The very rustlings of the wind in the trees recorded, to his ear, the moans of lust or pain.

At night he dreamed continuously of succubi and incubi, reinforced by the dead bodies of his victims. They took the forms of larvae which attacked his genitals and sucked his blood till it spurted in all directions. His own groans rang in his head like the screams of children calling for their mothers and begging for mercy. Then he would crawl from his bed and fling himself prostrate before a crucifix.

PRIVILEGE

Towards the end of this period the country people fled when they caught sight of his tall, brooding figure riding down a forest track or across the fields. The villages, when he passed through them, lay silent and deserted. No one ventured to denounce the Lord of Rais. For he could have had any peasant who did so hanged out of hand. As for the richer folk, including the Duke himself, they had no wish to quarrel with this financially almost ruined magnate until they had made quite certain he had no more land to sell.

The Church alone had nothing to lose by bringing the sacrilegious scoundrel to justice. The highly respected Bishop of Nantes began to watch his still wealthy parishioner very closely. The worthy prelate did not have long to wait.

In the spring of 1440 Gilles sold his lordship of the demesne of St. Etienne de Mer Morte to a certain Guillaume le Ferron, who sent his brother Jean, a tonsured cleric, to take the property over. On Whit-Sunday Jean le Ferron attended mass in the parish church of St. Etienne. Suddenly the Marshal, sword in hand and followed by two hundred men-at-arms, burst in among the terrified congregation. Flourishing his weapon over the head of Le Ferron, who happened to be kneeling, the terrible Baron demanded his instant submission. On receiving it in the most abject terms, the intruder had the unfortunate priest dragged off forthwith to the castle which Guillaume le Ferron had just bought. There Gilles first despatched Jean le Ferron under close guard to Tiffauges, then lowered the portcullis of the St. Etienne castle and prepared for a siege.

He thus committed two serious crimes of which both secular and canon law were bound to take notice. He had not only levied troops without the consent of his overlord, the Duke, but also profaned a consecrated edifice by seizing there the sacred person of a duly constituted servant of the Church. The Bishop of Nantes, with some difficulty, persuaded Jean V of Brittany to send one force to storm the castle of St. Etienne with a view to arresting its illegal occupant and another to rescue Jean le Ferron from the Tiffauges stronghold. But the Lord of Rais had by this time moved from St. Etienne to his fortified manor-house at Machecoul.

Meanwhile the Bishop himself set about collecting the evidence of the Marshal's already notorious magical practices, including rape, sodomy and homicide. In just over a month the now shocked and enraged prelate had all the testimony he needed for canonical action. His whole diocese was at once ordered to take steps to bring the malefactor before the Cathedral Chapter.

Gilles either felt that he could not resist, from a mere manorhouse in open country, so strong a force as that sent to arrest him, or else he believed that he might still be able to placate the Duke and secure immunity from the Chapter by confession. In any case he surrendered immediately to the Bishop's notary. That functionary searched the manorial residence from top to bottom. He found bloodstained boys' shirts, calcined bones and ashes which Prelati had not had time to get rid of. The Marshal and such of his associates as had not already deserted him were transported, in chains, to the gaol at Nantes.

The trial, by two courts at once, civil and ecclesiastical, opened on the 19th September 1440, a Monday. But the civil officers took little part in the proceedings. The secular arm confined itself to passing the sentence of death, which no priest, by canonical law, could utter. The prisoner at first adopted a haughty and abusive attitude, questioning in vain the competence and good faith of his judges and the witnesses against him. The main counts in the indictment were the rape and murder of hundreds of little children, the practice of sorcery and black magic and the sacrilege at St. Etienne.

Gilles contemptuously declined to defend himself. He would not answer any questions. He simply reiterated his previous scurrilous invectives. The Bishop, after consultation with the Inquisitor present, then passed sentence of excommunication.

On resumption of the proceedings next day everyone in the court was amazed to see the formidable Lord of Rais enter with bent head and clasped hands, in the attitude of a penitent. He now stated, in a low tone, that he recognised the competence of his judges and begged pardon for his offences. The sentence of excommunication was thereupon cancelled, as the law required.

But in order to ensure that the culprit's necessarily ensuing public confession should be precise and genuine, torture was decreed. Gilles successfully appealed for this ordeal to be put off till the next day. Meanwhile he confessed privately to the Bishop of St. Brieuc and the Breton State Chancellor. Prelati also confessed, in his patron's presence, to these officers. When the Italian was dismissed, de Rais took a significantly sentimental leave of him. 'Farewell, dear Francesco,' he is reported to have said. 'We shall never see each other again in this world. But you may be sure that we shall be happy together in paradise. Pray for me and I shall pray for you.'

These words were probably spoken as much for the ears of the Bishop and the Chancellor as for Prelati's. The Marshal may or may not have been sure, by this time, that he was doomed. Most likely his mercurial temperament still oscillated between hope and despair.

It was noticed that on this day and thereafter he seemed to have aged by twenty years. He looked haggard and, for the first time in his life, carelessly dressed. His sunken eyes burned as if in fever. He trembled incessantly, shaking his fingers in the gesture afterwards imagined by Shakespeare for Lady Macbeth. Yet it was in a steady tone, that, for hours on end, he recited the sombre catalogue of his crimes. Their details, of which he did not omit the minutest, occasionally elicited brief groans from the horrified audience.

No one present had ever heard anything like it. The judges, appalled, crossed themselves repeatedly. The Bishop of Nantes, at one point in the confession, rose and veiled the face of the image of the crucified Christ.

When the prisoner had ended his unprecedentedly dreadful narrative, he dropped to his knees and prayed aloud for the mercy and forgiveness of his Redeemer. Then he turned to face the vast, silent assembly of spectators. 'Parents of those whom I so cruelly put to death, pray for me!' he cried, beating his forehead against the stone paving of the hall.

A typically medieval incident then occurred. The Bishop of Nantes left his high seat, walked to the almost prostrate prisoner, raised him to his feet and embraced him. 'Pray thou,' he adjured the sobbing, shuddering penitent, 'that the just and terrible anger of Almighty God may be appeased. Weep, thou madman, that thy tears may wash away the pollutions of the charnel-house within thee.' Everyone in court knelt. A long, deep-toned murmur of supplication for the salvation of the soul of Gilles de Rais filled the enormous building.

Two days later final sentences were passed. The ecclesiastical court recognised the accused to have been guilty of heresy, apostasy and the conjuration of demons. The punishment for each of these sins was excommunication. But in consideration of the prisoner's repentance he would be received back into the bosom of the Church. The civil court condemned him to death and the confiscation of all his property in retribution for the hundreds of abductions and murders of children he had committed. Prelati and the Marshal's other accomplices were at the same time ordered to be hanged, like himself, in flames.

The Lord of Rais retained his penitent attitude to the end. At the combined stakes and gallows he consoled, embraced and prayed for his only fellow-sufferer, Prelati. His other companions in crime seem to have escaped after sentence. The Marshal himself perished without showing any signs of fear, either of his painful death or of what might follow it. Meanwhile the huge concourse of spectators intoned the solemn supplicatory Latin of Psalm CXXX, *De Profundis Clamavi*.

In the history of sexual excess during the Christian era the case of Gilles de Rais is unique. Never before nor since did anyone perpetrate such monstrous aberrations of the reproductive instinct on so tremendous a scale, repent of them with such apparent sincerity and die for them with such courage. After allowance has been made for every possible exaggeration and surrender to dramatic effect by the chroniclers of the time the main facts remain as certain as they seem inexplicable. They will not fit the hypothesis of either hypocritical blackguardism or temporary insanity on the part of the accused. Up to the death of Joan of Arc he had behaved like an honourable and sensible soldier by the standards of his day. Thereafter for eight years he deliberately engaged in acts as vilely degrading as his vivid imagination could conceive. Yet very soon after his arrest and incarceration his conduct became that of a pious Christian. It remained so up to and during his execution.

Historians in general have inclined to believe either that Gilles was the relatively innocent victim of a huge conspiracy by Jean V and the Bishop of Nantes to get hold of the last of his lands or that he was a convinced Satanist to the very end. In the first view all the evidence must have been faked but the prisoner realised that he could not escape the machinations of his enemies and confessed in order to shorten a hopeless struggle. The second opinion holds that the witnesses told the truth, that the Duke and the Bishop were honest and that the confession was a cynical mockery of Christianity by a fanatic who believed that he would thereby please the Devil whom he worshipped.

An adequately close examination of all the documents concerned and all the ingeniously detailed arguments since advanced on various hypotheses by modern theorists, especially psychiatrists and experts in medical jurisprudence, would fill a massive volume. It could only be written by a specialist in the byways of medieval history, demonology and sexual aberration. The foregoing brief outline omits many particulars of much interest. The purpose of its inclusion in the present work was only to attempt a reinforcement of its main thesis by a peculiarly striking instance of the results of a policy of confining the erotic impulse, on religious grounds, solely to a duly authorised propagation of the species within the bonds of matrimony.

An impartial study of the facts of medieval life seems to prove that such repression can only lead at best to a licence in the sexual field exceeding that under more liberal dispensations. At worst the persecution of amorous inclination by a bigoted theocracy may inaugurate, as in the case of the Lord of Rais, a recklessly ferocious perversity repulsive to even the most enthusiastic advocate of complete freedom for people to do as they please with their generative organs.

iii. EPILOGUE

The consequences of restriction are illustrated in the patristic age, i.e. before the year 1000, by the endless complaints of Christian prelates, like that of Boniface about the eighth-century English, of the 'lechery and adultery' of whole communities. By no means all of this behaviour can be ascribed to innocent savagery such as that of Tahitians when the first missionaries arrived or that of the seventh-century Queen of Ulster solemnly exposing her private parts to the hero Cu Chulainn, simply as an act of courtesy. This last episode is related to have occurred long after the introduction of Christianity to the country.

Superstition, from the start, fought a losing battle against the imperatives of erotic passion. In the first Christian epics the knights no more hesitate to copulate, by force if necessary, with unguarded or captive women and girls, than did the Homeric suitors of Penelope with the female attendants in her palace. The Ithacan princes only spared the queen because marriage was an essential preliminary to acquisition of her wealth.

The Christian clergy themselves, both high and low in rank, joined to a considerable extent in the general zeal for illicit fornication. The tenth century pope John XII was tried for adultery and incest, like his successor John XIII in 1415. Bishops took mistresses. Abbots installed harems. Parish priests were often regarded by their flocks as dangerous to the villagers' wives. Wandering or mendicant friars soon gained a similar reputation. The confessional, in particular, afforded daily temptation to the confessor. He had to listen to exciting stories of sexual misdemeanour by fair penitents who went into the frankest details of their experiences. For they had been taught to regard the cleric in question as, in virtue of his profession alone, a bloodless eunuch. Some of these young females, no doubt, deliberately set out to tease him. But others were quite innocent. In either case it would be easy for the priest to withhold absolution unless his repentant sinner submitted to the lust she had consciously or unconsciously aroused in him.

Nor was he always obliged to resort to this blunt expedient. Stories were current even in the earlier period of how such reverend fathers achieved their ends by carefully graduated stages. They were bound by canonical law to ascertain the precise nature of the sin confessed. Their questions could be most readily answered, by relatively inarticulate penitents, through pantomime. The ensuing charade might well lead to an unexpected substitution of the tonsured observer for the absent lover.

As for the friars who called, by invitation or design, to confess women and girls in private houses while the menfolk were away, no modern traveller in vacuum cleaners or washing-machines would ever get off to such a flying start with a personable young housewife, daughter or maid. For in medieval society the monk had much of the social prestige which in later times enabled gentlemen to talk shopgirls and domestic staff into fornication without offering them the slightest mercenary consideration for the surrender. Not all the friars were much better educated than their victims. But they all had the gift of the gab and were much more used to dealing with strangers. Above all, they were supposed by most of the lay population to be in daily direct communication with heaven. If the worst came to the worst, they could always affirm, like certain Mormon chiefs in the nineteenth century, that a supernatural vision had ordained the physical intimacy proposed. The reasons given for this command, if asked for at all by the prospective partner, were apt to be tied up in an impenetrable jungle of dog-Latin and pseudo-philosophical or pietistic jargon. The enquirer would either be quite overawed by such gabble or conclude that an ordeal which she understood perfectly well and which after all had its agreeable side would be preferable to being deafened by sermons out of church.

Even male adulterers who came to confess might be forced to reveal the name and address of the woman with whom they had sinned. For she would in all probability turn out to be a useful addition to the confessor's call-book.

As already mentioned, some monasteries, like the lay landowners, exercised the *jus primae noctis* without bothering to trouble the outside world for their sexual entertainment. The brides who obeyed their summons to the sacred building sometimes even brought presents with them. In fact a would-be seducer in those days would have been better advised to join the Church rather than the Army, in spite of the frequent opportunities for rape offered by military service. At any rate he was likely to live longer.

Trade, since comparatively few women were engaged in it or respected it, would be well down on the bright young man's list of possible future careers. It tended also, even more then than now, to be decidedly nerve-racking. The prevalence of fraud and robbery in the unsettled state of the times, the high risks of the slow and ill-found transport and the distinct perils of suing for debt people better off than oneself, let alone the great lords, made a merchant's life on the whole a hard and anxious one. The common labourer had better chances, actually, of going in wholeheartedly for fornication. For no one cared what he did among 'villeins' of his own sort, so long as he kept his hands off the property and persons of others.

But the youthful aspirant to amorous conquests might think more than twice about taking up medicine. The circumstances of that profession favoured success in casual love-affairs nearly as much as did the life of a friar. There is far less proof, however, that doctors took advantage of their authority to the extent that the clergy did. As both were equally unpopular with talkative sceptics and were equally exposed to calumny, the scarcity of scandal about medicos is remarkable. The oath of Hippocrates apparently meant more in the Middle Ages than subscription to the Creed and the Ten Commandments. The generally detested lawyers were also more often ridiculed for pomposity and unscrupulous money-grubbing than for violating the chastity of their clients.

Yet the general conclusion about the effects of medieval privilege on morals must include the view that it precipitated many individuals into debaucheries which they might otherwise never have dreamed of. Official repression of eroticism, moreover, led to orgies far more strange than those of mortification. Of these last habits flagellation began as self-torture and often ended in self-stimulation. But other masochisms practised by those who took ecclesiastical prohibitions too seriously caused both men and women to rack, roast and even hang themselves. The whole repertory of post-classical torments, on a rising scale from the hair-shirt, was ransacked to prove that those who voluntarily underwent them agreed with the fanatics that the human body, so far from being indulged, should be chastised up to the limit of endurance.

The boot made of soaked parchment contracted with heat and slowly blistered the flesh. The 'wedge' broke thighbones. The flayer's knife removed strips of skin from the abdomen and buttocks. The thumbscrew and the cupfuls of burning brandy splashed in the face were occasionally added to the ritual scourgings, fastings and freezings. A few monks and higher-ranking churchmen castrated themselves, as did Origen, for long the most influential of Christian theologians, in the third century. Nor were these self-castigators by any means only the tonsured.

Finally, the age offered nonconformist intellectuals little scope for meditation and enquiry except in theology. Heresies, therefore, of every kind proliferated, especially before the rise of overwhelming secular power among the orthodox priesthood of the thirteenth century. But the divagations from orthodoxy continued sporadically right up to the Reformation itself, which split all Christendom in two. The points upon which such heretics chose to differ from the generally accepted dogma seem to the modern mind usually trivial enough. But they sometimes involved, as in the case of the Cathars in early thirteenth-century Provence, a morality which most thinkers today would consider definitely superior to the obstinately narrow tenets officially promulgated by the medieval popes. Now and then a heresy would claim a greater degree of sexual freedom or, like the Czech Hussite sect of the Taborites in the fifteenth century, full emancipation for women. The adherents of such doctrines would be at once accused, as were the 'Bulgars', i.e. Manichees, of abominable sexual practices. But whether or not they explicitly demanded modification of the tabus on love-making, the restlessness which dictated their defiance of the ruling hierarchs can plausibly be argued to have arisen, fundamentally, from the unnatural restraint required by the Church in these matters.

The occasional indulgence permitted by the bishops, as at festivals and in carnival time, never proved to be enough to satisfy those who lacked the wealth or the courage to make arbitrary use of their generative mechanism. It is fairly safe to deduce from the evidence of more or less organised lasciviousness current among all classes, but especially the privileged, in the Middle Ages that a majority of citizens remained far from accepting in their hearts the rule of their religion that physical love must play as little part as possible in their lives. For it is clear enough that they did not even bar it from their main preoccupations. Certainly very few laymen indeed, perhaps fewer than at the present time, seriously aimed at the clerical ideal of sending it into permanent exile.

XI   Eastern Glamour

MOST people know that the Near East cradled the first centuries of civilisation. A good many know that Orientals still understand better how to get the most out of the sex instinct than Occidentals do. The influence of the hot lands of Asia Minor and of Egypt in this respect reached European communities almost as soon as they began to live in walled cities. Cretans and Myceneans, followed by Greeks and Italians, took a great deal of interest in Eastern erotic refinements. When the Roman Empire became Christian it had long since learnt most of what its oriental and African citizens had to teach of *luxuria*. In the moral chaos of that epoch it was not, after all, so surprising that the first Fathers of the new Church, itself born in an East which could be as austere as it was generally licentious, felt that an essential preliminary to the acquisition of converts must be an all-out assault on the persistent mania for amorous enjoyment.

Initially, they succeeded, up to a point. The best spirits of the age saw that peace and sobriety, to say the least of it, were ideals that went together and promised the restoration of a more reasonable mode of life than they percieved among those not yet baptised. These missionaries were tough and fought hard. But they were few. The barbarians flooding in from every direction were innumerable. After a few years the plan to chain up Aphrodite—or Ashtaroth—for ever proved impracticable. The evangelists could do no more than prevent the goddess from running absolutely wild. In this perfectly justifiable task genuine Christians have been engaged ever since. But they have gone too far at times in their zeal to convince congregations that fornication is the root of all evil.

EASTERN GLAMOUR

The medieval millennium was at many periods and places such a time. Pronounced rebellion against clerical tyranny in the sexual field, and certain other factors already stressed in these pages, often gave prelates all over Europe plenty of excuses for severity. They repeatedly behaved with a vindictive cruelty, as in the suppression of 'heresies', which their more easy-going opponents did not show. But towards the end of the period they learned, taught by sheer experience of the inutility of fanatical violence, to be more tolerant. After the great schism and the bitter religious warfare of the sixteenth and seventeenth centuries, it was the Protestants rather than the Catholics who flogged Venus to the bone. By the nineteen hundreds the pendulum began to swing back again. The process, no doubt, will last as long as humanity itself. Its beginning, however, in the early Middle Ages, reveals a facet of peculiar interest, namely the impact of Asian and African eroticism upon the Europe of those days.

Ever since the Romans had occupied Egypt and Asia Minor the characteristic sexual habits of the Levant had been affecting other regions bordering on the Mediterranean. Of such customs the chief were the treatment of women, girls and boys as mere playthings, the seclusion and voluminous garments of females, the harems of the rich, the widespread homosexuality, the precocious puberty and the morbid addiction to amativeness caused by a hot climate, involving much more idleness and mendicity than in the West.

The entire life of Jesus of Nazareth had been spent in Palestine, in the south-east corner of the inland sea, very close to the sites of the first walled cities of antique Mesopotamia. The first Christians came thence, carrying with them the devotion to ideas of the supernatural, the austere mysticism and humility, which were the obverse of the arrogant, passionate carnality of those lands.

Spreading west, they found manners and morals to be still familiar to them in many ways. For ever since the very foundation of the Empire, a generation before the birth of Christ, the flood of oriental notions, which had been resisted to some extent under the preceding Republic, had been gaining ground in Greece and Italy. Yet basically western psychology was very different. The independence of outlook was not only due to Greek culture. In the early fifth century B.C. that spirit had defied the 'Persian apparatus', as Horace long afterwards called Asiatic luxury and tyranny. But in addition the Teutonic migrations from the north had brought in a cult of rugged individualism resembling that for which such men as Cato had stood in Republican times. It was much more reckless than his, however, more like that of American pioneers in the early nineteenth century. The Christian Fathers, therefore, had to meet a situation which, in Italy at least, promised less than that in regions, including much of Europe, further east.

But the political and economic confusion that followed the collapse of the pagan emperors favoured the doctrinaires of a religion which preached absolute submission to a heavenly power determined upon order and the suppression of fraud and ferocity. The gospel made an immediate appeal to westerners long accustomed to the theoretically benevolent despotism of the later, deified Caesars. Not one of the latter, however, it was remembered by the more learned members of the new bishops' audiences, had sacrificed his own son to prove that he was prepared to redeem the world from its misery.

Nevertheless, a public welcome for a fresh start under the banner of the Trinity was one thing. Private inclination was quite another. The uncompromising oriental cult of the organs of sex was rooted far back in the primitive, originally agricultural religions of the dawn of specifically human, i.e. consciously speculative, mentality. Such rituals had already gone too deep to be forgotten. It proved relatively easy for the Fathers to bring into disrepute the cultivation of the reproductive instinct for its own sake, involving all sorts of refinements and perversions unnecessary for simple procreation. It was much harder for the Christian standard-bearers to eradicate the age-old impulse to give free rein to straightforward appetite whenever and wherever time and place—which the historically minded poet Swinburne in the late nineteenth century considered so important in these matters—seemed to forecast satisfaction.

Christianity could never quite overcome this disposition, as old as mankind itself. The Church tried every expedient, from argument to terror, calculated to lock out Venus Pandemos, the

EASTERN GLAMOUR

greatest rival in its view to the Celestial Virgin, for ever. But, though barred from the door, she constantly returned, as the heathen satirists had so often prophesied, through the window.

Yet success did attend the bishops' efforts to get the theory accepted, especially where boys and girls, as contrasted with married men and women, were concerned. The Asian view of sodomy as a peccadillo was not only rejected, as a sin, by canon law, but rendered positively criminal. The seduction of virgins, other than those purchased in the slave-market for the purpose, had always been considered a serious offence in most communities, whether civilised or savage, all over the world. For virgins were a species of capital which could be relied on for a substantial return by its first owner—the father—so long as it remained intact. He would lose money if his daughter lost her maidenhead prior to marriage. For the pride of masculine lust in general regards an uncontaminated object as more desirable than second-hand or hundredth-hand goods. Only rarely, as for instance in ancient Corinth and eighteenth-century Paris, is the experienced courtesan preferred. In medieval times, as always in the East, the virgin commanded a high price. As a rule it fell abruptly if she fell from virtue.

The Christian Church, as we have seen, also regarded virgins with a respect bordering upon the absurd. But this attitude arose, of course, from ideas the very reverse of carnal. The Fathers adored virgins because they refrained, for the time being at any rate, from the deadly sin of fornication. They were the 'brides of Christ' and for that reason sacrosanct. This coincidence of view between an orthodox churchman and his ideological enemy, the first prizing untouched girls as symbols of a disembodied spirit and the second competing for them as more exciting bodies than those already experimented with, has its humorous side, the central figure being in most cases, despite all the lyric poets who have ever lived, so very far from a suitable incarnation of either Aphrodite or the Mother of Jesus.

However that may be, violations of the Sixth Commandment were regarded more leniently by ecclesiastics—though of course still sternly reprehended—than violations of chaste maidens. An erring husband could certainly be forgiven if he repented. An erring wife did not escape so easily. But she could still hope for rehabilitation after due penitence. For the priests were much concerned to maintain the stability of family life, which they rightly conceived as the foundation of that firm social order they were trying to promote. What they did not see was the fact that matrimonial steadiness has less to do with occasional erotic aberrations than with psychological compatibility. They did recognise, however, that natural jealousy in either partner could be trusted to keep adultery from becoming too scandalous. Fear of the *crime passionnel*, common and unpunished in the East and frequent though punishable in the West, would usually, it was felt, hold infringements of the marriage bond within reasonable limits.

All the same, if the medieval collections of *facetiae* are to be taken literally, adultery was very prevalent in the European Middle Ages. The stories, of course, were meant to entertain and no doubt exploited the delight most people feel in hearing about the discomfiture of others, in this case deceived husbands. The demand for this pleasure was probably met more by invention than by true report. But quite a large proportion of tales convince the reader that they are transcripts of experience, if only by reason of the oddity of their details, fact being so often stranger than fiction. Moreover, documentary evidence, especially concerning the socially prominent, remains almost as plentiful in the history of love as in that of war, largely because physical violence was frequently initiated by adulterous conduct.

Accordingly, down to the rise of Arab power in the eighth century, and its prolonged influence on Europe, the relations between the sexes customary from Damascus to Illyria, taking in the Byzantine Empire on the way, were reflected more than dimly in the freer societies of Christian Italy, Gaul and Spain. The main difference was that the bishops officially imposed a sexual discipline on the turbulent populations of the West much tighter than the oriental religions, of which Christianity had originally been one, ever troubled to force upon Easterners mostly under the effective control of absolute lay monarchs.

Mohammed had been born about 568. By the beginning of the eighth century those who professed the religion he had founded as 'Islam' had expanded from Asia Minor to India in the East and across North Africa to Ceuta in the West. In the year 711 the Berber chieftain Tarik was summoned across the Straits of Gibraltar into Spain by the political enemies of Roderic, King of the Visigoths, to assist in the latter's overthrow. This purpose was duly performed by the allies. But Tarik had sent word to his overlord in Africa that there were possibilities of plunder over the water. In two years the fanatical Muslims made short work of the hopelessly divided and tepidly Christian occupants of the country. The invaders subdued it from Gibraltar to Toledo, whence they crossed the Pyrenees in search of further conquests. At Poitiers in 732, however, they were disastrously defeated by the able Frankish ruler Charles Martel, Charlemagne's grandfather. The main body of the Mohammedan forces then returned to consolidate Arab power in the peninsula.

The cultural superiority of Muslims over Christians at this date and for another two hundred years was marked. They were more learned in science and philosophy, more artistic, more just and generous, more industrious and sensible. Above all, they were quite as individualistic, by tribal tradition, as the contemporary Franks of central Europe.

So versatile and rational a people naturally brought with them into that alien continent an idea of carnal love as uninhibited by religious tabu as any ancient Greek's and actually a good deal more refined than his. For the first time the Goths of Spain heard of an ideal which in their tongue, when they eagerly adopted the concept in the tenth century, came to be called chivalry. The Arab amorist, as his highly developed poetry showed, regarded his women—more than one could of course be possessed by any individual who could afford it—with a consideration extended to them by no other nation of oriental origin. The sentiment amounted to a passionate adoration, generally limited, however, to physical characteristics. It carried mystical overtones, in the same way as the later Christian cult of the Virgin Mary, though no Arab supposed his mistress to be a goddess. He thought of her simply as projecting so overwhelming a material beauty that it seemed to comprise the whole secret of the universe.

It is true that these first Eastern conquerors of Europeans were religious fanatics. To them the Christians appeared as barbarous unbelieving savages, to be exterminated in the name of Allah, the one real God, who had no use for them. He would never admit them to his paradise, a garden, significantly enough, of innumerable virgin *houris*, whose maidenheads were miraculously renewed as fast as the faithful could dispose of them. This eternity of copulation could not have formed a stronger contrast with the blissful passivity among sexless angels conducting an endless litany, which the Christians contemplated. Most of them abhorred the Muslim vision. But for some time converts to it far outnumbered the few who left mosque for basilica.

The African 'Saracens', as the medieval Christians called the Arabs, deriving the word from the latter's own term for 'easterners', were at an even earlier date, the middle of the seventh century, raiding Sicily. In the eighth century an expedition from Alexandria sacked Syracuse. In the ninth organised Saracen settlements were set up in the island, which at once began to change its cultural character. The brief revival of classical learning in Charlemagne's time expanded to take in the science of erotics introduced by the Muslims.

Then Moors from Spain took Panormus and all Sicily became an emirate. Syracuse fell to it in 878. The same historical pattern emerged as in Spain. Civil wars raged. Christians surrendered to oriental sexual habits. Much fraternisation between conquerors and conquered became the vogue. By the middle of the tenth century the island could be regarded as an important outpost of Islam, though never comparable in wealth and power with Cordova at the same period. During the next hundred years Christian reconquest, again as in Spain at this time, got under way. But it registered a more real and lasting success than on the other, the western, side of the Mediterranean. As early as 1090 Count Roger the Norman had won back Sicily for Christianity.

But meanwhile Islamic culture had taken firm root. In architecture and in literature, in science and in social refinement, above all in the relations between the sexes, the passionate devotion to and respect for feminine youth and beauty, the Muslim masters had surpassed their subjects and eventual pupils. The native Sicilians still spoke Greek in those days. But they had forgotten the liberal traditions of Hellas. The Normans, when they came, fell under the same spell of chivalry as had fascinated the Visigoths of Spain. The Mohammedan religion, Mohammedan law and military organisation, were more than tolerated by the Northmen, who studied, admired and retained them in practical use. At the same time the new rulers introduced French and English, Italian and Hebrew settlers. Until the end of the twelfth century the island enjoyed an enlightened despotism. It grew to be by far the most cosmopolitan centre of civilisation in Europe, quite equalling in intellectual brilliance Spain and Provence. The Court of Roger was full of eunuchs and courtesans. But it also swarmed with philosophers, poets and artists of every description, race and creed.

In 1194 the crown passed to the Holy Roman Empire. The second emperor, Frederick II, acceded in 1198 as a minor. By 1220 he had restored the indulgent policy of Roger. Saracens and Jews were no longer heretics. To strictly orthodox Christians, therefore, their emperor appeared as little better than a 'Saracen' himself. But opinions varied so considerably that nearly all Christendom split into two parties, standing for pope and emperor respectively. In Italy the so called Ghibellines exalted Frederick to almost divine status. The opposing faction, the Guelfs, including Dante, named him Antichrist.

But neither side could deny his exceptional intelligence and versatility as a human being. They called him familiarly *stupor mundi*, the wonder of the world. He was very highly sexed even for those days and maintained a huge harem staffed by eunuchs. But this intense physical energy and ardour was paralleled in his mind. He feared no novelty and welcomed, like Leonardo da Vinci and the fashionable intellectuals of the twentieth century, the most bizarre theories and works of art, if they seemed to have any real life in them. He adored scholars, spoke six languages, wrote good poetry, studied mathematics, philosophy, zoology, medicine and architecture. He personally set forth, like Napoleon, a new code of laws. It was adopted in Sicily in 1231, when he was thirty-seven.

Red-bearded, prematurely bald and rather short-sighted, he nevertheless charmed everyone he met by his good humour and wit. After his death many people were inconsolable. A legend arose that this colossal fornicator, patron of the arts and benevolent autocrat had remained indestructible. He was sitting in a cave in Germany before a stone table, through which his russet beard had grown, waiting to restore to the Holy Roman Empire the peace and prosperity he alone could bestow upon it. The story was afterwards transferred, under ecclesiastical influence —for none of the contemporary popes liked Frederick—to his namesake and grandfather, the emperor Frederick Barbarossa I (1123-90), who also had a red beard and was a very decent fellow, but a bit of a pedant and puritan in morals. In fact this earlier Frederick was a much more typical medieval German than his restless, dazzling and Priapean grandson.

Frederick II had looked for a moment like fusing the civilisations of east and west for good. This dream, if it had ever settled down into permanent and invincible reality, would not only have cut out much religious, political and social strife during the next few centuries, including our own, but would in all probability have removed the ticklish question of sensible erotic behaviour from the field of controversy for ever.

But as the thirteenth century advanced the popes asserted their irresistible power over the polyglot intellectuals of a dozen racial strains. Italian ousted Greek and Arabic as the chief vernaculars, outside Spain, of southern Europe. The nostalgia for Frederick (d. 1250) did result in the popular revolution known as the Sicilian Vespers, which took place in 1282. According to tradition one of the hated French men-at-arms in the service of Charles of Anjou, then king of Sicily, indecently assaulted a Sicilian girl in a church near Palermo at the hour of vespers. Her first shrieks brought fifty swords from their scabbards. The whole town rose. Thousands of Frenchmen were massacred before another king, Peter of Aragon, replaced Charles. But under the Aragonese dynasty the island never regained its cultural prestige. For a couple of generations it had stood as the third most effective agent—after the Spanish Moors and the Saracens of Syria—in the promotion for Christian Europe of a more reasonable attitude to life in general and the loves of men and women in particular.

Meanwhile, in Spain, the bigots on both sides had been at a standstill ever since the tenth century. By that time the sophisticated Moorish culture had reached its height in the great city of Cordova under the poet-caliph Abdurrahman III. The Arabs were rapidly abandoning the Koran for manuals of a more practical character. These were concerned with architecture and music, literature and mathematics, medicine and navigation, agriculture and, especially, erotics. The relaxing Muslims took this last science very seriously. They gave it a much more complex structure, both in theory and execution, than had ever been known in Europe since Crete and Mycenae went up in flames.

In the rest of the continent, even in the eastern lands ruled by Byzantium, five centuries of Christian theocracy had obscured the oriental philosophy and practice of profane love which had been so familiar to the last of the heathen plutocrats. The spirit of these exotic refinements, which now re-entered the West, also began to control, in particular, plastic art, letters, metaphysics and scientific research. This change accounts to a considerable extent for the eccentricity of medieval as compared with classical civilisation. The imaginative extravagance and inconsequence of the former, one might almost say its surrealism, gave it the rich and startling variety of a drug-induced dream. Whether or not the drug was Christianity would require a volume to discuss. But the dream certainly, as Goethe remarked of the 'perverse angel' Bettina von Brentano, both fascinates and exasperates. Just as that intellectual madcap burst into the calm German sage's mind and blood like an unpredictable fairy with a taste for silly practical jokes, so the Middle Ages, sandwiched between the degeneration of Athens as interpreted by Rome and the liberal vigour of the Renaissance, has the air of a wild intruder into the logical process of history. Medieval love, from the tenth century onwards, partakes fully of this definitely romantic development.

The Arab poets who settled in Spain had long since given up the traditional themes of desert horsemen. They favoured almost exclusively subjects drawn from sexual experience. For them love was the highest form of happiness, directly related to feminine physical charms, which were far too delicate and mysterious in their operation to be lost in the mindless exercise of bestial rut. They constituted, accordingly, on this view, an ideal object of ingenious speculation and regulation. The Sufi mystics who accompanied the North African invaders of Spain regarded amorous experiment as necessary to the comprehension of God, a bridge, in short, leading to truth. Rejection of a lover by a woman represented the difficulties which intelligence encounters in its efforts to understand divinity. Subtlety in the sexual act itself corresponded with the mental agility not only desirable but actually compulsory in the study of theology.

Ibn-Darrach, for example, (d. 976) writes of his lady: 'She has set wide the gates of passion to an orchard of which I may taste but the beauty and the perfume. I am no wandering beast of the field, to take a garden for my pasture.'

The Visigoth women to whom this conception of love was first introduced—for the Arabs brought few of their native concubines with them—took to it with remarkable rapidity, facility and, one may suppose, astonishment and relief as well as delight. At all times women have detested the brief and clumsy embraces natural to males untutored in what the Sufis called 'the science of hearts'. But such disappointed ladies have not always been in a position, let alone encouraged, to say so. In a generation or two, therefore, feminine influence, as never before in Europe, began to play a leading part in the rehabilitation of amativeness against official Christian disapproval. It is scarcely too much to declare that emancipation of the 'fair' sex first started, though the road to fulfilment was to prove long and hard, in Moorish Spain.

Certain conventional limits, however, were employed by the Arabs in writing or speaking of women. Licentious verses (*baleik*) were indeed commonly composed and circulated. Their imagery was unmistakable. But it was not blunt. The Christians were not so squeamish. From the first they called a spade a spade. They described exactly, in the language of the street-corner, what they lusted for. There was no such language in Arabic. Even today an Arab camel-driver's obscene curses are couched in flowery phrases, with picturesque circumlocutions for the identification of the sexual organs.

Allah's prophet also forbade the representation in graphic art of the forms of human beings. This prohibition came to be disregarded to some extent, though never in the least suggestively, by the eleventh century. A similar reluctance to carve or paint the nude attractively can be observed throughout the Middle Ages or at least as far as the early fifteenth century. Nothing is more striking in artistic history than the Renaissance leap in the other direction. But until then the puritanisms of Christendom and Islam were comparable in this respect only.

For about the year 1100 the troubadours of Provence had already begun to be more outspoken than their Arab models across the Pyrenees. The First Crusade of 1096 was also taking Europeans into Asia Minor, for reasons as much concerned with the reputed wealth of that region as with the Holy Sepulchre. In Syria they learned, among other things, more about that love which their Church so heartily condemned. Thus oriental eroticism, so ardent under its veil of fanciful rhetoric, so realistic for all its ceremony, was taking fresh root in the West at this time. For nearly half a millennium it had almost been forgotten.

Such considerations may or may not have occurred to Pope Urban II when, impelled by political and commercial as well as religious motives, he started the militant rush to Palestine. It is also quite possible that the powerful Order of Cistercians in Burgundy, about the same time, initiated the reconquest of Spain from the Moors partly because they wished to eradicate what they probably considered sexual mania in that peninsula. But of course both these enterprises had the reverse effect. They undoubtedly reinforced the psychological revolution against clerical domination of sexual relations. The rebels had been more or less active ever since St. Anthony was tempted by seductive demons in the Egyptian desert. The insurrection burst into renewed fervour as more and more Christians got to know the Saracen 'demons' better at both ends of the Mediterranean. Like modern Russians who are never quite the same after living in the West for a while, the French, German and English knights returned from these campaigns with almost unrecognisably broadened minds.

As might have been expected, the Spanish kings at that date were not in the least concerned to expel the Moors, who had taught them so many of the graces of civilisation, including in particular how to get the most out of the procreative instinct. The kings regularly fought each other as much as they fought against or even alongside the emirs, simply to extend their political power. They imitated Muslim polygamy and luxury with the heartiest relish, even after the ideal of getting rid of the 'infidels' had been publicly proclaimed under Burgundian pressure. In the twelfth century King Alfonso VII of Castile received the pious Louis VII of France in the presence of a perfect horde of wives and concubines. The King of Aragon spent quite half his time seducing other peoples' consorts. According to the troubadour Guiraut de Luc he even violated nuns. Physical love in fact, in both its loftiest and basest aspects, ruled Spain all through the Middle Ages, thanks to the Arabs. The amorous passion flourished only slightly less in the regions invaded by the Crusaders, where its cult was so far more ancient. But in Asia Minor and the Levant fanatical austerity equal to that of any Western ecclesiastic could be found more often than at the other end of the Mediterranean.

The Crusaders discovered Byzantium itself to be semi-oriental, with all that this adjective implies in the field of erotics. The emperors kept concubines and so did all the rich men. The city's prosperous industry of popular fiction had been mainly concerned with adultery long before a similar trade began to thrive in the West. Many Byzantine plots were taken over by the Italian and French compilers. The Eastern Empire still covered nearly half the Asian peninsula extending into the Mediterranean, and all the seaboard, the Turks being confined to the centre of this area. Palestine was held by the Fatimite Caliphs for the moment. But Islamic habits and customs, devoted to 'houris' whether on earth or in paradise, prevailed further north and west, even crossing the Aegean Sea. As in Spain, the Christian knights were the more tempted to adopt the ideas of their opponents about love for the reason that most of the Western warriors soon came to admire the Muslims' relatively sophisticated conversation as much as their prowess and honourable conduct in battle.

The sack of an oriental city, when the harems were assaulted like European nunneries on similar occasions, would no doubt be represented in terms calculated to make the stay-at-homes, even those who had taken part in comparable exploits during Western raids and campaigns, lick their lips. For the wives and daughters of the Saracens, the returned lord of the manor would be sure to emphasise, did not in the least resemble the timid, smelly, lean, fish-blooded and inexperienced convent-dwellers. They were women of spirit, living in luxury, learned in lechery and, of course, all of staggering beauty.

EASTERN GLAMOUR

A story by Jules Lemaître (1853-1914) regales his readers with the following paragraphs about a Crusader in a harem. They give the essence of this popular myth. Messire Ory kicks open the 'door' leading to the womens' quarters.

'There they were,' the author continues, 'lying among cushions on a carpet thick as turf, plump creatures with painted faces, swathed in brilliantly coloured silks. The light was dim, softened by panes of stained glass, in this place of damnation. Perfumes of poisonous sweetness rose in spirals of blue smoke from the firepans.

'The most beautiful of the women writhed to Ory's feet, weeping and moaning in the Saracenic tongue. She wreathed her arms about him and mingled caresses and languishing looks of diabolical power with her supplications. Ory could not understand her words. But he knew well enough that this heathen wished to lead him into temptation. He was aware of nothing but her material and earthly beauty, fleshy, amber-hued, smelling like honey, and those almond-shaped eyes that were so black under their heavy lids.'

Messire Ory did not, of course, yield to the seductive Saracen. For one thing, he had his chaplain with him. For another, he had sworn to be true to his lady-love in France. And for still another, this story was published at a period when even in France really ambitious writers could not afford to disregard the sexual code officially in force among Christian monogamists. So this highly fictitious crusader merely kicked the unfortunate girl and rushed out of this 'place of damnation' behind his perspiring chaplain. It is to be feared that his example was not often followed in real life.

Jerusalem fell to Godfrey de Bouillon, leader of the Western knights, in 1099. Thereafter many of them settled in the country and changed some of their habits to those, including open concubinage, of Islam. The Christians who returned home imported, as a rule, a strong spirit of sexual licence to reinforce the existent erotic restlessness in Europe. Troubadours like Guilhem IX of Poitiers and many other amorous adventurers enthusiastically joined a second Crusade, hoping for novel experiences in the warmer, more liberal atmosphere of the passionate East. The new Latin Kingdom of Jerusalem and several Frankish principalities elsewhere in the Holy Land remained nominally Christian. But they lived in even more oriental fashion than the Byzantines, who could now teach them little about the art of love. The constant communication between Europe and Asia which then arose began steadily to loosen the still fairly firm grip of the occidental Church upon the libidinously given.

But during the twelfth century, at the very time when Moorish influence on the West had done its lasting work, the Franks in the Levant started degenerating in a military sense. The alternations of silken voluptuousness and arduous battles among themselves, in chain-mail, over burning deserts, decimated the men. Political power passed to their wives and daughters. But these ladies could not control the brigandage, centred on the crusaders' castles, and spreading throughout the conquered lands, which gave Saladin his chance.

In 1187 Jerusalem passed under the control of that astute Sultan of Egypt. He had united the Muslims at last to deal with the intolerable anarchy of their eastern lands. But expeditions continued to be sent from Europe until the end of the thirteenth century, when the western Christians finally evacuated Syria. They brought a lot of the native girls back with them, mostly dancers. It was at this period that they became common and socially influential in Europe. The story by Balzac already referred to illustrates this feature of medieval society at the time. It was increased by a regular organisation of the slave-trade in Asian, Egyptian and Moorish women, who were bought even by priests.

But for two centuries now the West had known intimately how orientals lived, what views they held of the relations between the sexes, or between men and boys for that matter, and with what arguments those opinions were supported. Venice at that date was the great emporium for such exchanges. The Venetian women were more highly prized, more accomplished, more high-spirited and better dressed than any others. It was the ambition of every adventurous young European male to embrace one of them at least once. They were believed superior even to a native Mohammedan, as combining the fair skin and red-gold hair so much admired in the Middle Ages with all the erotic lore and artistry of a 'Saracen'.

EASTERN GLAMOUR

It was a Venetian, Marco Polo, too, who introduced Europe to the luxury of even more distant oriental lands than those which bordered the Mediterranean. His accounts of his travels in China proved to the Christians that they were a mere minority among the rich and civilised nations of the world. The subjects of the Sung emperors of Hangchow, which stood on lagoons like Venice but was far bigger, had never heard of clerically imposed sexual restraint. They raised their eyebrows with polite incredulity at Marco's tales of life in Europe. That continent would perhaps have grown uncomfortably conscious of a certain provincialism in religion if the Tartar Empire had not collapsed about 1350, causing a xenophobia in China which cut off communications for several centuries, during which, moreover, hostile Islam lay across the frontier between Christendom and regions of the earth which had not to contend with tabus on love.

Yet the lessons from the East were never again forgotten. They remained indelible in the European mind, though they could make little practical headway against the overwhelming secular power which the popes had acquired in the continent, in addition to their spiritual prestige, during the very period when the western settlers in the Levant lost theirs.

The fourteenth century began, nevertheless, with a notable increase of material luxury and the sensuality of all kinds which tends to accompany relatively sudden prosperity. For the eviction of the crusaders from Syria had opened up the trade routes to Asia again after nearly a millennium of practically ceaseless disorder and warfare of every description. Only pirates and brigands had then seemed able to make a decent living out of inter-continental mercantile traffic. But now silks and satins, perfumes and cosmetics, poured into Italy and central Europe—Spain already had them—together with a hundred varieties of aphrodisiacs from the rhinoceros horn, said to be that of the Christian symbol of virginity, the unicorn, to ginseng, esteemed on account of its forked root, which bears a distant resemblance to the phallus, cantharides and strychnine.

The ground was thus well prepared for that unprecedented outburst of the worship of the senses, as well as of intellectual and artistic energy, which marked the Renaissance. That soil only needed one more fertiliser, the large-scale rediscovery of pagan libertinism which started early in the following century, the fifteenth and last, strictly speaking, of typically medieval life. Thereafter the 'moral poison of the infidels' which had begun to spread to European veins first in Spain and then in the Levant, reached the lifeblood of the Church itself.

There was another reason why the crusades in particular, as well as the general prevalence of warfare, encouraged the amorous freethinkers, especially the women, of the Middle Ages. Wives and daughters in all social classes, long before the First Crusade, had been obliged to lament, for the best part of their lives, the absence of husbands and lovers on apparently endless campaigns far from home. A good many of the less naturally pious girls and matrons thus abandoned consoled themselves with such males as they could find. These would be mainly domestic servants, foreigners, vagabonds, cripples, monks and friars, middle-aged merchants, prisoners, escaped or otherwise, and bandits. But this state of affairs grew far worse when departure for the Holy Land, either on military service or on pilgrimage, both carrying great social and spiritual prestige, became the mode during the twelfth and thirteenth centuries.

Lonely and lascivious ladies soon made their appearance as heroines of the stock themes of popular story-telling. In real life many husbands and lovers, in the absence of reasonably fast facilities for communication, did happen to return very unexpectedly and sometimes unrecognisably. This fact undoubtedly lent spice and drama to the fiction retailed. It is also beyond question that these general circumstances help to account for the remarkable decay of conventional sexual morality with which churchmen were confronted in the fourteenth century. The degeneration sometimes saddened them, sometimes infected them and sometimes roused them to righteous wrath. But always, if they were honest, they had to recognise that all the hard work put in for so many centuries to suppress unruly amativeness had failed to stem the permanent tide of rebellion, now rising to a flood.

There was nothing for it but to compromise, to be tactful and charitable, while holding fast to the important Christian doctrine that carnality was the devil's pitchfork to damnation. But by the time this judicious policy had got fairly under way the Middle Ages had ended and the Renaissance, closely followed by the Reformation, was upon them.

The predecessors of the new age had included Abdurrahman III in Cordova, Saladin in Syria and Frederick II in Sicily. They were all representatives of the oriental outlook in matters of sex which had so deeply influenced pagan Greece and Rome and their Christian heirs, the populations of medieval Europe. Henceforth revolt against persecution of the erotic impulse was to take a form more dependent upon the classical tradition of the West, from the intellectual brilliance of Themistocles and Alcibiades, both morally unstable highbrows, to the sceptical urbanity of Horace, a kind-hearted cultivator of simplicity who nevertheless had no real interest in ethics, than upon models originally out of Asia.

But the glamour of the East never quite lost its fascination for the rebels. It can be traced through the ages of Titian and Louis Quatorze to its definite revival in the eighteenth century, to say nothing of later times. Medieval man had known it still better. Consciously or unconsciously he always felt its attraction. His Bible showed little of its sensual side and he never tried, like a Hollywood film director, to give it one. Prophets and apostles were recalcitrant to such a mould. But the remarkable proportions of sexual preoccupation in the Middle Ages would in all probability have been less exceptional without such close and durable contacts with the men and women of infidel Islam and the atmosphere from which that faith, so accommodating from a libertine standpoint, came to seduce the western world.

XII Pornography

HERMAS'S story of the second century about the shepherd and the twelve virgins with whom he spent the night in a cave and who stripped off their clothing to make a bed for him is clearly intended to excite the reader. But just as evidently the romantic scene so easily imagined behind the words carries allegorical overtones. It is probable that the twelve maidens whose garments the shepherd, i.e. Everyman, receives represent twelve moral ideas of heavenly origin, perhaps related to the signs of the zodiac. He is to clothe himself in future with certain virtues. Christian pornography began, thus early in its history, to disguise itself in transcendental or sentimental robes. It continued to do so from time to time until late in the eighteen hundreds, when heroes and heroines who transgressed the current sexual code were designed to attract sympathy simply by their physical beauty, misfortunes or social courage.

This rather sly pathetic fallacy, as it must always seem to the strictly orthodox, was repeated in a different though still pastoral form at the beginning of the third century by no less a personage than a Greek bishop, one Longus, author of the enormously popular indecent romance *Daphnis and Chloe*. This tale recounts the initiation into love of a couple of rustic foundlings at a very tender age. The style is highly literate. But its rhetorical charm and conventional set speeches cannot conceal the element which accounts for its success from that day to this. The prurient interest felt by adults in the clumsy and tentative approaches to copulation by partners on the very threshold of puberty is cunningly titillated. The rest is merely artistic decoration.

The innocent pair, though reciprocating each other's love and enjoying perfect freedom in the open fields, do not manage to consummate their desires. There is a reference to pederasty in the attempt of the parasite Gnatho to seduce Daphnis, who is fifteen. The latter is also given a lesson in love by an obliging girl named Lycenium. She is quite satisfied with her experiment. But Chloe, in spite of all this new knowledge imparted to her boyfriend, remains a virgin. Longus, after all, was a bishop addressing Christians. It is not until the children discover their aristocratic parents and marry that 'Daphnis acted as he had been instructed by Lycenium. Then Chloe, for the first time, understood that their former diversions in the woods had been only shepherds' frolics'.

The pornographic nudge, last of a long series, is here once more unmistakable. But it must be admitted that at this period the many Christian novels written in Greek concentrated mainly on hair-raising adventures to maintain suspense. The invariably erotic background is generalised. Such frank details as occasionally crop up would not have been considered particularly thrilling by contemporary readers, though they were sometimes excised by nineteenth-century editors. Until a much later date than that of Longus, coinciding with the cultural rebirth of the eleventh century, little deliberately scabrous treatment was given to the theme of love by writers of fiction.

The recording of fact, however, was much bolder. St. Gregory of Tours (538-594) paints a devastating picture of the sexual behaviour of the Franks, whose nominally Christian empire occupied in the sixth century what is now France and parts of Germany, Switzerland and Austria. Gregory, a sometimes injudicious but never disingenuous cleric and statesman, tried hard to be impartial in dealing with the barbarous chieftains who surrounded him. They maintained their ancient customs, in which polygamy loomed large, under the veneer of an apparatus of ecclesiastical hierarchy which had the greatest difficulty in controlling their ferocious instincts. The kings and their courtiers married and remarried even oftener than modern film-stars, without as a rule troubling about the formality of divorce. Concubines of all descriptions swarmed. Their intrigues and jealousies made history in positively Turkish style. Some of them had been carried off from nunneries.

It was in vain, for instance, that St. Germain, bishop of Paris, had King Haribert excommunicated for bigamy and sacrilege. Haribert couldn't have cared less. He stuck arrogantly to his two queens, one of whom had been a nun. King Chilperic had several consorts at once, of whom Fredegond, according to Gregory, was a woman of great beauty, high intelligence and utterly unscrupulous character. The saint's chronicle is filled with accounts of her shameless plots, adulteries and murders. She started by trapping the king, already her lover, into marriage with her. A certain bishop who should have known better connived at her persuasion of the Queen *in situ* to act as godmother to her own— the queen's—daughter. A relationship was thus established between mother and daughter which prevented the unhappy lady, who was not well versed in canon law, from remaining married to Chilperic, the child's father. He had the nerve to exile the bishop for abuse of his functions. But he married Fredegond.

Incest was also a common crime among the Frankish nobility. Some bishops, like Praetextatus of Rouen, were weak enough to condone the sin. For the ostentatious wealth and violence of the chieftains and perhaps their well attested conviviality, a sort of rude, jocular charm they exercised in their cups, seduced more than one prelate. Bishop Bertram of Bordeaux, of Teutonic blood himself, went in for concubines and other peoples' wives on an extensive scale. He was even said to be one of the formidable Fredegond's lovers.

Other high-ranking ecclesiastics could not stop the right of asylum in the churches from leading to revels by the refugees and their friends and servants in the sanctuary so obtained. Such debauches often assumed scandalous proportions. Gregory records (Book V) 'bloodshed, drunkenness and vanities, including the theft of pictures and ornaments in the church by male and female attendants'. He adds that a certain Leudast, a former Count of Tours, but excommunicated, held absolute orgies in the basilica of St. Hilaire, where he lived in sanctuary. 'He was frequently surprised in adulterous acts under the holy portico itself.' (*Et adulteriis saepe infra ipsam sanctam porticum deprehensus est.*)

PORNOGRAPHY

St. Gregory, no bigot, came of a good Gallo-Roman family himself. He administered his rowdy diocese firmly and honestly. He felt the greatest disgust at the prevalence of so much coarse profligacy in a formerly civilised country. But he had to be tactful. In fact he may have carried this policy a little too far. To a modern mind he seems to have been unduly lenient to the crimes of kings and nobles who in other ways protected and supported the Church. But he had no mercy at all on those, like Chilperic, who infringed clerical privilege.

No trace appears in the saint's history of any very special condemnation of erotic licence. It was not until some centuries later, by the year 1000 at earliest, when the secular power of the priesthood had greatly increased, that it ventured to preach an ever growing exhortation to restraint, amounting finally to persecution, in this field. In the sixth century, at any rate, it still remained too dangerous to treat as 'heretics' important persons who saw no harm in *luxuria* but otherwise subscribed to orthodox doctrine. All the bishops could do was disapprove and in flagrant cases excommunicate. As the only educated men available for the job of restoring order to Europe they were much more concerned with that arduous task than with pursuing wenchers and harlots. At a later date, of course, they applied to heretics such terms of abuse as that noted by Admiral Nelson in the phrase 'a term of endearment among sailors'. A hundred years after this definition a sociologist might have added 'undergraduates'. An early twentieth-century wit remarked that a Cambridge man is 'a fellow who wears filthy, grey flannel bags and calls his best friend a bugger'.

As already noted, the name of the Bulgarians, who were converted to Christianity in the ninth century and preferred the Eastern to the Western Church, lent itself to some deplorable punning among the adherents of the latter. '*Illos hereticos,*' observes a contemporary chronicler, '*Quos Franci bugeros appellant*'. Heretics of any kind soon came to be commonly accused of every form of libidinous depravity, including that of homosexuality. For this practice was viewed as peculiarly infamous by expounders of a dogma which, however grudgingly, allowed Christians to enjoy sexual pleasure only in order to propagate legitimate offspring.

St. Gregory was a serious and, within his lights, conscientious historian. But naturally fiction, both in prose and verse, if mainly at this period the latter, continued the heathen tradition of two kinds of narrative, the popular and the high-flown. The street-corner story-tellers and the courtly bards alike would have been inhuman if they had not set love between men and women, as well as conflict between men, in the position of a chief ingredient of their concoctions.

The ephemeral popular literature of this type during the first eight hundred years of the Christian era has nearly all perished. But later productions of the same sort give a fair idea of what it must have been like. Gross and downright in expression, much concerned with deceived husbands, perhaps it had even then adopted a somewhat sardonic tone about priests and great lords. But much of it, no doubt, was meant to be edifying. It would certainly deal, under ecclesiastical inspiration, with the legends of saints, martyrs and other holy personages who successfully shamed the devil.

The tenth-century German nun Hrotswitha wrote, in Latin, a series of quite remarkable plays strongly influenced by the pagan Roman dramatist Terence (c. 190-c. 159 B.C.). But she is a good deal more outspoken than her heathen model about the tender passion. Where he treats it perfunctorily she positively hammers it. Some of her scenes are set in brothels. One represents a cemetery where a lover interrogates the sexton. The intruder wishes to dig up his mistress's corpse. Go ahead, says the sexton. She's not putrid yet. You'll find her still in fair condition for fornication. Ha, cries the lover, as he seizes a spade, Now I can offer that bitch all the insults I please! (*Abutere, ut licet.—Nunc in mea situm est potestate quantislibet iniuriis te velim lacessere.*)

Hrotswitha's range of interests also far exceeds that of Terence in directions other than that of necrophily. Even in the depths of central Europe she knew a lot about the magnificence of the contemporary Court of Cordova and its vices. One of her tragedies describes how a chaste young Christian prince of Galicia (in northern Spain) rejected the amorous advances of the Caliph, who had taken him prisoner. The cruel Moor, incensed by this obstinate behaviour, beheaded his royal captive.

PORNOGRAPHY

Terence's women, again, are always weak and sentimental, easily seduced. The uncompromising German nun entirely rejects so absurd a view of her sex. In a riotous comedy she presents a fool of a pagan Roman general who is reduced by magical art to fondling pots and pans under the impression that they are Christian virgins whom he has captured. The girls watch him from behind a curtain, hardly able to stifle their laughter. On discovery of the hoax he orders them to be stripped naked by his soldiers, preparatory to a promiscuous orgy. But their clothes simply won't come off. As fast as they are torn down they slide up again. For God himself, with all his saints and angels, is now taking a hand in the matter and the heathen is utterly discomfited.

In a tragi-comedy the plot of many a subsequent tale is first unfolded when an exuberant visitor to a brothel calls for the best-looking girl in the house and is introduced to his long-lost daughter.

Hrotswitha also wrote narrative poetry. In one of these effusions a certain St. Gandolf is killed, like Agamemnon, by his adulterous wife. When miracles occur at his tomb she is described as caring no more for them than if they were so many farts. (*Mirabilia non secus ut ventris crepitum existimavit.*) Thereupon she is punished by being made to go on farting incessantly for the rest of her life.

Such crude vigour, expressed however in quite elegant Latinity, is less evident in the more sophisticated of the early medieval epics. The most famous and immediately appreciated of the love-stories invented in the Middle Ages, the tale of Tristram and Iseult, may have originated in Ireland during the period of its occupation by the Vikings of the ninth century. The various short lays, inspired by the conception of an adulterous relationship between, probably, a Pictish warrior and a Scandinavian princess, were eventually given a single epic form by the English *trouvère* (troubadour) Thomas, living in the twelfth century.

This production, of which only fragments survive, was translated into German by Gottfried von Strassburg early in the following century. His verses, together with some relatively minor poems on the same theme, were later turned into prose and incorporated with the final version of the Arthurian legend. That myth was also basically an account of adulterous adventures, those of the originally French knight Lancelot, the highly amorous and much married hero of a twelfth-century folk tale, and Guinevere, the wife of an invented king of Britain. Sir Thomas Malory (d. 1471) compiled his *Morte Darthur* in English from this prose source.

Sexual passion is of course the root from which all fictitious narrative, good, bad and indifferent, arises. But it is highly significant that in the millennium of the most persistent official repression of amativeness by Christian Europeans, from the fifth to the fifteenth century, the whole spirit of the poetry and prose then most universally admired glorified rebellion against the principle of marital fidelity so rigorously commanded by the Church. Unfaithful wives had been fiercely persecuted, for obvious reasons, long before the Christian era. All administrators saw that family life must be upheld if social order was to be preserved. The natural jealousy of the dominant male did the rest. But no one then dreamed of imposing legal or religious penalties on a husband's love-affairs with women not married to him, let alone a bachelor's or widower's seduction of someone else's wife.

The surviving lyrical poetry of the central Middle Ages has been collected in the so called *Cambridge Songs* stored in manuscript form at the Library of that university. The manuscript dates from the middle of the eleventh century. But most of the songs were composed about a hundred years earlier. Many have been erased by bigots at various dates on account of their indecent contents and phrasing. But about half of those the fanatics did not meddle with are far from pious in tone.

They are generally written in the liturgical metres best known to the masses of the people. One gay story of marital infidelity derives much of its comic effect from the mock solemnity with which it could be intoned. The sonorous beginning runs:

> *Advertite,*
> *omnes populi,*
> *ridiculum*
> *et audite quomodo*
> *suevum mulier*
> *et ipse illam*
> *defraudaret.*

PORNOGRAPHY

It goes on, in the same organ-like structure of strophes, in which one expects, but does not get, the periodical ringing 'Alleluia!', to tell how a Swabian merchant's wife, during his two years' absence abroad, became pregnant. She told her husband, on his return, that some snow which she had swallowed while thirsty had done the trick. The husband pretended to believe her, but on his next voyage sold the 'snow-child' for a good round sum. When he came back he told his wife that the boy had 'melted away' on a sun-scorched sandbank where the ship had been wrecked. He thus turned the tables, with a wit peculiarly medieval, on the adulteress, who could not have failed to realise that her cock-and-bull story had not deceived him.

The *Carmina Burana*, so called from their having been long preserved in a Bavarian abbey of Benedictines, date from the twelfth and thirteenth centuries. The manuscript contains lewd love-songs, also in the metres of hymnology. The verses vary from the riotous to the humorous, pathetic and satirical. All deliver more or less good-humoured attacks on a greedy hypocritical sensualist, 'Bishop Golias',* a purely mythical personage, said to be the 'master' of the dissipated 'wandering scholars' who composed these ballads. For this reason a metre frequently used was called 'Goliardic'. It became a favourite in light verse. The lilt is thunderous.

> Aestuans intrinsecus ira vehementi,
> in amaritudine loquor meae menti,
> Factus de materia levis elementi,
> folio sum similis de quo ludunt venti.†

This is the most celebrated poem in medieval Latin. It was written in the twelfth century by the so called 'Archpoet', a German minstrel at the Court of the Archbishop of Cologne. The defiant address of a mock-penitent, it describes him as 'devoted to Venus. Whatever she commands is a pleasure. She never dwells in craven hearts'. But he sardonically begs the Archbishop's pardon for 'committing adultery in my heart with girls I cannot win to in the flesh'. 'It is a most arduous task,' he sighs,

---

*Cf. p. 47.
†'Stormy seas within me and rage there's no allaying
to my mind all secretly do speak a bitter saying.
Made I am of elements so weightless and a-straying,
my course is like a leaf's drift with which the winds go playing.'

with a grin, 'to be pure in mind at the sight of a maid. We young men cannot endure hard laws. We cannot help desiring tender bodies. . . .* All roads lead to the couch of Venus . . . let him whose mind is conscious of no sin cast a stone at me . . . spare this penitent.'

In the original this stuff is superbly elegant, pointed, passionate and yet obviously a leg-pull throughout. It is moreover so phrased as to seem at the end a real repentance laid at the feet of the bard's master. One is reminded, by the sense, of modern Communists recanting their capitalist shortcomings. But it is very doubtful indeed whether any Communist of any nationality ever wrote anything so highly civilised as this magnificently condescending apologia, comparable with anything by Burns or Heine in the same line. The Archbishop must have admired it, if he wasn't a perfect dolt. There is no reason to suppose that he was.

Such is one of the most brilliant blows ever struck by a medieval rebel against the 'unco guid'. In a more literate age it would have had great social effect. But in the twelfth century the 'miracle plays', in which saints were treated with jocose familiarity, and the popular epics and prose tales were probably more influential. For no sooner had the priests made a positive fetish of the Sixth Commandment than the poets began to see visions of noble dames who transgressed it.

Adultery, so far as literature was concerned, became a still more imperative fashion than in pagan times. It was felt to be a specially vivid reflection of life. Undoubtedly the marriage conventions of the day encouraged illicit love-making. For girls were then married off, if possible, as soon as they reached puberty. No one dreamed of consulting the wishes of a child of twelve or thirteen in so important a matter, or even, in exceptional cases, of asking a comparatively illiterate and sequestered young woman of twenty odd what she felt about the husband chosen for her. Accordingly, in nine marriages out of ten wives found themselves tied for life to man at least twice and often three times their age, whom they scarcely knew and consequently feared as much as they had previously feared their father. They

* Cf. p. 48.

were miraculously lucky, therefore, if as soon as this stranger, with whom they were too young to have really desired sexual intimacy, brusquely introduced them to it, they did not begin to wonder whether it wouldn't be more fun with someone else.

Consequently, a very great deal of medieval fiction, prose or verse, light or heavy, idealised the relatively mature wife and the enterprising gentleman, whether or not married himself, who became her lover. For this situation, as even pagan story-tellers had found, in all ages, all over the world, allowed innumerable motives for those secret intrigues, adventures and escapades of a romantic and sometimes bloody character which everyone, law-abiding or otherwise, enjoys reading about. In heathen times the thrills had been provided only by suspicious husbands or male relatives. Under the Christian dispensation the hostility of the powerful ecclesiastical hierarchy could also be expected. It could, further, rally to its already formidable aid that of quite half the lay population, those who, for one reason or another, found it expedient, or in accordance with a personal outlook, to censure sexual divagations from the norm of matrimony.

A special element in the thought of the Christian Middle Ages reinforced in a most unanticipated manner the tendency of contemporary literature to make tragedy or comedy out of passionate or merely licentious attachments between married women and men not their husbands. The notion of chivalry, a respectful and tender courtesy, a polite ritual, a generally protective attitude, in masculine dealings with adult females on ordinary occasions, had first arisen among orientals and in particular Muslims. This unfamiliar behaviour had originally been encountered by Europeans on the southern and eastern outskirts of the imperial dominions of ancient Rome, in Asia Minor, in North Africa and, after the conquest of most of Spain by Arabs in the eighth century, in that peninsula.

The descendants of the savages who had swooped from the forests of northern Europe to dismember the Roman Empire began by being amused. They guffawed at the spectacle of towering athletes in all the terrific panoply of war bowing to salute in adoration frail little shrinking feminine creatures voluminously veiled in silks, whom the warriors could have raped in a matter of seconds. But in the course of time the Christians grew fascinated by the sight and started to imitate it, at first, no doubt, in burlesque fashion. But later the virtues of merciful magnanimity which had occasionally astonished their ancestors in contact with southern cultures appeared to the followers of the Cross as one of the brightest mirrors of the beneficence of heaven. Was not Christ compassionate? And even more so his Mother?

The cult of the Virgin Mary—after all, she was a married woman too—assumed more and more conspicuous proportions. It soon became the mode to lend its mysticism to purely mundane idolatry of suitably high-born and therefore dignified and remote ladies. The latter thereupon reciprocated by acting, in the preliminary stages of such an affair at any rate, as much like the —of course youthful—Mother of God as their education, training and natural gifts of intelligence and imagination permitted. The pose of prostration at the feet of such glorified females linked up with the masochism of penitents and ascetics already prevalent even among the laity. This whole social attitude was codified in 1255 by the Styrian *minnesinger* Ulrich von Lichtenstein in his poem *Frauendienst* ('Service to Women'), relating the absurd feats he performed at the behest of his ladylove, including dressing up as a leper. By this time the solemn worship expected of a 'perfect lover' had degenerated into antics which recalled alternately the cloister and the theatre.

But nearly two hundred years before, towards the end of the eleventh century, the situation had given rise to an altogether extraordinary type of poetry, far better worth the name than Ulrich's. The productions of the so called *troubadours* ('inventors') were by turns grossly licentious and intensely devotional. Their verses reached a very high standard of technical accomplishment, were often deeply erudite and repeatedly incisive and pictorially epigrammatic to a degree unknown in Europe since the times of Juvenal and Martial. These compositions, by no means all composed by kings, princes and their aristocratic friends, have had a decisive influence on the nature of European lyric ever since, from the masterpieces of Dante to those of Ezra Pound.

The word *troubadour* is Provençal for 'finder' (*trouveur* or *trouvère* in northern France). The poet was so called because he 'invented' phrases and metres not previously familiar. But he

PORNOGRAPHY

also knew how to 'find' the mistresses, whether or not he ever managed to seduce them, without whom he could neither live nor write nor sing. From the very start he had the reputation of 'roaming through the land to deceive ladies' by his impassioned hymns to their beauty and virtue. Such was the fame of Guilhem IX (b. 1071), Count of Poitiers and Duke of Aquitaine, as well as that of King Richard I, the 'Lion-hearted', of England nearly a century later. The best English historian of Guilhem's time, the monk William of Malmesbury, called the Frenchman 'stupid and wanton' (*fatuus et lubricus*) and credits him with the foundation of an 'abbey of debauchery', perhaps resembling that of the notorious 'Beast' Aleister Crowley (d. 1947) in Sicily. The hagiographer Jaufré Gros similarly declares that the Count-Duke was 'the enemy of all chastity and virtue'.

He could in fact be boastfully facetious, if also nobly melancholy, at times. He writes, for example:

> 'They call me infallible master.
> She who has me for a night desires
> to have me again on the morrow.
>
> So great an expert am I at the trade, I could earn
> my living at it, I swear, in any market.'

and again, even more crudely:

> 'Ay, one hundred and eighty-eight times
> I fucked* 'em, as you shall hear shortly.
> I nearly burst baldric and harness. Nor can I tell
> the great weariness I had of it after 'twas done.'

It was no wonder that Guilhem died at fifty-six, after a sad valediction in these terms:

> 'All is laid waste that I loved best,
> pastimes of the bold and proud.
> So be it, if God wills,
> and may he take me to himself.
>
> Friends, I beg you, after my death
> come, do me all the honour that you can.
> Gladness we knew together and gaieties
> both far away and in my own domain.'

---

* In Provençal *fotei* (French *foutis*, Latin *futui*.)

These two poems, written by the same man, are not so different in tone as they appear at first sight. Guilhem, a typical troubadour, resembles Yeats in his aristocratic capacity to switch easily from coarse, downright vernacular to the most delicate and subtle brooding in highly sophisticated language. A good deal of troubadour poetry was the first in history to modulate religious emotion, in this case mariolatry, into the sighs and affectations of forlorn love, so often uttered since that time by Petrarch, the sonneteers of the Renaissance and the seventeenth-century madrigal writers. But many of the twelfth-century lyrics, like those of Villon three hundred years later, have a modern ring in their preoccupation with nature, violence and sexual lust. They also seem modern in their occasional obscurity, due paradoxically enough to an equally modern quest for concision. Their frequent vulgarity, too, is sometimes to be referred to this aim.

As already suggested, adultery had always been an ingredient in the great military epics of the earlier Middle Ages. But it had not been treated at length or in detail. The troubadours in their brief songs addressed mainly to a femine audience gave a central position to an illicit relationship with a woman. They derived all their other ideas, directly or indirectly, from it. The effect upon European literature and thus upon the characteristically European view of love between the sexes was immediate and decisive. This influence culminated eventually in Shakespeare himself, who can be, by turns, as slyly or brutally lascivious and as sorrowfully refined as Guilhem.

Robert Briffault in *Les Troubadours et le Sentiment Romanesque* (Editions du Chêne, Paris, 1945, pp. 79-80) distinguishes these literary innovations as follows:

> 'The canons of passion were formulated with amazing pedantry. Each individual sigh and heart-beat, the "cruelty" of the fair lady, the "despair" of the lover and the concession, at certain times and places, of "favours" doled out at fixed intervals and limited in duration according to a methodically graduated scale, were all anticipated in accordance with an erotic formulary, to fall short of which would have been a gross lack of courtesy. The various situations which may arise in the course of a love-affair, the emotions proper to each one

of them and the problems that some of them might present were the subjects of treatises and set disputes closely imitated from the debates of scholastic theology. Knotty points were referred to recognised authorities whose judgments were used to codify the body of love-law. The society of the castles of Languedoc (Provence) devoted their fastidious leisure to these discussions on "questions of love" with much the same fervour as the guests of the Hôtel Rambouillet and of Mdlle de Scudéry's drawing-room were to apply at a later time to the pursuit of wit and good taste. Such were the gatherings which gave themselves or were given the name of the "Courts of Love". Their actual staging is a trifling matter for us today. A subject of much greater interest is the amplitude, the formality and the incredible seriousness which characterised these whimsical disputes on psychology in the twelfth century.'

The troubadours' love-poetry itself constituted a form of protest against the condemnation of lubricity by the Christian Church. Such opposition was at times cunningly concealed in the style familiar from hymns to the Virgin Mary. The novelty of the verses, to the still half barbarous descendants of the invaders of the Roman Empire, consisted in their being addressed openly to a mortal being. The ancestors of the listeners had regarded erotic lays as formulae of incantation to cast a spell over the woman thus courted. The author was accordingly liable to prosecution as a wizard. The Viking bard Ottar the Black, for instance, was condemned to death for dedicating a song to the daughter of King Olaf. In one of the numerous variants of the story of Tristram, adopted by Tennyson in *The Last Tournament*, the hero is killed by King Mark for having sung a love lyric to Iseult.

But in twelfth-century Provence such semi-savages were enthralled by the inheritors of a Gallo-Roman civilisation which had not forgotten Propertius. Nor were men like Guilhem and his successors ignorant of the refined poetic conventions of contemporary Moorish Spain.

There, for two hundred years already, the Arabs had been freely expressing in elaborate verse every feature, both material and spiritual, of sexual intercourse. They raved of the breasts, the hips and the reproductive organs of their mistresses as wildly, within a dozen varieties of tricky metre, as they related these glories to those of the Muslim paradise. Moorish prestige stood high in Europe at this time, even among inquisitive churchmen. For the Arabs were not only connoisseurs of amorous delight. They were leading the way in poetry, music, mathematics, astronomy, geography, chemistry, medicine and metaphysics. Moorish sensuality, moreover, was tempered with mysticism. The learned philosopher Ali-ibn-Hazm of Cordova had written: 'Love is often a matter at first of jest and frivolity. But it may become extremely serious and solemn.' So much, the first troubadours must undoubtedly have thought, for the misogyny of Paul of Tarsus and Clement of Alexandria!

It is certain that the Arab invaders of Spain brought few feminine companions with them. Accordingly, the Hispano-Gothic women with whom they staffed their palaces must have played a considerable part in this development of Arabic poetry, which was to exert so momentous an influence on European history. For these ladies disposed of a culture and a social liberty far exceeding those of the average Muslim female. They had brought these advantages with them long ago. For in the Gothic north of the continent the sexes had been, even in the age of Tacitus, on much more familiar terms with each other than in the partially orientalised Mediterranean south. Consequently, a boisterous conviviality, as well as erudite discussion of abstract themes, came to be common in the mixed society of Moorish Spain in its heyday, from the tenth to the twelfth century. In contemporary Christian lands the sexes never met in this way.

This state of affairs in Spain perhaps helped to induce some Muslim poets, notably Ibn-Guzman of Cordova (1078-1160) to share the opinion of the troubadours beyond the Pyrenees that true passion cannot flourish unless it is adulterous. Ibn-Guzman jeers at pious fakirs and gets into trouble with the police, just as did many of the minstrels who wandered about Provence and indeed Spain itself. The troubadour Arnaud de Marsan, for instance, boasts of having gained the love of a daughter of King Alfonso VII of Castile. That monarch, incidentally, like King Henry VIII of England, possessed no less than six more or less legitimate wives, one of them a Muslim princess from Seville, to say nothing of a well stocked harem.

The more than half Moorish character of the Spanish Courts at this time in fact strongly influenced, like the societies the crusaders found in Syria, the growing restlessness of the other parts of Christian Europe under the ecclesiastical tabus on erotic freedom. The troubadour Arnault Daniel, a friend of King Richard I of England and much admired by Dante, who, however, calls him 'the lustful', observes: 'I have never left the Court of Aragon without desiring, the next day, to return there with a single bound.' As Arnault wrote nothing but love-poetry and never seems to have thought of anything but young women, the inference is obvious.

Gaucelm Faidit, another Provençal troubadour, had a row with the King of Aragon himself about a lady. The sovereign, according to a colleague of Gaucelm's, one Guiraut de Luc, specialised in violating nuns. Some of the most reckless of these peripatetic and licentious bards were actually monks, like the Rabelaisian Peire de Vic of Montauban, who got a Priory out of the Aragonese king. Peire Roger, in the time he could spare from verse and love making, was nothing less than a Canon of Clermont. How such men reconciled their roving amours with their priestly functions seems a bit of a mystery to modern minds. It does prove, however, as does much other evidence, that the medieval Church contained large numbers of bold spirits who lived pretty much like laymen and gave only lip-service to their dogma. In any case the troubadours were all extremely clever and the clerical hierarchy, as already noted, was now deliberately exercising a tolerant policy, at least towards its more able members.

But it was not to be so, in Provence, much longer. The elegance and luxury of the southern lords, who shaved carefully and parted their hair, had already struck the uncouth and hirsute nobility of the north as being no better than the ostentation of so many effeminate actors who did not deserve their luck. In addition, the growing power of the French bishops saw in the headlong amativeness, the oriental interests and general self-indulgence of this large region of Christian Europe a threat to both the spiritual and the secular ambitions of the orthodox priesthood. For Provence and its 'Courts of Love' extended from Aragon to the Loire, far beyond the bounds of the modern district that bears the name. How much longer were its swarms of dandified poets and courtly fops to ridicule piety as prudery and the stern enforcement of chastity as vulgar jealousy? Worse still, might not the wealth and cosmopolitan outlook of the Provençal barons, if allowed to increase still further, easily come to enslave the very kingdom of Christ itself to the infidels?

The south of France had always been and still is a part of Europe peculiarly susceptible to a very close alliance of eroticism and intelligence, not so consistently evident elsewhere. The Greeks colonised the coast early. The Romans preferred its milder climate to their own. It was the first of their provinces to become thoroughly civilised. In the later stages of the Empire Gallo-Romans were better administered and at the same time more refined in their sensual gratifications than native Italians. This promising or sinister—according to one's personal philosophy—situation began to annoy Christians as early as the fifth century. The German theologian Salvian, who died at Marseilles about 490, declared that 'all Aquitaine is nothing better than a huge brothel'. He went on to curse, in the exaggerated style of those days, resembling that of nineteenth-century Socialists, the cynical wickedness of the over-educated owners of the great estates. (*De Gubernatione Dei*, VI, 72. VII, 16, 27.)

But as time went on both the Church and the lay lords learnt wisdom. The former concluded that it could not afford to ignore the opulence of these nominal but generous Christians. The latter defended themselves from moral criticism by representing amorous relationships as noble. Their system of apologetics, as full of subtle distinctions as any plea advanced in the schools of theology, could not, they proclaimed, be considered in the slightest degree scandalous. The scandal appeared, rather, in the coarse behaviour of jealous husbands and the brutish, unregulated copulation of the lower social orders.

All the same, not to refer again to Guilhem IX of Poitiers, later troubadours often came to the point with disconcerting abruptness. The usually elegiac Cercamon writes: 'Pray God that one day I shall clasp her in my arms and watch her strip herself for bed.' And again: 'Here can I not live long nor there hold out without embracing her or grasping her naked at my side in a curtained chamber.' Bernard of Ventadorn, a scullion's son who rose to be the lover of Eleanor of Aquitaine, wife of King Henry II of England, exclaims: 'I think I shall die unless my fair one invites me thither where she is wont to repose, that I may kiss and caress and strain in my arms her white, plump, smooth body.' Bertram de Born, Lord of Hauteford (1180-1205) wrote of Matilda, Eleanor's daughter: 'The more one disrobes her, the more grows inclination and desire. Her dazzling bosom turns night into day. When the eye looks lower the whole world seems alight. How good it is to hold that blooming and supple form naked in one's arms!' Peire Vidal (1175-1215), a self-confessed scatterbrained type, approaches an unknown lady with the observation, in exquisite verse: 'If ever we find ourselves together undressed it will go better with me than if I were Sir Richard of the Lion's Heart.'

Such quotations could be multiplied *ad lib*. They ring the changes upon almost every possible aspect of the meeting of lovers 'within the alcove', when the lady 'unveils her graceful shape by lamplight'. Arnault Daniel goes even further than the Count of Poitiers in nine whole stanzas, too long to cite here, of erotic scatology.

No medieval literature, in fact, registers so bold and frank a protest as did the troubadours against the harsh repression of free thought and free love by the Christian doctrinaires. The ideals of the singers of Provence seemed novel at the time. But in reality their visions looked back to Athens as much as forward to the Italian Renaissance. They were backed by the very weapons of intricate intellectual argument and mystical sentiment which the Church itself employed. They were therefore felt to be so dangerous that St. Bernard of Clairvaux (1090-1153), the very embodiment of professional monasticism in the Middle Ages, and his friend King Louis VII of France (1121-1180), the very incarnation of lay religiosity in that period, determined to bring the heedless inhabitants of the Midi to reason. But the century ended before the decisive step was taken in this connection.

The scepticism of the Provençal lords had caused them to welcome heretics. Of these the chief were the Cathars ('puritans' in

Greek), who denounced the corruption of the orthodox prelates and preached humility and poverty. The sect was centred at Albi in Provence. In 1209 Pope Innocent III declared a crusade against the 'Albigenses'. The barons and bishops of northern France and Germany descended upon the region with half a million men-at-arms, including the ruffian Simon IV de Montfort, father of the famous English statesman and soldier who became Earl of Leicester under Henry III. Simon and his associates wiped out the entire civilisation of Provence with fire and sword. According to a contemporary chronicle the country could only show, of its native inhabitants, 'men and women entirely naked, without even their privy parts covered'.

More than three hundred towns and two hundred castles were burned. All their inmates were massacred. 'Mutilated bodies and intestines,' the chronicle adds, 'were strewn about the public squares as if they had rained down from heaven.' Simon de Montfort, like any ancient tyrant of Assyria or Egypt, gouged out his captives' eyes and cut off their noses. The camp-followers carried off whole droves of girls, forcing them to walk by stabbing them with pikes. The Cistercian monks drowned the shrieks of their tortured, burned, hanged and stoned victims of both sexes by intoning the hymn 'Veni, Creator Spiritus'.

For eight years the ferocious slaughter and plunder raged monotonously on. But in 1218 a stone flung by a woman from the ramparts of Toulouse killed Simon de Montfort. Eventually Count Raimon VII of that city brought in Spanish troops to reconquer most of the denuded and ravaged lands of the once gay and learned Courts of Love. But the real spirit of the troubadours had died in that fearful holocaust. Their successors, of whom Petrarch was the most eminent, never again seriously challenged the supremacy of medieval religious fanaticism. The Inquisition, founded by St. Dominic and Queen Blanche of Castile soon after the Albigensian Crusade, saw to that.

Tertullian had considered sexual love to be the essence of sin and woman to be 'the gate of hell'. Ambrose thought chastity more important than the doctrines of the Christian faith. 'The lightest strain upon our chastity is harder for us to bear than death,' Tertullian added. And again: 'The kingdom of heaven is the eunuch's fatherland.' Ambrose actually opines that the extinction of the human race is preferable to its propagation through sin. (*Exhortation to Virginity*). 'Married persons,' he wrote in the same *Exhortation*, 'should blush for the state in which they live.' Clement of Alexandria went one better. 'Every woman,' he exclaims in his *Pedagogue*, II, 2 'should be overwhelmed with shame at the thought that she is a woman.'

But these extravagant pronouncements of the Fathers never succeeded in suppressing the deepest of human impulses, on occasion more urgent even than hunger. The Albigensian Crusade imposed its horrors on the rebels in vain. The private conduct of medieval man, not recorded in writing, did not change after 1218. Poets like the thirteenth-century Italian Sordello, who usually celebrated the Virgin in their verses, were often renowned libertines after working hours. It would be an exaggeration to say that hypocrisy entered literature in the twelve hundreds. But it certainly entered life a good deal more noticeably than it had in less vigorous periods of the Christian imperative.

Giovanni Boccaccio (1313-1375) observes in his *Trattatello in Laude di Dante* (X. 12) that the greatest and profoundest of Italian poets was 'very lewd, not only during his youth, but also even after he had reached an advanced age'. The underground revolt, in fact, never ceased from the beginning of the fifth century to the end of the fifteenth. By then it had come out into the open. The most incisive spirits of the following centuries, if they were not cynical enough to compromise, often fell, like Galileo, before priestly intolerance. But even more often, like Voltaire and Goethe, they successfully defied it. The outcome of the struggle has not yet been definitely decided. Men and women of genius are still socially persecuted if their private lives do not conform with conventional Christian standards. Those who are not fanatics on either side are driven to conclude that the basic conflict between an artificial code of moral austerity on the one hand and the instinctive incorrigibility of human nature on the other must be eternal.

The medieval literary mind took more naturally to verse than to prose. So far as its sexual interests were concerned, the realistic attitude so evident from other surviving monuments of that period could more easily be concealed from ecclesiastical censors and inquisitors in the rhetoric of mystical ecstasy and the obscure mythological allusions then considered proper to metrical composition. Nevertheless, prose tales, more suitable for mass consumption than epics about knights and princesses, were continually written down or passed from mouth to mouth, first in Latin, then, from the eleventh century onwards, in the main vernaculars of Europe. Most of the extant stories are in French or Italian.

In northern France (Picardy) for instance, the charming thirteenth-century tale of *Aucassin et Nicolette* shows clearly enough the attitude of persons of the middle and, *a fortiori*, lower social classes to the prelates' policy of sex-starvation. 'What am I to do in paradise?' exclaims the 'amorous' Aucassin. 'The only people who go to paradise are those of whom I will tell you. Old priests go there, and the halt and the maimed and such as stay crouching day and night in front of altars and under the vaults of hollow crypts. And there go pilgrims in their old threadbare mantles and the ragged and those who go barefoot and shoeless and die of hunger and thirst and poverty. Such are they who go to paradise. What have I to do with them? I would rather go to hell. For to hell go the clerks with fat purses and the handsome cavaliers who die in the jousts or fighting gallantly, the valiant men-at-arms and the true men. With these I would rather go. And there go the fair courtly ladies who have two or three friends besides their barons. And there go all the gold, the silver, the vair and the grey pelisses. And there go the minstrels and the jugglers and the kings of the world. With these I would rather go, if I may take my most sweet friend Nicolette with me.'

But such boyishly improper sentiments were not taken very seriously even by the relatively fierce clergy of the north. In the south they were even more indulgent, passing without a qualm the farces and comic narratives, mostly about marital infidelity, but also sometimes hinting strongly at the advantage taken by priests of their sacred office to seduce unmarried girls. Such stories reached a high literary level in Boccaccio's *Decameron*, a collection of a hundred short novels. They are ostensibly related by a party of seven ladies and three gentlemen, all young and gay, who had retired to a villa near Florence to escape from the Black Death of 1348. The author himself, a learned humanist, openly confesses to having committed adultery. He is no Christian idealist and not in the least afraid of the grossest allusions to the material aspects of fornication.

One of the shortest and most licentious of the *Decameron* items, the Fourth Tale of the Fifth Day, told by a male narrator, is so characteristic of Boccaccio's delicate humour that a few passages may be quoted. Its title, like those of all the rest, is merely a synopsis. 'Ricciardo Manardi is discovered by Messer Lizio da Valbona with his daughter, whom Ricciardo marries, remaining on good terms with the father.'

Caterina da Valbona, as summer is coming on, persuades her mother to let her sleep on the balcony, 'where I could listen to the nightingale'. Ricciardo of course climbs up to the balcony 'and was greeted quietly but with the greatest delight by the girl. After many kisses they lay down together and took delight and pleasure of each other almost the whole night, making the nightingale sing many times.' At last they slept 'Caterina with her right arm round Ricciardo's neck and her left hand holding the thing which you ladies are so ashamed to mention among men.' At dawn the father said to himself: 'Let us see how the nightingale made Caterina sleep last night.' He entered the girl's room, saw the lovers sleeping together naked on the balcony and without interrupting them went back to the matrimonial bedchamber and said to his wife: 'Come and see how fond your daughter is of the nightingale. She has caught it and is still holding it in her hand.' The parents then contemplated the scene together, still without waking the couple. Said the father: 'Well, since she has caught him, he shall be hers ... he shall marry her ... he'll soon find he has put his nightingale into his own cage, not anybody else's.' He then woke the young man and quietly discussed the situation with him. Meanwhile 'Caterina loosed her hold of the nightingale ... and without getting out of bed Ricciardo took her as his wife in the parents' presence.' After the parents had departed 'the two young people ... since they had not travelled more than six miles that night, went on another two.' A more formal wedding then took place and Ricciardo 'for a long time in peace and quietness hunted birds with her day and night as much as he pleased.'

Boccaccio also, like most popular entertainers of his day, attacked the clergy with the greatest coolness. In one story, lifted in part from the Roman satirist Petronius, who flourished under Nero, a stout and elderly abbot finds it more convenient, while copulating with his girl-friend, for her to assume the superior position. He is seen in these circumstances by one of his monks, who had also enjoyed the girl. The monk is thus enabled to blackmail his chief into releasing him from the vexatious penance that dignitary had already imposed upon him.

Again, we hear of a merchant in Paris who considered it a shame that his Jewish friend Abraham, a splendid fellow, was not a Christian. Abraham agrees to visit Rome with a view to conversion. On arrival he was duly impressed, though only by the enormous amount of 'lechery and sodomy' prevalent in the Holy City. But this discovery did the trick. Abraham, on his return to Paris, told his friend that if Christianity could flourish as it did when its most important representatives behaved so badly, it must be true, and he would gladly accept baptism.

In France the short humorous story, with its emphatic erotic colouring, culminated in the *Cent Nouvelles Nouvelles*, a collection attributed to Antoine de la Salle (1388-1462). This author may also have written the celebrated farce *Maître Pathelin*, about lascivious lawyers, and the significantly titled *Quinze Joies de Mariage*, revealing the secrets of married libertines. In England the fourteenth-century balladists, including Chaucer, were particularly down on clerics, their strictures ranging from embittered invective to sardonic contempt. Chaucer's naïve, rather than obscene, references to the sexual organs are scattered throughout his works. His older contemporary Langland, in the allegorical *Piers Plowman*, repeatedly uses the seduction metaphor, complaining, for example:

'How Wrong against his'—Peace's—'will had his wife taken
and how he ravished Rose, Reginald's love,
and Margaret of her maidenhood.'

But the most outspoken critic of both the monastic Orders and the secular clergy was the Florentine Poggio Bracciolini, already so often mentioned in these pages. His indecent satirical tales in Latin, called *Facetiae*, mainly about the failings of the priesthood, were written early in the fifteenth century. By then it was no longer so dangerous as it had once been to twit the

Church. But Poggio did more. His *Dialogue Against Hypocrites* covers the ecclesiastical hierarchy with ferocious and scurrilous abuse. This composition was in its turn outpaced by his disputes with the contemporary scholars Filelfo and Valla, who hit back in kind. These polemics dragged in every sexual perversion either of the three learned contestants had ever found referred to in Juvenal, Petronius or Martial. All Italy laughed, fumed or blushed, for years on end, over the reckless devilries invented on each side. The facts that even bishops guffawed, that Pope Nicholas V employed Poggio to ridicule the anti-pope Felix and that the genially foul-mouthed scholar ended his days as Chancellor and Historiographer to the Republic of Florence are proof enough that the long medieval battle for at least open debate on what is or is not disgusting and sinful in the sexual field had finally been won.

In all these works the evidence is overwhelming that ordinary Europeans felt themselves to be in the thick of a conflict between the spirit and the flesh. This preoccupation is most vividly apparent in the strangely beautiful and haunting poems of François Villon (b. 1431), by common consent the most important figure in French literature before the Renaissance. A born vagabond and rebel, he knew himself, from the first, to be in peril from the Holy Willies of the day. He writes ruefully:

'A Frenchman I—a thing I hate—
of Pontoise, Paris. So soon or late
a six-foot rope will be my fate
and my neck will feel my arse's weight.'

He is sure that no one really cares about anything but wine and women. What do we do with all the money we make, he asks. He answers immediately in the cynical refrain:

Tout aux tavernes et aux filles.

Yet he loves his mother, is boundlessly generous and laments the ugliness and cruelty of the world at large. He is deeply sympathetic with the plight of elderly whores and describes it in perhaps his most famous piece, 'The Fair Armourer', i.e. the former wife or daughter of a maker of armour. She catalogues the carnal attractions she possessed thirty years ago in luscious detail.

> 'With tiny breasts and haunches plump,
> projecting, clean-cut, right for the job
> of amorous encounter, beauteous, broad—'

and the 'pretty little garden' she had between her 'big, firm thighs.' She contrasts all these glories with the horror of her present appearance in even greater detail. She ends with a 'Phew!' (Fy!) for the once 'pretty little garden'.

The ballad he sent to his friend 'Fat Margot,' on whom he perhaps really attended as a ponce, is even more boldly scabrous. He describes how he brought her clients' meals and if they paid well asked them to come back as soon as they felt 'in rut' again. The refrain of the four stanzas runs:

> 'Here in this brothel where we hold our state.'

After a quarrel and reconciliation with Margot she

> 'farts me full loud,
> all puffed like a poisonous beetle ...
> and at morn when her guts are a-rattle
> mounts me to save her fine fruitage.
> Underneath I squeak like a floor-board, make myself flat,
> while her lust knocks me utterly out ...'

The bitterness of a frustrated intellectual determined to shock by posing as the vilest of human specimens is unmistakable.

But François, though he never misses a chance to curse priests and monks of every description, remains deeply devoted to God the Father, the Holy Virgin and all the saints in the calendar. He is a Christian all right. But he does not believe that heaven will damn to all eternity irremediable human foibles like 'rutting' and thieving. What he can't stand is sentimentality and its derivatives, the falsely romantic, artificial sexual ardour of the rich and the mumbo-jumbo of purely religious mysticism.

Villon resembles Euripides in his alternations of savage acidity and exquisite pathos. His pictures, sketched by a poet of genius who was also a merciless realist, clearly reveal what was going on in medieval society as it merged into the Renaissance. The revolt against the tyranny of the tonsured had reached its climax. Throughout the surviving European literature of the previous millennium the surge can be traced, from ripple to thunder, of the wave on which Aphrodite still rides, and will ride for ever, against the rocks.

XIII Censors

THE first Christians lived in a society permeated from one end of the Mediterranean basin to the other by oriental sex-cults. These systems explored exhaustively the innumerable ways in which erotic enjoyment could be obtained and enhanced under the most various conditions. Consequently, the early Fathers, in considering what they were to do about the prime practical object of the Pauline lectures, i.e. the drastic disciplining of the procreative impulse, had a great deal of information to go on concerning the heathen practices in the opposite direction.

Arnobius in particular, an African rhetorician writing at the beginning of the fourth century, gave his fellow-theologians the requisite data in no less than seven separate books 'Against the Heathen', describing the libidinous perversions of this instinct then current. He stressed especially those which, through the wicked sophistry of their advocates, might appeal to Christians. As one of these he instanced the *coitus per os* or *fellatio*, i.e. the introduction of the penis into a partner's mouth. This habit is mentioned by several Roman authors. The epigrammatist Martial, for example, lists it as the third of the assaults with which he threatens trespassers in his garden. The other two are rape if the offender is a woman and *coitus per anum*, generally though not always translated 'sodomy', if a boy. Grown men are to be subjected to the *coitus per os*.

According to the Fourth Gospel Christ's human nature was the vehicle for the self-revelation of the *Logos*, the 'word' of God. Words come from the mouth. Accordingly, Arnobius seems to have imagined that *fellatio* might be represented to the Christians as an act symbolic of a dogma central to their beliefs.

Bizarre as this fancy may appear to the modern mind, it is no more so than many other weirdly rambling arguments by medieval theologians.

The question of whores and their place in a Christian State also came up at an early stage. It was clear that their obstinately flourishing trade constituted a serious menace to the spread of St. Paul's ideas. On the other hand Jesus had been kind to Mary Magdalene. He seemed more than once to have compared harlots favourably with the pompous hypocrites of his day, the Scribes, the Pharisees and the Sadducees. Most of the Fathers, however, decided that every effort should be made to convert these female 'hosts of Midian' to a proper way of thinking. Basil, Bishop of Caesarea in Syria during the fourth century, started 'homes of refuge' for them. Other prominent Christians followed his example during the next few generations. In the sixth century the former actress Theodora, who became the wife of the emperor Justinian, set up a hostel for those who had once been her associates.

Closely connected with these early measures, an equally long, strenuous and fruitless campaign was undertaken to stamp out the age-old mania for dancing. For this amusement was considered, with good reason, to be one of the main incitements to sexual profligacy. At the very beginning of the fourth century the Provincial Synod of Elvira in Granada forbade women to keep nocturnal watches in churchyards. For these gatherings, ostensibly called to pray for the dead, constantly degenerated. They turned first to a ritual trampling down of the evil spirits supposed to haunt cemeteries and then, as these rhythmic movements heated the blood, to frenzied gambols and lewd exhibitionism which attracted male onlookers. 'Disgraceful' orgies of promiscuous eroticism followed.

The Fathers were greatly helped in their raids on amativeness by the conception of heresy. This term, derived from Greek, has the root meaning of 'choice'. The Christians applied it from the start to any divergence from their main stream of thought. Orthodoxy being regarded as the divinely ordained depository of truth, it was permissible to attack 'heretics' with the utmost rigour of moral indignation. For if they were not extirpated they would cheat the whole world into being damned for ever.

But the average man finds it rather difficult to follow theological controversy. So the quickest way to enlist his support was to accuse those named as heretics of being addicted to abnormal use of their sexual organs. This kind of behaviour, even in those erotically carefree days, was relatively uncommon among the masses of the people and therefore easy to brand as disgusting and contemptible.

The second century Gnostics taught that God might be 'known'. The third century Manichees did not believe in the divinity of Christ. Many other sects of varying degrees of reasonableness arose in the subsequent stages of medieval civilisation. Some, like the thirteenth century Cathars, were quite admirable in their sturdy realism. But one and all were denounced as homosexuals. The Manichees, who were supposed to have reached Europe through Bulgaria, had the distinction, as we have seen, of fathering the popular synonym for a practitioner of their alleged habits. They were called in French *bougres* and in English *buggers*.

But unluckily for the Christian clergy this weapon of propaganda proved two-edged. People who had previously only the vaguest notion of 'buggery' and would never in the ordinary course of events have thought of perpetrating this form of coitus, had it suddenly and vividly brought to their attention. Moreover, the ascetics themselves, then regarded as the most noble of Christians, both the men who abjured female society and the women who abjured male, were almost at once most painfully tempted by the allurements of 'unnatural vice'.

There had been a time, during the first two Christian centuries, when the exaltation of the sincerest converts had reached such heights that they positively sought the enticements of an opportunity for normal copulation in order, triumphantly, to defy them. Aspirants to sanctity competed for the honour of sleeping 'sinlessly' with nude virgins, while the latter, for their part, reciprocated as best they could. But this system, called *agapetism*, from a Greek word for the kind of non-sensual love we now name Platonic, soon broke down. Scandals and complaints multiplied. Orders were issued for this sort of transcendence of the flesh to stop.

The principle of sheer repression, mainly by the scourge, took its place. This expedient succeeded to a certain extent in the monasteries and nunneries. But here too it was found in due course that the whip could be an aphrodisiac. Meanwhile the laity, in the rural districts especially, continued to remain pretty generally heretical in the sense of not bothering much about sexual restraint. Phallic worship still went on in the villages. Even statues of saints were sometimes provided with a conspicuous male organ. No doubt an ancestral memory of the once ubiquitous garden-god Priapus lingered in these rustic communities.

By the sixth century the priestly censors had called in the majesty of law. In Gaul the Merovingian Councils were set up. They derived their name from Merovech, a king of the first Frankish dynasty who was said to have fought against Attila's Huns in the middle of the fifth century. The Councils passed a number of laws forbidding the clergy to get drunk and recommending sexual continence. In 533 the Orléans councillors suppressed the Order of Deaconesses. It had been started to give girls a chance of making a career in the Church. But unfortunately the young women had been found to constitute a temptation not only to their male opposite numbers, the deacons, but also to older priests who should have known better. The Franks, in fact, seem to have been as incorrigibly bent on fun and games as their modern descendants. In 586 the Synod of Auxerre, a cathedral town in central France, had to prohibit the use of churches and nunneries as dance-halls.

But it was in England, even then a country as notable for its puritans as for the coarseness of its debauchery, that the famous Penitentials were first promulgated. These were collections of pronouncements intended for the guidance of confessors in estimating the penances to be imposed for an extraordinarily large number of sins, mainly of an erotic nature. The bulky Anglo-Saxon Penitentials were soon copied in other lands and constantly re-edited.

The version produced by the Northumbrian historian and theologian Bede (672-735) exceeded all others in the quantity of its ordinances and the minuteness of its details. For a simple fornication he prescribed a year's fast. Adultery was punished by from two to seven years, according to its circumstances, on bread and water. But under King Canute, a very severe critic of such conduct, culprits lost not only the right to marry again, but also, perhaps to render such a contingency rather less likely, their noses and ears.

Even the confession of licentious thoughts carried disagreeable penalties, generally forty days' fast.

Bede was also very down on masturbation, a practice then almost unknown in the non-Christian, polygamous world, but very frequent in Europe. He gave this matter no less than twenty-five paragraphs, noting the various methods of 'self-abuse' employed and grading its punishments with reference to the persons confessing it. Their ages, ranks and professions had to be considered, as well as the place in which the offence was committed—it happened pretty often in church apparently—and the mental activities which accompanied performance.

A layman could get forty days of fasting and psalm-singing for this sin, clerics more. Sodomy and bestiality rated twenty-two paragraphs in Bede's Penitential, again demanding attention to the age and social position of the offender, the type of person or animal involved as partner and the method of procedure. Life penances might be imposed in cases regarded as peculiarly obnoxious.

But these two perversions were interpreted much more widely in the Middle Ages than today. The term sodomy was often applied to what would be called bestiality in the twentieth century and *vice versa*. Moreover, anyone having carnal intercourse with a Jew or an infidel was liable to be convicted of bestiality, since such individuals were regarded by the orthodox as less than human. On the other hand fornication with a nun was treated as incest on the ground that such women were the sisters of all mankind. Such couplings could also be characterised as adultery, the nun being a 'bride of Christ'.

Further legal chastisements were ordained by the Penitentials for those who kissed each other, wrote or read lascivious books, sang wanton ditties, danced suggestively, wore indecent clothing, bathed with the opposite sex, watched lewd theatrical entertainments or hung about in churches after midnight. For these big, shadowy buildings, always open, were much frequented by loose characters for nocturnal assignations and even orgies.

Severe as these regulations were, they could not compare with the ferocity of earlier punishments. Under the first Christian emperors convicted panders had melted lead poured down their throats. In the reign of Valentinian I (fourth century) sodomites (in the modern sense) were burnt alive. In 390 Theodosius I proclaimed: 'All persons who have the shameful custom of condemning a man's body, acting the part of a woman's, to the sufferance of an alien sex, for they appear not to be different from women, shall expiate a crime of this kind in avenging flames in the sight of the people.' All through the Middle Ages proved homosexuals were formally sentenced to this type of execution. But it was rarely carried out. For such offenders were always tried in ecclesiastical courts, which could not officially authorise the death of a criminal, though they could, at discretion, hand him over to the secular arm to be burned or hanged. As a rule they would not do so except in such shocking cases as that of Gilles de Rais, dealt with in Chapter X of the present work.

All the same, though the clergy did not normally kill homosexuals, they pursued such persons with a peculiar hatred, as guilty of one of the four *clamantia peccata*, 'sins which cried to high heaven'. This odium dated from that felt by the ancient Hebrews for their political foes the Canaanites, who had male as well as female prostitutes attached to their temples. The antisodomy crusade also derived its ruthlessness, of course, from the prevalence of this practice, almost from the start of Christianity, among celibate priests and monks.

St. Ecgbert, Archbishop of York in the eighth century, and a brother of King Eadberht of Northumbria, corresponded with such eminent prelates as St. Boniface, the Englishman who converted the Germans to Christianity, Alcuin, the Archbishop's own fellow-townsman and Charlemagne's favourite English theologian, and finally Bede of the Penitentials. In 729 Ecgbert himself composed a book of canonical writings which is even more explicit than Bede's on the subject of early medieval prurience.

An adulterous bishop is there condemned to a fast of no less than twelve years, accompanied by almsgiving in bulk, tears and prayers. The question should also be considered of depriving him of his diocese. A fornicating priest must fast for three years and thereafter two days a week for three years. If his partner is a nun seven years are the minimum. But even if he is only guilty of lascivious talk or ejaculating semen involuntarily at the mere sight of a woman, he is to fast for twenty days. They are increased to a hundred if he permits such self-pollution of set purpose (*propria voluntate*). If he experiences a night emission while asleep he must get up and sing a psalm, followed the next day by thirty prostrations, apparently of oriental type (*maxillam suam ad terram inclinet*). Again, if he has encouraged such a nocturnal vision (*si volens in somno moechatus sit*) the psalms to be sung must be twenty-four, or the whole psaltery if this affair happened in church. An eleventh-century editor, however, allows the choice between ten psalms and a thousand self-inflicted lashes and so on in proportion. It seems a strange ratio and one can only speculate as to the reason for it.

If a priest kisses a woman lasciviously he must fast twenty days or forty if the contact is accompanied by ejaculation. Licentious meditation leading to self-pollution (*si polluatur cogitationis voluntate*) carries a week's penance, three weeks if the penitent actually masturbated (*tactu manus*) on such an occasion.

Night emissions had formed the subject of anxious debate between the highest prelates in Christendom over a hundred years before Ecgbert wrote his canonicals. At the end of the sixth century St. Augustine II, converter of southern England and first Archbishop of Canterbury, enquired of Pope Gregory I whether a priest so 'polluted' would be entitled to officiate at mass the following day. The reply was that it all depended. If the ejaculation could be proved to result from natural infirmity, the priest need only pray and ask God to forgive him. If, however, the polluted one could be shown to have consumed too much wine and highly spiced food the day before, he could only officiate if it were found absolutely necessary for him to do so. But first he must pray, sing psalms and distribute charitable gifts. But if, finally, he had been indulging in licentious meditations before retiring to rest, he must not on any account officiate at mass next day. Instead, he must make a full confession and undergo the penance prescribed, i.e. the singing of seven psalms, with a knee-bend at the end of each verse, followed by a day's fast on bread and water or thirty psalms with knee-bends as specified.

Habitual fornication by a beneficed priest may be penalised by fasts of twelve months, three years or ten years, according to circumstances. The last phrase might mean anything from the number of times intercourse took place over a certain period to the total number of partners or the degree of enthusiasm, fraud or violence with which the act might be sought or practised. Deacons and monks were let off more lightly, with three years' fasting. But if a child is born as a result of such behaviour, the bishop or other judicial authority may increase the penance at his discretion. Lay brothers will have to fast twelve months for the same sin, three years if a child is fathered and seven years if the sinner destroys the infant. A fornicating nun may be liable to anything from three to seven years' fasting.

Laymen who seduce another layman's wife or daughter must fast one year or three if a child is born. But, oddly enough, if the sinner is a bachelor, a fast of as much as ten years may be imposed. This severity was probably intended to promote early marriages and thus, in the Archbishop's view, to reduce the general incidence of lust. By way of comparison, incest with a mother, sister or daughter carried a punishment of twelve years' fasting.

Bestiality, which St. Ecgbert seems to restrict to the modern sense of the word, incurs a heavy maximum penalty, from seven to ten years' fast. Extenuating circumstances depend on the type of penitent and species of animal involved. They may lop the sentence to as little as a hundred days. It may be conjectured perhaps that an imbecile who uses a creature of little value would get off lightly. For *fellatio* (*qui in os semen effuderit*), the sin which so worried Arnobius, a fast of seven years is prescribed. A householder who seduces his maidservant (*verna sua*) will be in for a year's fast. If a child is born, he must free it from serfdom (*redimat eum*) and put in another year's fast.

Little boys who have unnatural coition forced upon them (*si parvus puer a majori opprimatur in coitu*) are punished, charitably enough, by only five days' fasting. But if the child did not resist such an assault, the penalty is increased to twenty days. This is also the figure for boy masturbators. But grown men may get as much as a hundred days for this offence, presumably if it is habitual or especially shameless.

A husband having intercourse with a menstruating wife is due for forty days. The strange habit, no doubt homoeopathic in origin, of drinking one's own blood or semen, is penalised by five years' abstinence from all but the bare minimum of food required for subsistence. The sentence for fornication in a church is, again rather strangely, left to the bishop's discretion. But this concession cannot mean that such sacrilege would not be punished with great severity. Homosexual congress carried to extremes (*si coiverit*) incurs, like the most offensive forms of bestiality, ten years' fasting. But boys committing this sin are merely 'suspended', presumably what we should call 'bound over'. Beasts which are 'polluted' by a man must be killed and the carcass thrown to dogs. But if there is any doubt about the matter the animal need not be slaughtered. On the other hand a person habitually practising bestiality as well as fornication is condemned to fast in a monastery for the rest of his life, if such conduct can be clearly proved against him (*si valde multa commiscuit*).

No one should ever contemplate a woman naked, even his own wife. If a husband proves impotent, the wife can desert him and marry another. No woman, the Archbishop writes boldly, counter to the common opinion of his time, should be married against her will. Nor need she stay with a husband if she returns to him the bride-price he paid for her. If he declines to accept the sum she may be permitted to enter a convent.

In some Penitentials a fast of as much as seven years is prescribed for a husband who copulates with his wife 'like a dog', i.e. in the attitude of animals so engaged. For this posture was considered to provide an excessive amount of pleasure for the partners. But if he actually commits sodomy upon her he is to fast for the rest of his life and suffer excommunication. Conjugal relations on a Sunday, even after dark, are punished by three days' fasting. Legitimate sexual intercourse is also to be omitted for forty days before Easter, seven days before Whitsun and fourteen days before Christmas. No one, in any case, is to go to church, at any time, after marital congress, without washing. Menstruating women, even nuns, who attend divine service in that condition, must fast for twenty days.

Whoever 'weakens' (*imbecillitatem intulerit*) another's genitals or wounds them must pay for the appropriate medical treatment and fast for from two to three days or twelve months if the injury proves incurable. There seems to be a reference to witchcraft here. For the Archbishop goes on to prescribe seven years' fast for a woman who performs the act of coition with 'poison' (*si cum venefico coeat*) and three years for any female who mixes a male's sperm with food in order to increase the sexual attractions of a woman who eats from the dish so prepared.

It gradually becomes clear, as one reads on through St. Ecgbert's Canonicals, that they have the character of case-law. Sins and penances appear to have been jotted down just as they came to the compiler's notice, in the very reverse of orderly fashion. In Book II, moreover, the penalties begin to vary considerably.

Bestiality and homosexuality by adults are now thought worthy of seven, ten or fifteen years' fasting. Yet in certain cases, presumably mild, the penalty is one year for a layman and two for a monk. Elsewhere three years only are recommended for sodomy between laymen. A kiss or embrace between partners of opposite sex entails a month's fast. But if accompanied by improper contacts (*contactu eius inverecundo ad carnem*) three months are prescribed.

Habitual masturbation carries three years, as does also habitual fornication (without any reference to circumstances). A single act of masturbation is punished on one page by four meatless days. Yet elsewhere, if the offender is a young boy he gets a month, if a man forty days. The mere desire to fornicate should be expiated, in proportion to its strength and duration, by twenty to forty days. An adulterous wife is due for three years, but only one if she simply masturbates with the idea of extra-marital intercourse in mind (*si ipsa eundem modum secum fornicandi imitetur*). Those who practise *fellatio* (*qui semen ori inmittat*) get seven years. But some consider, the Saint adds, that this is the worst of crimes and should entail lifelong penance.

Incest with a mother is punished in Book II by a fifteen years' fast, with a sister or daughter by from seven to twelve years. Brothers who commit sodomy with each other must abstain from meat for fifteen years. A mother who seduces a son under the age of puberty gets three years. Impure thoughts should be combatted by engaging in certain—unspecified—penances until the thoughts are forgotten. An unsuccessful attempt to seduce a woman should be atoned for by a week's fast.

In the case of sexual intercourse between a monk and a woman of the laity, he must fast for three years and she for two. If a layman seduces a nun, he is only due for two years, but she for three. Both are to fast for four years if a child is born and for seven years if they kill it. At one point St. Ecgbert condemns a habitually homosexual bishop to fourteen years' fasting, a priest to twelve, a deacon to ten, a subdeacon to eight, a clerk to seven and a layman to five. A monk seducing a nun is in for four years, but for seven if he has intercourse with a woman of the laity, although this last figure was only three on a previous page.

So the long, complex catalogue goes on, growing more and more confused, as revisions, alterations, repetitions, afterthoughts, new subdivisions and fresh hypotheses pile up. The Archbishop obviously wearied of his self-imposed task pretty often, forgot what he had said before or was faced with hitherto unprecedented cases. But he does end by firmly and triumphantly laying it down, once and for all, without the slightest hesitation, that a bishop who fornicates with cattle must fast eight years for a single offence and ten years for more than one. Priests, deacons and clerks, however, who perform such acts, are let off with five, three and two years respectively.

Confessors were instructed in later manuals to question very closely penitents who admitted sexual misbehaviour. As already noted in the foregoing pages this latitude exposed the priest to great temptation in some cases, especially if the sinner were young, attractive and shy. Precisely what, in what order, did he or she or the partner concerned actually do in consummating the offence, what were the prevailing conditions and environment and what feelings and physiological reactions were concurrently observed by the penitent in his or her own person and that of the other, if any? The answers to such queries might well heat the blood even of an anchorite. Unless the confessor were very experienced in such matters or of naturally sluggish imagination, he would need considerable fortitude to maintain his equanimity. The evidence is clear that many not only grew excited but proceeded to commit sins which themselves entailed confession and penitence—in theory.

Bishop Burchard of Worms (d. 1025) gives some interesting examples of such interrogations, along a particular line of enquiry, in a *Decretum* which also includes the appropriate penalties for affirmative replies.

'Have you done,' the confessor is to demand in a typically exhaustive paragraph, 'what certain women are wont to do, contriving a certain engine or mechanical device in the form of the male sexual organ, the dimensions being calculated to give you pleasure, and binding it to your own or another woman's pudenda, and have you thus committed fornication with other evilly disposed women or they, using the same or some other apparatus, with yourself?'

Admission of such a proceeding would be followed by the imposition of five years' fasting at 'all legitimate Church festivals'.

'Have you done,' he is to repeat inexorably, 'what certain women are wont to do, sitting upon the aforesaid instrument or some other device of similar construction, and thus committing fornication upon yourself in solitude?'

If the penitent confesses to having arranged a private indulgence of her prurience in this way she is to fast for one year.

The Bishop leaves no legal loophole for evasion in this matter. For he adds: 'Any woman using any fornicating instrument whatever, either alone or in company with another woman, must fast for three years, the first on bread and water only.' He thus, perhaps inadvertently, varies the penalties already prescribed, as indeed he does again on a later page, where four years are mentioned. Nuns are of course given heavier sentences, no less than seven years, if they adopt such artifices for 'Lesbian' coition.

The somewhat later Compendium of Canon Law deals among many other matters with the punishments for such 'heresy' as involves sexual practices offensive to the Church. Since all heretics of any kind were accused of these sooner or later, the bishops had to work at least double time in their efforts to stamp out unorthodox Christians, to say nothing of the varieties of infidels.

Heretics could be excommunicated, deprived of Christian burial and excluded from the monastic Orders. This last punishment fell heavily upon those numerous persons who wanted to be monks or nuns, either to obtain a little peace and quiet in such troublous times, or simply to enjoy the opportunities for more or less discreet debauchery which they confidently hoped would occur. Sometimes, of course, candidates had their eyes on both amenities. It would be peculiarly distressing for them if, owing to some trumped up charge of having said or done the wrong thing at the wrong time, they were permanently ruled out of these coveted institutions.

In Canon Law sacrilege included the seduction of a nun and simony. The latter sin usually meant the selling of Church property. But it also covered the use of a 'holy object', such as the Host, for erotic satisfaction. We have already seen that this ultimate blasphemy could occur during celebrations of the Black Mass. The pollution of ecclesiastical vestments, vessels and furniture in the same way would also be simoniac. The improper use of consecrated ground fell into the same category. So that favourite device of lustful priests, the drugging of nuns or female parishioners with Communion wine preparatory to taking possession of their persons behind the altar, would be a double offence. Simony would be committed in tampering with the wine. Sacrilege as well as simony would be perpetrated in fornicating on holy ground. If a nun were the victim a third sin, that of incest with a 'bride of Christ', would occur simultaneously with the other two.

The crime of incest, incidentally, covered a husband's sexual intercourse with a relative of his wife and her copulation with a relative of his own. The penalty was withdrawal of the right to ordinary conjugal congress. As to sodomy, the Compendium defines *sodomia perfecta* as the unnatural (*non servato debito sexu*) coition of a couple either male or female. 'Imperfect' sodomy, not otherwise specified, is declared not liable to retribution under Canon Law. This freedom is also accorded to bestiality, a matter not for the ecclesiastical but for the civil courts. But homosexuals might be deprived by the Church not only of the Eucharist, through excommunication, but also of their wives if the latter could be regarded as innocent. For an odd feature of medieval society, in strong contrast with that of modern times, was the rarity of lay bachelor sodomites and the frequency of this practice among married men. Theologians were so down on it that most addicts defended themselves from persecution by marrying as soon as possible and keeping their main sexual interests secret. In any case bisexuality, an inheritance from classical times, was then much more prevalent than today. Though the secular arm was in theory authorised to burn convicted sodomites or bury them alive, such executions, as already noted, were only carried out in highly spectacular cases.

As early as the eighth century the Church had found it necessary to condemn the sophistry of penitents who substituted alms-giving for fasting in observing their sentences. Unfortunately the clergy themselves were not always proof against corruption by wealthy sinners who, after admitting various lapses from chastity, subscribed generously to ecclesiastical funds instead of giving up their hearty meals as ordered by their confessors. Some bishops even began to extort fines from people too poor or too mean to bribe them in this way.

One most profitable expedient, very popular with rural deans and archdeacons in connivance with the local lord of the manor, was the *leyrwite*, a fine for unchastity which could be inflicted on a serf if he or she thus 'wasted' the masters' property. If, for example, a girl serf should prove to have been 'unchaste of her body', the lord would lose the *merchet* or payment due to him on the marriage of a female serf, since no one would marry her if she were known to be of loose character. The man or men responsible for the girl's conduct would then have to pay the lord's lost *merchet* in the form of a *leyrwite* disbursed in the ecclesiastical court.

In medieval society, accordingly, a system of allegedly sacred law narrowed down sexual activities, as well as a great many others which seem to any modern moralist quite harmless, in an intolerably restrictive manner. It was no wonder that people resorted to every expedient to evade such regulations. The wonder is that so many believed implicitly in their divine authority and sheepishly obeyed them if there seemed no other way out of the scourging, fasting and psalm-singing they imposed. In the monasteries and nunneries, no doubt, supervisors were officially supposed to see to it that the punishments duly took place. But there must have been a lot of deliberate blindness to evasion of them even in such closely packed communities. As for the laity, it is hard to imagine who could have enforced the penalties on a householder, whose will was law in his own home. But probably something must be allowed for the innocent human pride in acquiring a reputation for virtuous repentance by refusing second helpings at dinner and being careful to make a great deal of noise in private by ostentatious prayers, tears, chanting and self-flagellation.

The absurdly wide interpretation of incest must have given a great many perfectly decent people awful headaches. Until 1215 one could marry neither one's first nor one's seventh cousin. In that year, however, Pope Innocent III kindly permitted the marriage of third cousins and beyond. Prior to that date any cousins who married would 'riot in the bed of consanguinity'. But of course special dispensations could be granted to 'grave and noble persons' who were willing to pay for them.

The commonalty were another matter. In the small villages where most of the population lived these prohibitions often meant that one had to pack up and travel in order to seek a wife or husband, since everyone in the district was quite likely to come within the unlawful degrees.

Nor, according to the Code of the emperor Justinian, the so called *Novellae Constitutiones* (sixth century), could a man marry a woman for whom he had stood godfather, thus adopting a 'spiritual' relationship to her. We have seen how the Frankish queen Fredegond tricked her predecessor out of the throne by invoking one of the numerous extensions of this law. For various other connections of this type, e.g. that of a sponsor and the child of another sponsor, were also made illegal. As for marriage to a Jew or a Mohammedan, such a proceeding, as already noted, was considered equivalent to bestiality.

But if a couple did manage to marry without incurring penalties under ecclesiastical or civil law they were still subject to vexing supervision by the clergy. Weddings took place throughout the Middle Ages on the church doorstep, never inside the building. But the subsequent meal did, tables being set out in the nave, where pews had not yet been introduced. After eating and drinking its fill the wedding procession, not accompanied by the priest, repaired to the house of the bride's father to stoke up with a second banquet, followed by dancing.

When the newly married pair eventually retired, all the guests who could squeeze into the matrimonial chamber followed them, helped them to undress and executed a number of more or less decorous fertility rites. As soon as husband and wife were safely bedded, the priest reappeared, blessed and drank with them, drenched them and their bed with holy water, filled the room with incense to dispel demons bent on rendering the bridegroom impotent or the bride barren or both and wound up by recommending the now thoroughly bemused principals to spend their first night together in prayer and fasting. Sometimes they were prohibited from copulating for at least three days.

This interval of abstinence was popularly known as the 'Tobias Nights'. In the apocryphal Book of Tobit,* a Jewish novel probably first written in Greek about 250 B.C., a Samarian named Tobias was sent by his blind father Tobit to fetch money Tobit had left with a friend. Tobias met on his journey a girl named Sara who told him a strange story. She had been married seven times, but was still a virgin. On each of her wedding nights an incubus had turned up and strangled her husband before he could exercise his conjugal rights. Tobias, after consulting the archangel Raphael, decided to try his luck. He married the girl, but on the wedding night, instead of embracing her, smoked the heart and liver of a fish, praying hard the while, as advised by the archangel. The smoke drove the incubus away and the bride and groom lived happily ever after.

According to a twelfth-century divine named Alberich, married couples who indulge in sexual intercourse during Lent or on holidays are plunged after death into a lake of melted lead, burning pitch and resin, situated in an otherwise unoccupied district of hell.

But offences much more serious in modern eyes than exercising conjugal rights on Sunday evenings were committed with impunity by the clergy, especially the senior ecclesiastics. We

* See p. 116.

have already seen (p. 93) that in 1299 a French knight whose daughter had been seduced by the Bishop of Orléans finally despaired of having the exalted culprit brought to justice. After all other measures had failed he took the law into his own hands and murdered the fellow, with what further result is not recorded. But it is likely enough that the daring avenger escaped arrest for this probably justifiable homicide.

St. Thomas à Becket, when a priest was brought before him for raping a girl and murdering her father, who had tried to intervene, simply had the tonsured ruffian removed to another benefice. For the Church considered its executive officers the only effective authorities who stood between administrative order and utter chaos. Their sacrosanct character, therefore, had to be bolstered up at almost any cost. The manifest injustice of this attitude deepened to more or less secret defiance, as time went on, the already rooted resentment by medieval man of the only too frequent excesses and arrogance of his priesthood.

As the secular power of the papacy increased, rising to almost unquestioned dominance in the twelfth century, heresy hunts were stepped up. Those who wished to think out problems, especially questions of sexual morality, for themselves, were subjected to resolutely organised persecution. In former centuries their suppression, together with that of the cranks and escapists who always flourish in times of political uncertainty, had been relatively easy. The brains and learning had been mostly on the orthodox side.

But now a culture not exclusively drawn from the Christian scriptures was beginning to make itself felt. The impact of Mohammedan civilisation had been formidable, not only in Spain, for two hundred years. The Arabs understood more of Aristotle's empirical and speculative philosophy and of Alexandrian scientific research than the Christians did. Scholars in Byzantium and Asia Minor, Sicily and Provence, were gradually finding out, like John P. Wanamaker in the nineteenth century, that 'they didn't know everything down in Judee'. To Pope Innocent III in 1199 the position looked dangerous.

He issued a decree which led to the foundation of the Holy Inquisition. He massacred the most obstinate of the Provençal heretics in the so called Albigensian Crusade. He hammered at

Islam in Syria and connived at the sack of Constantinople by the Eastern Crusaders. By the thirteenth century those who disagreed in any way with Rome were regularly being burned alive, over a slow fire, after torture. The property of these victims was always confiscated by the Church.

Turbulent lords in the outlying regions of Christendom were severely disciplined. In 1285 an English knight abducted a couple of young nuns from the Wilton convent for his harem. He was excommunicated, a penalty which deprived him of all civil rights, whipped for three weeks in the parish church, the market-place and the neighbouring church of Shaftesbury, ordered to fast for several months and wear no shirt for three years. Nor would he be allowed the usual dress and insignia of a knight, but only 'apparel of a russet colour,' till he had spent three years on pilgrimage in Palestine.

But the still officially celibate clergy themselves continued to give trouble by their persistent lasciviousness. The notably humane Franciscan preacher Berthold von Regensburg told a thirteenth-century congregation that women were perfectly entitled under canon law to resist priestly ravishers. When he was in Brussels, he said, a poor working girl confessed to him that she had made the nose of one of these supposedly sacrosanct satyrs bleed, while defending her virtue in a fist fight with him. Other priests to whom she admitted this dreadful deed had imposed the penance of a pilgrimage to Rome by way of atonement. 'But,' Berthold went on, 'I told the poor child on my own authority that in such circumstances she could strike any priest as hard as she could and it would be no sin.' In any case, the preacher added, the Brussels confessors had no business to enforce such a severe penalty. For Pope Alexander III, one of the best of the medieval pontiffs, had decreed in the last half of the twelfth century that women and children could be absolved by their bishops for the offence of striking a priest.

As for the punishment of libidinous clerics themselves there was little serious question of any such thing in the thirteenth century. Pardons could readily be obtained for public and persistent concubinage, for committing an abortion on a woman seduced by the abortionist himself and for corrupting nuns. A case is noted, in the Formulary of the Papal Penitentials issued at this time, of a monk whose sin in once beating a nun he had seduced was considered more serious than his incestuous 'pollution of a bride of Christ'. Again, a deacon who lives with a concubine, ostensibly his servant, is granted absolution forthwith. But if he dares to marry her he will be remorselessly prosecuted.

Protests against this state of affairs by conscientious prelates like Bishop Grosseteste made no difference. The Roman Curia flung dispensations and indulgences about as if they were handbills. Some pardons, however, could be justified by common morality, such as that of a youth who castrated an older man when the latter tried by force to commit anal coition upon him. In another case two brothers were excused for having similarly emasculated the ravisher of their sister. Such primitive retaliations were pretty common in those days, even against priests, some of whom were 'unmanned' or even killed by their indignant parishioners.

A more amusing case, to the thirteenth-century mind, was that of a canon who died of fright after being given a light beating by his more austere travelling companion for introducing a whore into their bedroom. Another anecdote in this Penitentiary relates that a certain layman had been flirting or romping (*procabatur*, which perhaps means here a kind of street-corner horseplay) with the daughter of his hostess, prior to retiring to the bedroom he had been allotted in the house, where he was a guest. While subsequently urinating there he was terrified by the male members of the establishment, who rushed into the chamber flourishing weapons. They threatened to deprive him of his exposed member unless he married the girl immediately. Such a wedding, in the absence of a priest, but before witnesses, would be quite valid under medieval law, as in the case reported in the last chapter, where Boccaccio's story of the 'nightingale' was noted. In the present instance the wretched man complied under duress. But he never touched the young woman afterwards and applied to the ecclesiastical court for annulment of the ceremony on the ground that there were no impartial persons in attendance. But the court declined to adjudicate on this difficult problem. It was passed on to the civil authorities, with what result is not recorded.

The Penitentiary lists example after example proving that

ecclesiastics could do pretty well what they liked so long as they did not marry. Prosperous laymen could also obtain absolution fairly frequently for sexual misconduct. But one enterprising gentleman was not so lucky. After copulating with the mother of a girl cousin (degree not specified) of his wife, he went on to apply the same treatment to the girl herself, who was only twelve. Both he and the child's mother were ordered by the ecclesiastical court to 'remain chaste for evermore' besides doing prolonged and disagreeable penance. The question of what does or does not constitute 'chastity' was debated in exhaustive and scabrous detail by the celibate judges. It seems to have been decided, perhaps with an eye to the 'agapetism' of earlier centuries, that the marriage of persons who had previously made a vow of chastity could be permitted on the understanding that full consummation was not contemplated, if the parties pleaded that otherwise 'incontinence' would result.

Celibacy was in fact, as the Fathers themselves admitted, of post-apostolic origin. Jesus of Nazareth had taught a refined type of Judaism in this field. St. Peter himself was married. So was Tertullian. St. Paul never dreamed of prohibiting the marriage of priests. The decree that all clergy of whatever rank were to be celibate was issued by Pope Siricius in 385. But this rule never obtained in the Eastern Church. Consequently, far less scandalous sexual depravity among priests occurred under that dispensation than in the West.

This carelessly confident underestimation of the invincibility of the procreative impulse was perhaps from an administrative point of view the most fatal shortcoming of the medieval Church. It led in the fourteenth century to an exacerbation of lay revolt against clerical oppression in this respect. The rebellion was by then in full flood. It was never again to abate, though in the sixteenth century it took a milder form, rather of sceptical contempt than of moral indignation.

The morally respectable English poet John Gower (1330-1408) openly wrote that prelates encouraged the vices of the laity in order to enrich themselves with the bribes that would then be forthcoming from the sinners with a view to evading penance. Gower's contemporary William Langland inveighs with equal frankness in the satirical vision of his *Piers Plowman*, which runs to seven thousand lines, against ecclesiastical abuses and the rapacity of the friars in particular. The slightly older and very earnest religious reformer John Wyclif was of the same opinion. His followers, known as Lollards from their habit of singing in a low key (the word is connected with 'lullaby') went about chanting such doggerel as:

'For a simple fornication
twenty shillings he shall pay
and then have an absolution
and all the year usen it forth he may.'

Chaucer lived at the same time. He returns again and again to this theme. The English were certainly to the fore in those days, as they were often to be in later ages, as champions of democratic common sense versus outmoded despotic cruelty.

The average 'indulgence' cost fourpence, alternatively a drink in a tavern, the cancellation of a gambling debt, the payment for a prostitute or in the case of young men or women the simple offer to the confessor's lust of the penitent's own body. Everyone was bribable, especially the 'summoners' or clerical spies who reported transgressors to the ecclesiastical courts. Chaucer defines them in the Prologue to the Friar's Tale.

'A somnour is a runner up and down
with mandementz for fornicacioun.'

Persons named by the summoners could often escape sentence by informing against others financially better off who could be relied on for hard cash. It was really no wonder that the Bishop of Exeter called the behaviour of such blackmailing 'somnours', who particularly persecuted women, 'damnable presumption'. However, busy people who could not avoid, in this way, being sent on long pilgrimages to atone for their sins, could always hire others less hard-working to impersonate them. Such masquerades attracted poverty-stricken and/or lazy individuals, who could thus see something of the world free of charge and in tolerable conditions. For pilgrims were usually respected and well entertained on their supposedly pious journeys. The stay-at-homes on their routes would generally feel sorry for them and appreciate their 'repentance'.

It need only be added that, despite the Inquisition, the

deliberate multiplication of offences under the heresy heading, the summoners and all the other desperate measures promoted by the Church, including the most appalling visions of damned souls in hell, the end of the fifteenth century saw cases of sexual misbehaviour equalling in number all the other crimes dealt with by both ecclesiastical and civil courts. For by then the latter, owing to the increasing defiance of canonical law and order, had come to the assistance of the bishops in trying persons accused of unauthorised erotic activities.

XIV   Conclusion

THE matrimonial experiences of the distinguished British statesman Lord Melbourne (1779-1848) were unfortunate. In 1836 his appearance as a co-respondent in the Divorce Court did not improve his already strained relations with King William IV. Nevertheless, Melbourne benefited his country by his actions and the young queen Victoria by his advice much more than might have been expected. For he said and did many things in his life outside the House and Buckingham Palace which scandalised conventional society. One of his somewhat Wildean witticisms was to the effect that he didn't know what the world would come to if religion began to interfere with peoples' private affairs.

He might have instanced medieval history, very largely a record of such interference. From end to end of the period the Christian Church cannot fairly be said to have improved European sexual behaviour much beyond the point it had reached in the last years of the pagan Roman Empire. On the whole the continent was happier, under the Antonine emperors at least (first and second centuries) as officially subservient to Jupiter than throughout the Christian Middle Ages, a millennium which Lord Melbourne would certainly not have liked at any stage of its development.

Yet, though life may have been less insecure and oppressive under Trajan and Marcus Aurelius than under Justinian or even Charlemagne, to say nothing of the long despotism of the papacy, the great *pax romana* of the heathens remained comparatively dull. No art was produced to match the grandeur of Romanesque and Gothic architecture. No literature equalled the comedy and

CONCLUSION

satire of Boccaccio and Chaucer, the nobility of Dante or the lyrical ardour of Petrarch and the troubadours. The sumptuous splendours and gaieties of the colourful, spectacular ages of feudalism, its luxuriant decline and the extravagant, rollicking courtiers and merchant princes of the fifteenth century far outdid, even in taste, the traditional sobriety of pagan Roman manners, unaffected by the decadent vulgarity of the more notorious emperors and their satellites.

Compared with the twilight of the older religions the medieval morning of Christianity drew a furious energy from the very spirit of revolt against the tyranny of its Church. The excesses of the carnivals, the professional jesters and the lower ranks of the clergy—for with a few glaring exceptions the higher prelates stood very much on their dignity—the more or less secret societies of witches, crypto-pagans and other heretics, the ubiquitous harlots and the irrepressible strolling players, wandering scholars and tellers of improper stories, all in one way or another flourished the banner of Venus, so to speak, in the face of priestly asceticism.

But even the saintly mystics owed their gravely magnificent visions to a basis they would have repudiated with detestation if they could have recognised it. For the exaltation of all religious monomania is fundamentally akin to that of sexual passion. In fact, to a psychologist's eye, pious ecstasy in all its manifestations carries every sign of both the fierce and the tender aspects of the procreative impulse.

If Aphrodite or Venus, Astarte or Ashtaroth or Cotytto, could have been taken for granted, as in former times, by Christendom, there would have been no such thing as what is now called typically medieval civilisation. The sly or boisterous humour of its popular farces is on the whole narrower in range than that of their classical predecessors. The Christians' obsession with sex, forced upon them by ecclesiastical policy, so that the plays and tales of the Middle Ages ride the topics of adultery and seduction to death, inflicts a certain childishness on their comedies, which never approach the sophistication of either earlier or later times. On the other hand, neither before nor since the medieval era has the fastidious spirituality of the ideals of chivalry been rivalled, born as it was through a transcendence of oriental sensuality by the cult of the Virgin Mary, itself an ultimate goal, if ever there was one, of true love.

But man is the most highly sexed of all animals. It will always be impossible to thwart the erotic instincts of humanity without causing a distress so dire as to be mortal if it is not met by rebellion. Fortunately for later ages the naturally defiant Western mentality, after nearly perishing as the barbarians closed in, proved stubborn enough to face and overcome the challenge of a perverse bigotry. The strength of the insurgents won because it was unconscious, a deep, amoral urge, not, as the priests proclaimed, a deliberate flouting of decency.

The question why this point of Christian orthodoxy was not simply laughed out of court as soon as it was announced has been much debated. Some psychologists have supposed that religion itself, any religion which involves fear of the supernatural, is rooted in the terror which children feel when they are disciplined by their parents. It is assumed that the infant then longs for a superhuman parent, one who will reward as well as punish them. This figure will be almighty and omniscient, therefore will be obeyed however cruel or absurd the orders issued may be.

As regards Christianity in particular, this school of thought declares that the clerical insistence upon the basically evil nature of women was accepted in this example on account of the innate tendency of the child to resent its mother. For she is the parent most regularly in contact with it. But one may well ask why, if this is so, the whole world did not immediately become Christian in the sense of being as sexually inhibited as a saint of the Dark Ages. As nothing of the sort happened even in Europe itself the theory looks dubious. In fact deeply religious men nearly always revere their mothers. St. Augustine of Hippo adored his though he thought that involuntary erections of the penis proved that 'nature' was sinful. D. H. Lawrence, too, whose 'dark gods' were as real to him as Christ to Augustine, loved his mother far more than any of the women he deliberately sought out, while pursuing his theories, in later life.

It appears much more probable that the very intensity of the orgasm achieved as the result of erotic action frightened people. It was an experience, like that of a hostile god's attack, which

CONCLUSION

they could not control or resist. On these grounds classical and even Eastern philosophers, not only Plato but also Buddha, condemned the positive cultivation of lust, as opposed to its occasional indulgence in harmless circumstances. But they did not, like the Christians, consider all seminal ejaculation and even the very idea of it as reprehensible enough to deserve severe punishment unless initiated—with due reluctance, one must imagine—for the devout purpose, enjoined by God, of keeping the earth populated.

The obstinate survival into modern times of phallic cults alongside those of the vintage in grape-growing countries gives some support to the hypothesis that the sexual orgasm, like intoxication by wine, was regarded in primitive ages as a manifestation of supernatural power, affecting all human beings without their being able to do anything about it. The impulse to worship what can give so much pleasure, as well as pain when frustrated—the 'bitter-sweet' Eros of the ancient Greek poets—perhaps remained a perfectly innocent combination of desire and anxiety or even terror until its ubiquitous and overwhelming possession of mankind brought it under fire from elderly lawgivers, the 'too severe old men' of whom Catullus complained to Lesbia.

For administrators who had lost their capacity for or much of their interest in carnal excitement may well have judged that it took up too much of their group's time, reducing their military and commercial prospects. The notion of guilt in this connection may have arisen in some such way, receiving a tremendous fillip when St. Paul pinpointed fornication as the root of all evil, therefore shameful and squalid. It is true that most pre-Christian languages, including Greek and Latin, stigmatise the 'private parts' as something to be ashamed of. But this synonym seems just as likely to derive from the need to protect, and so to cover, such important organs, a need felt by all savages as well as the civilised. The belief that one ought to be humiliated by the recognition of these anatomical features as channels for the flow of fertilising liquid and urine appears artificial by comparison.

In any case horror of the sexual act is not only characteristic of some pre-Christian sects like the Essenes but grew very slowly even under Christianity. Such outlying European regions as

Germany and Russia, to say nothing of Spanish subservience to Islam for nearly eight centuries, resisted conversion for periods between seven and nine hundred years. Even at the centres of medieval Christendom in Italy and France the opposition to Pauline austerity proved formidable. Defiance was never suppressed, though persecution of it raged far more fiercely than that which accounted for the Christians martyred by the pagans.

This ferocity nearly proved fatal to the religion which was ultimately to triumph in Europe. At the turn of the twelfth and thirteenth centuries the defeat of the theoretically monogamous but persistently dissolute crusaders by the practically polygamous but otherwise relatively puritanical Muslims shook Christendom to its foundations. Subsequently the Mohammedans almost succeeded, again and again, in taking over the West. It is significant that they were halted for ever in the sixteenth century. For by that time the official European attitude to Venus had become more reasonable. It accorded better then with what Christ himself seems to have felt in his rare references to the fair and frail, who 'loved much' and against whom 'he that is without sin among you, let him first cast a stone at her'.

The remarkable proliferation of sexual perversions among the clergy of the Christian Middle Ages, especially the monks, from flagellation and sodomy to bestiality, was directly due to the senseless enforcement of celibacy. Those who suffered under this prohibition but were not bold enough to evade it openly, or cheat or bribe their way out of it, did not constitute a majority, many as they were. Yet even of this minority a sizeable group unquestionably found erotic satisfaction in a variety of abnormal practices.

'When the desires of men,' the historian H. C. Lea wrote thirty years ago, 'are once tempted to seek through unlawful means the relief denied them by artificial rules ... unbridled passions are no longer restrained by a law which has been broken or a conscience which has lost its power. The records of the Middle Ages are accordingly full of the evidences that indiscriminate licence of the worst kind prevailed throughout every rank of the hierarchy.' He adds elsewhere: 'The Church issued countless commands of chastity and tacitly connived at their perpetual infraction.'

CONCLUSION

The even more shocking masochism in monasteries and nunneries had the same source. Nuns proved their contempt for the natural interests of young women by scarring their faces and cutting off their breasts as well as their hair. An Alexandrian nun actually blinded herself after being told by a male visitor that she had beautiful eyes. Others deliberately burned or freezed themselves. Some put on masculine clothing so as to appear unattractive to the opposite sex, with the unfortunate result in some cases that they were solicited by their own.

It is true that the best of the monks, of the Benedictines especially, preserved civilisation by their cultivation of the virtues of charity and scholarly, educational and even medical industry. But at the same time their excessive arrogance, what Gibbon called their 'intolerant and inflexible zeal', began to corrupt the very values that in other ways they saved from extinction. Their admirable energy, in fact, was largely wasted in artificial exercises, many of which would be regarded as futile by liberal churchmen today. The world at that time needed communities of would-be saints less than it needed schools of common sense. Perhaps there have always been too many of the former and too few of the latter, even in the present age.

On the whole the military Orders of monks, those of the Hospitallers and the Templars, as well as the Order of Teutonic Knights in Prussia, though not those in Spain and Portugal, had a better reputation, despite the great scandal of alleged sodomy among the Templars. Their dissolution at the beginning of the fourteenth century seems really to have been due to political jealousies rather than to any revelation of sexual licence among them.

The nunneries, too, had more promising activities to be proud of than prayer, penances and perversions. The inmates were taught nursing, cookery, plastic art, literature and music. But the twelfth century experiment of double establishments, with monks on one side of a dividing wall and nuns on the other, proved a disaster, as already noted (p. 89).

At the Dissolution in England under King Henry VIII the bones of new-born infants were found all over the place in convents, even in the privies. For it was not so easy for nuns as it was for monks and priests to have bastards adopted. Yet the risks of infanticide could not have been greater. It was a capital offence under civil law throughout the Middle Ages, since children dying unbaptised were doomed to everlasting perdition under the orthodox rule. Mothers convicted of exterminating an unwanted child were burned or buried alive, usually after impalement.

The pagans had not supposed either abortion of the foetus or destruction of a born infant, e.g. by exposure, to be a crime at all. They regarded the unconscious embryo in the womb as simply a part of the mother, like fruit on a tree. If she cut it away or dissolved it, as if it were some sort of tumour, that was her affair. But the Christians, for the first time in history, attached sanctity to human life from its beginning. The early Fathers, however, differed as to the point when annihilation of the conceptus became murder. Tertullian insisted that this was the case as soon as the rudiments of a second life started in the ovum. Augustine contended that only a properly formed and animate foetus could be the subject of lethal assault. His view was eventually embodied in Canon Law, though excised in later times.

Less fanatical Christians, members of the ordinary lay public or persons who submitted to the tonsure for more selfish reasons than a true vocation, reacted in more subtle ways, consciously or unconsciously, to the restrictions imposed by the Church on the lusts of the flesh. They sought to escape from their sufferings as intimidated individuals by combining as artists, for example as sculptors, writers or actors, to mock the omnipotent clerical hierarchy rather than chance the dangers of conspiring against it. Or else they flung themselves exuberantly into the joyous crowds celebrating the duly authorised religious festivals. There they could feel, for once, boldly irresponsible, forgetful of frowning moral censors and the awful menace of eternal, excruciating enslavement in hell. Their frenzied dancing, yelling and licentious romping burst from an identical psychological source, the longing to break away from the tormented self. The perverse asceticism of the saints had no other fundamental origin. But while the latter tried to repress their dread of sin by depersonalising pain, the former strove to stifle their private misery or forebodings of it by a loss of self-consciousness in pleasure.

CONCLUSION

Another weapon of revolt gleams in the very striking medieval sense of humour. Its tenderly teasing character rarely degenerated, though it had plenty of excuse to do so, into the bitterly satirical epigrams typical of less rigorously constrained epochs. The magnates who enjoyed, even at times revered, the impudence and absurd antics of their jesters, were in their turn seeking relief from the crushing solemnity of their public lives in the shadow of ecclesiastical severity. Laughter was perhaps never again so effective a destroyer of the pretensions of tyrants as in those days. It kept the post-heathen and pre-Renaissance millennium sane in the midst of more factors making for ruin and madness than have ever afflicted the western world before or since those thousand years.

But of course there remained a darker side to the rebellion of lay 'heretics' against what Lord Melbourne would have called impertinent interference with their private lives. Any decent woman who repelled the advances of a lascivious priest was liable to find herself run in for Manicheeism or some other doctrine condemned by the orthodox. She would be lucky if she had not to meet, in addition, a charge of witchcraft. But the numerous sects of anti-sacerdotal moralists were hunted down with equally merciless rigour. The brutish massacre of the Albigenses by order of Pope Innocent III in Provence extinguished a culture, that of the troubadours, far ahead of its day in refinement. Such naïvely puritanical nudists as the Brethren of the Free Spirit in Germany and the Adamites of Bohemia were wiped out by armoured papal troops with the most atrocious cruelty. These Central European mystics and their families went to their deaths by fire or sword laughing and singing. Such a mood is recorded of very few of the relatively more civilised men, women and children who fell victims to ecclesiastical ferocity in that period.

It is remarkable, by the way, that the Teutonic races in their comparatively cold climate were even then irresistibly addicted to nakedness in the open air. It is a habit typically expressive of revolt against official oppression. The Latins of southern Europe in their much sunnier atmosphere scarcely ever adopted such a custom. Yet the history of the always voluminously clad desert peoples proves that dryness and heat are as productive of resentful as of gay reactions.

In 1412, however, on the 11th October, a certain friar named Antonio started a nudist cult at Fermo in the Marches of Italy, not far from the Adriatic coast. He declared himself to be an incarnation of God the Father and Christ and announced that he would lead all true Christians to Jerusalem. Some twenty men and women, perhaps mainly from curiosity, followed this heavenly visitant as far as the river Tenna. There he made them all strip to the skin and baptised them. After this ceremony they all returned to Fermo, naked as the day they were born, 'without even drawers on' (*etiam sine tarabolis*), and paraded the city, presumably to obtain further recruits. Riots of course ensued. The Bishop's vicar ordered the exhibitionists to cool off still further in gaol, till they returned to a more Christian way of thinking. It is not stated how they were punished. But probably, as they were too few to constitute a serious rebellion, they were let off with the usual penances for mild and transitory forms of heresy.

The Lollards, the Hussites and the Taborites were rooted out more bloodily in the last two centuries of the Middle Ages. But other less conspicuous insurgents survived till this fermenting sore in the orthodox body of a recklessly rigid Church finally burst in the Reformation movement of the early fifteen hundreds. The schism that ensued proved far more drastic than that between Rome and Constantinople at the end of the fourth century which merely marked the distinction of oriental and occidental religious thought. That break had not, in other words, been a revolution from within, on intellectual premisses, but the consolidation of an already existent cultural difference. It did not require long wars, as the logically based Reformation did, to ensure its permanence.

The more northerly nudists, incidentally, severely tested the continence of the clerics sent to deal with them. In the twelfth century the Abbot of Harvengt in Flanders complained that in the summer people went about the streets of the town, on their ordinary business, in a state of entire nakedness, without even a loincloth. They alleged, in reply to the protests of their clergy, that they had to keep cool somehow. The scandalised abbot's emissaries were calmly told to return to their prayers. Nothing else seems to have happened. No doubt the phlegmatic and pig-

CONCLUSION

headed Flemings were not so easily excited as southern Europeans. Even today, after all that has happened since the twelfth century, their English cousins remain on the whole as singularly incurious as the Netherlanders themselves about public revelations of nudity. Not long ago a party of stalwart Dutch girls stripped to the waist on a crowded beach at Brighton, while drying after a swim, without apparently arousing much interest among the family parties of bathers within a yard of them.

As regards other forms of heresy, the cults of witchcraft and satanism, with their mainly erotic preoccupations, naturally attracted the sternest disciplines of the Church. But it was not until the Counter-Reformation movement of the sixteenth and seventeenth centuries that, for obvious reasons, the priestly rage in this direction touched positively pathological heights. The very widespread medieval practice of bestiality has sometimes been accounted for as derived from the witches' orgiastic assemblies. For the presiding debauchee on these occasions would often be disguised as an animal. But it appears more reasonable to follow the early twentieth-century psychiatrist Alexis Forel in relating the acts in question to the childish traits in the typical mind of the Middle Ages. In the modern world this perversion is mostly confined to imbecile, lonely or ugly farm-hands, with little access to girls but plenty to the mares, cows, donkeys and goats in the stable, the poultry at the barn-door and the rabbits in the hutch, coition with these smaller creatures usually proving fatal to their continued existence.

In the case of medieval women, nuns in particular were addicted, for very evident reasons, to this aberration, which Forel considers quite harmless. The lapdogs or larger canine breeds kept at the convents, both for protection and to solace the ample leisure of the inmates, could be trained to lick the clitoris or actually to couple with their mistresses. Swans are also said to have been popular with the Ledas of the Middle Ages. There was, finally, the consideration that sexual indulgence with beasts would not normally lead to pregnancy, though of course horrifying legends of infants with birds' or horses' heads were current.

But an imaginary conception could often be believed to follow the extraordinary blasphemy in which both monks and nuns supposed themselves (while masturbating) to be copulating in quasi-religious ecstasy with the Virgin Mary, Jesus Christ, the Holy Ghost or God the Father. These sins would be represented to the confessor as having really occurred in a transcendental vision of mystical union with the Godhead. The lives of the saints both male and female which were read in the monasteries and nunneries contained accounts of such experiences, which were, however, always stressed as being purely spiritual. It would then be difficult for the listening priest, in view of the real or apparent sincerity of the naive or sophisticated penitent, to arrive at a just decision about penance. The confessor might even wonder whether such seeming proofs of sanctity required any atonement at all. He might judge that on the contrary they should be honoured as conferring exceptional distinction on the recipient of such intimate favours from heaven.

Almost the only variety of sexual abnormality not mentioned in medieval legal records or Penitentials is exhibitionism, a very frequent erotic mania in modern times. But the public exposure of the male or, more rarely, female, generative organs is usually accompanied by masturbation. Consequently, this latter sin was probably held to cover the merely incidental denuding of the private parts and this initial procedure was not separately catalogued or punished. In the Middle Ages an exhibitionist who did no more than show his 'pudenda' to feminine passers-by, even if he called special attention to the act, would doubtless only send both matrons and spinsters into fits of laughter, assuming that they took any notice at all of a sight then relatively common. Their ridicule would as a rule effectively prevent further aggression. If it didn't, the offender could always be reported for attempted rape. The affront to modesty in the circumstances of an age when this notion was very much more restricted than it is today would not of itself be actionable. After all, anyone could in those days go and watch professional comedians exhibiting a phallus, real or artificial, in the ordinary course of entertainment.

An attitude of genial contempt, rather than the rage of a modern controversialist, characterised the medieval revolt, determined as it was, against the hypocritical friars who debauched the wives and daughters of laymen and the so-called celibate

CONCLUSION

vicars who kept concubines. The literature and art of the day proves that this critical scorn also applied in large measure to the secular lords who rode rough-shod over the masses of the people, if not over the clergy. During the ostentatious fourteenth century many frantic proletarian outbursts against aristocratic privilege, especially in France and England, frightened the Governments of Europe. Nevertheless, the real enemies of traders, artisans and peasants were always conceived to be those who used their spiritual prestige for material ends, in particular the satisfaction of their erotic appetites.

Even twentieth-century European history, for example in Russia, Spain, Italy and Germany, not to mention the persistent anti-clericalism in France, proves that in times of revolution the clergy, however innocent, are the first to suffer. They are supposed, by simple-minded men with a grievance, to enjoy powers unfairly bestowed upon them by the structure and beliefs of specifically Christian society. Whether or not the revolutionaries subscribe to its religious dogma, they instinctively attack, more furiously than they do the comparatively remote and in the rebels' view cynical industrialists, landowners or other capitalists, the familiar black-clothed figures who profess charity and seem to uphold its opposite.

The basic incompatibility of religious with political ideals, making for more hypocrisy in priests than in politicians, the latter being materialists like the insurgents themselves and therefore better understood, inspires the odium. It is always unreasonable. Even in the Middle Ages most clerics were as decent as most laymen. But unfortunately for the former they were expected to be more decent, in the face of excessive temptation not to be anything of the kind. For their office itself, with its superimposed moral prestige, gave them opportunities which the average layman, not so supported, would find it hard to resist. The average medieval priest did resist them. It was the stupid bigotry of his professional superiors, as a class, that forced so gaudy a colouring upon the sexual history of the period.

Asceticism carried to extremes, as in the repulsive masochism of many of the best known saints, who deliberately lived in filth and pain throughout their existence, did not especially disgust populations scarcely yet conscious of the principles of sanitation and the inextricable mutual involvement of body and mind. The men and women of the Middle Ages had been conditioned by their preachers to be much more concerned with the dramatic act of sex and its perversions than with the dull routine of purely hygienic measures. If they had been familiarised with such regulations they would have hated them as much as modern pre-puberty children do. Doctors and men of science were generally despised as charlatans or feared as magicians all through the millennium. On the other hand the medieval laity, at any rate until the spread of sophistication in the fourteenth and fifteenth centuries, really admired the stinking and groaning saints of hagiography. But the villagers and citizens also loathed the lustful tyrants who so often descended upon them from the cloister or the presbytery.

The moral rebellion was of course founded, as already noted, on the profound instinct of humanity to reject, like Lord Melbourne, interference with so private a matter as carnal excitation. But this imperative could never have extended, even among savages, to participation in the absolute licence which all too many tonsured and secular authorities in those days allowed themselves. They were regarded, implacably, as 'guilty men' by their victims. But since there was no remedy in force, because wealth and weapons were overwhelmingly on the side of the hierarchies, the artists, merchants and farmers could only express their hostility in disdainful, malicious laughter.

This policy, the only one in fact open to them, succeeded. For by the end of the fifteenth century not only those soon to follow Luther but half Europe were determined to have done for ever with a theocracy so vulnerable by then to corruption of all kinds. The process had begun with the obtuse blunder of making 'chastity' the queen of all virtues. The struggle really only lasted so long because enough truly unselfish, reasonable and personally modest scholars and administrators, like St. Thomas Aquinas, Duns Scotus, La Tour-Landry and Philip of Burgundy existed among the clergy, knights, barons and princes to remind Christians that Christianity stood for ideals less impracticable and exclusive than permanent fetters on physical love.

The penances for concupiscence, in short, did not work. Fasting does not eliminate desire, as the saints Jerome and Anthony,

CONCLUSION

if they had sacrificed discretion to honesty, could have told their disciples. Scourging can actually exasperate the itch to copulate, as many a sincere but worried flagellant could have added. Pilgrimages only give the instinct a wider field in which to operate and pile exotic on familiar stimulations. Prayers and psalms become mechanical in no time, turning to a thin veneer of barely conscious babble overlaid upon thoughts of quite a different nature. Nor were the sermons emphasising the 'uncleanness' of women, their menstruations, foul-smelling emanations and blood-clotted births, any more use. Once a parishioner got out into the sunlight and saw a good-looking girl he forgot all about them. The same oblivion awaited his vicar's constant reminders about evacuation processes in both males and females, proving, as it had seemed at the time, that the flesh bred nothing but excrement and urine.

It was in vain that the Hebrew patriarch Reuben, following the Pythagoreans and Essenes, had given Christianity a lead in this fatal direction a hundred years or so before the birth of Christ. 'Evil are women,' he had written, 'overcome by the spirit of fornication more than men and in their heat they plot against men and by means of their adornment they deceive first their minds and by the glance of the eye instil the poison and then through the accomplished act take them captive ... guard your senses from every woman if you wish to be pure in mind.'

It was in vain that a sixth-century bishop had declared that women had no souls, while others affirmed that they would be unsexed on the Day of Judgment. It was in vain that women were excluded from all but the most inferior sacred functions, so that magnificent choral music was sung by eunuchs instead of sopranos. It was in vain that women were driven out of the most remunerative and respected secular occupations, so that they could neither, like Aspasia, assist legislators, nor, like Boadicea and Ayesha, Mohammed's chief wife, call warriors to battle for causes they believed just. It was in vain that canon law disabled feminine personal liberty and their rights to hold and dispose of property. For even during the medieval period itself and much more often afterwards women like Eleanor of Aquitaine and Blanche of Castile, to say nothing of dramatists like Hrotswitha and many other learned and able abbesses and ladies of the manor or many a stalwart housewife and inn-hostess, showed again and again that they could be the mental equals of men.

The Church would have done better to concentrate upon the view of Christianity held by Marcion, a wealthy shipowner trading mainly in the Black Sea. He was converted in the middle of the second century and eventually settled in Rome, where he founded his own community. Marcion believed that Christ had aimed at the substitution of gentleness and patience for cruelty and fury, the cultivation of love and forgiveness instead of hate and vengeance, the exercise of compassion and benevolence instead of selfish calculation.

These ideas were not new. They had been stressed by Chinese and Jewish religious leaders before Marcion's time and by Arabs after it, not to mention Socrates and Seneca. But these philosophers were heathens and therefore anathematised by the early Fathers, who drew attention rather to the militant activities of Jesus of Nazareth, his violent attacks on 'scribes', Pharisees, bankers and lawyers, his threats of hell-fire. Congenial as these diatribes were to the fierce temper of the early Christian era, their puerility in other respects made posthumous torment seem very remote and unreal, especially as it might be avoided by penitence.

Consequently, the moral advance represented by Christ and Marcion was retarded by the childish pedantry of disciples inconsistent enough to offer Christians escape from heavenly blackmail by the performance of certain more or less disagreeable ceremonies, which made no difference whatever in the end to the 'sinful' proclivities of the temporarily repentant. It would be easy to convict medieval theologians of arguing in a circle, postulating their points of ethical doctrine as if they were self-evident mathematical truths. But the scholars of the Middle Ages were not in a position, culturally, to realise that moral judgments arise from purely subjective emotion, which cannot prove the objective existence of its source. It is only today generally recognised that good and evil are matters of degree.

Thus for centuries after Tertullian's *'credo quia impossibile'*, implying a positive rejection of all scientific knowledge from serious discussion, there was 'scarcely a rule' according to the nineteenth-century Irish historian Lecky, 'which reason teaches

CONCLUSION

as essential for the attainment of abstract truth that theologians did not for centuries stigmatise as offensive to the Almighty'.

The British theologian Pelagius (360-420), whose followers Augustine suppressed in the fifth century, knew better. So did Pelagius's associate Julian, Bishop of Eclanum, a see in Apulia, who considered sexual desire perfectly innocent. It is involuntary, he declared, and the substance of flesh created by a beneficent deity must be good. He jocularly teased Augustine, for instance, about his saying that in paradise children would be begotten without concupiscence, just as fruit is shaken from trees.

These heretical clerics can now be seen to have been incontrovertibly right as against the orthodox fanatics who locked out love between the epochs of Tertullian and Savonarola. For sex, as Groucho Marx once remarked, quite in the spirit of Pelagius, is here to stay.

Select Bibliography

Historia Francorum, St. Gregory of Tours, Ed. Guadet and Tarnnue, 1836
Récits des Temps Mérovingiens, A. Thierry, 1841
Patrologiae Cursus Completus, Ed. J. P. Migne, 1850
La Piété du Moyen Age, L. G. A. de Martonne, 1855
Juris Canonici Compendium, F. L. M. Maupied, Ed. Migne, 1861
Les Artistes de l'Alsace Pendant le Moyen Age, C. Gérard, 1872
Demonialitas, L. M. Sinistrari (c. 1660), 1875
Histoire du Luxe, H. Baudrillart, 1878
Les Bouffons, A. Gazeau, 1882
Fous et Bouffons, P. Moreau, 1885
The Discoverie of Witchcraft, R. Scot (1487), Ed. Brinsley Nicholson, 1886
Le Moyen Age Médical, E. Dupouy, 1888
Là Bas, J. K. Huysmans, 1891
A Formulary of the Papal Penitentiary in the Thirteenth Century, Ed. H. C. Lea, 1892
Woman under Monasticism, L. Eckenstein, 1896
Les Incubes et les Succubes, J. Delassus, 1897
Das Geschlechtsleben in England, E. Duehren, 1901
The Medieval Stage, E. Chambers, 1903
Medieval Studies, G. G. Coulton, 1905/31
From St. Francis to Dante, G. G. Coulton, 1906
The Censorship of the Church of Rome, G. H. Putnam, 1906
La Prostitution du XIIIe au XVIIIe Siècle, L. Le Pileur, 1908
Geistige Ehen in Urchristentum, L. Stöcker, 1909
A Medieval Garner, G. G. Coulton, 1910
La Question Sexuelle, A. Forel, 1911

SELECT BIBLIOGRAPHY

Illuminated Manuscripts, J. A. Herbert, 1911
Die Prostitution, I. Bloch, 1912/25
Voyages aux Pays des Sculpteurs Romans, A. Forel, 1913
Moeurs Intimes du Passé, A. Cabanès, 1919
The Witch Cult in Western Europe, M. Murray, 1921
Le Procès Inquisitorial de Gilles de Rais, L. Hernandez, 1921
The Medieval Village, G. G. Coulton, 1925
History of Witchcraft and Demonology, M. Summers, 1926
Legacy of the Middle Ages, C. G. Crump and E. F. Jacob, 1926
Life and Work in Medieval Europe, P. Boissonade, 1927
Malleus Maleficarum, J. Sprenger and H. Institoris (1490), Ed. M. Summers, 1928
Social Control of Sex Expression, G. May, 1930
History of Sacerdotal Celibacy in the Christian Church, H. C. Lea, 1932
The Peasants' Revolt of 1381, G. G. Coulton, 1934
The Women of Early Christianity, L. Eckenstein, 1935
The Fool, E. Welsford, 1935
Sacrifice to Attis, W. A. Brend, 1936
Medieval People, E. Power, 1938
Christianity and Morals, E. Westermarck, 1939
Oeuvres de nos Imagiers Romans et Gothiques, J. de Borchgrave d' Altena, 1944
Les Troubadours et le Sentiment Romanesque, Robert Briffault, 1945
Witchcraft and Black Magic, M. Summers, 1946
La Sculpture en France, B. Champigneulle et L. Gischia, 1950
Religious Dances, E. L. Backman, 1952
The Devils of Loudun, A. Huxley, 1952
Les Arts Primitifs Francais, L. Gischia et L. Mazenod, 1953
Sex in History, G. R. Taylor, 1953
Secret Enemy, J. Cleugh, 1954
Ladies of the Harem, J. Cleugh, 1955
Gilles de Rais, R. Villeneuve, 1955
Federico II d'Hohenstaufen, E. Pontieri, 1957/8
Eros, A. Sutherland and P. Anderson, 1961
The Dark World of Witches, E. Maple, 1963

Index of Personal Names

(Characters from literature in italics)

Abdurrhaman III, Caliph, 236, 245
Abélard, 78
Abraham, a Jew of Paris, 268
Achilles, 45
Adalbert, Archbishop of Mainz, 77
Adam and Eve, 21-2, 49
Adonis, 55
Aethelstan, King, 108
Afra, St., 131
Agamemnon, 159, 251
Agnes, St., 9
Alberich, the theologian, 287
Albertus Magnus, 179
Alcibiades, 15, 245
Alcuin of York, 86, 277
Aldhelm, Bishop, 85
Alexander the Great, 118
Alexander III, Pope, 289
Alexander IV, Pope, 92, 108
Alexander VI, Pope, 15, 187, 193-4
Alfonso VII, King of Castile, 240, 260
Alfonso X, King of Castile and León, 136
Ali-ibn-Hazm, 260
Allah, the god, 233, 238
Amboise, the Lord of, 121
Ambrose, St., 264
Andrea, Professor Giovanni, 78
Andrea, Novella, 78
Andrew, St., 71
Andromache, 205
Andromeda, 50
Angelico, 28, 35
Anne, St., 50
Anouilh, Jean, 169
Antonio, Fra, 302
Anthony of Egypt, St., 83, 94, 112, 116, 239, 306
Anthony of Padua, St., 52
Aphrodite, the goddess, 14, 43, 158, 228, 231, 271, 295
Apollo, the god, 50, 115
Apollyon, 115
Apuleius, 102, 127
Archembald, Bishop, 81
Arderrn, John, 178
Aristophanes, 126-7, 155
Aristotle, 25, 151, 288
Arnobius, 272, 279
Arnold, Matthew, 15
Artaude du Puy, 61
Artemis, the goddess, 159
Arthur, King, 252
Arthur, Prince, 68
Arundel, Sir John, 97, 207
Ashtaroth, the goddess, 228, 295
Asmodeus, 113, 116
Aspasia, 307
Astarte, the goddess, 8, 295
Asterius, St., 37
Athanasius, St., 11, 84, 156
Athenagoras, 13

313

INDEX OF PERSONAL NAMES

Attila, 275
Attis, the god, 8
Aucassin, 266
Augustine of Hippo, St., 9, 11, 15, 42, 102, 114, 116, 134, 159, 296, 300, 309
Augustine of Canterbury, St., 84, 88, 278
Augustus Caesar, 118, 151
Ausonius, 146
Ayesha, wife of Mohammed, 307

Bacon, Roger, 179
Ball, John, 205
Balzac, 119, 123-4, 218, 242
Bartholomäus, the apprentice, 138
Bartolomeo di San Marco, 32
Basil the Great, Bishop of Caesarea, 37-8, 273
Baudelaire, 67
Bede, the Venerable, 85, 181, 275-7
Beelzebub, 209
Belch, Sir Toby, 82
Belial, 50
Benedetto, Alessandro, 191
Benedict, St., 83-4, 94
Berengaria of Navarre, Queen, 201
Bernard, St., 22, 25, 28, 263
Bernard of Ventadorn, 263
Berry, Duke of, 28
Berry, Duchess of, 49, 208
Berthold von Regensburg, 289
Bertram, Bishop of Bordeaux, 248
Bertram de Born, 263
Béthencourt, Jacques de, 186
Blanche of Castile, Queen, 201, 264, 307
Blois, Count of, 161-2
Boadicea, Queen, 307
Boccaccio, 17, 182, 194, 265-7, 290, 295
Boethius, 116
Borgia, Cesare, 193, 217
Bosch, Hieronymus, 23, 35

Botticelli, 28, 35
Boucher, 35
Brant, Sebastian, 61
Brennus, 173
Brentano, Bettina von, 237
Briffault, Robert, 258
Buddha, 297
Bueil, the Lord of, 119, 121
Bunyan, John, 115
Burchard, Bishop, 283
Burns, Robert, 254
Byron, Lord, 34, 67

Caillette, 61-2, 71
Caliban, 60
Canute, King, 276
Casanova, 153
Castracani, Castruccio, 42
Caterina da Valbona, 267
Cato, 330
Catullus, 127, 297
Cellini, Benvenuto, 108
Cercamon, 262
Charlemagne, 21, 47, 107, 137, 141, 162, 178, 200, 233-4, 277, 294
Charles of Anjou, King of Sicily, 236
Charles the Bald, King of the West Franks and Roman Emperor, 21
Charles the Bold, Duke of Burgundy, 43
Charles V, King of France, 60
Charles VI, King of France, 42, 49, 70, 208
Charles VII, King of France, 208, 211-2, 214
Charles VIII, King of France, 187, 191
Chaucer, 15, 67, 97, 102, 207 268, 292, 295
Chatterley, Lady, 169
Chilperic, King of the Franks, 248-9
Chloe, 246-7
Chrysostom, St., 11, 37, 58, 152

INDEX OF PERSONAL NAMES

Clarembald of Canterbury, 88
Claus, the jester, 63
Clement of Alexandria, 7-9, 11, 118, 156, 260, 265
Clement, Bishop of Rome, 155
Clement VI, Pope, 53, 55-6, 209
Columbus, 187
Conrad of Marburg, 108
Cornelius Celsus, 186
Constance, sister-in-law of King John, 68
Constantine, the Emperor, 14, 20
Cornille, Hierosme, 119, 122-3
Cotytto, the goddess, 295
Cronos, the god, 158
Crosbiter, Laurence, 137
Crowley, Aleister, 125, 257
Cu Chulainn, 223
Cupid, the god, 196
Curialis, 156
Cybele, the goddess, 8
Cyprian, St., 9-10, 133, 154

Dacher, Gebhard, 209
Dali, Salvador, 34
Danae, 50
Danderi, 68-9
Daniel, the prophet, 21-2
Daniel, Arnault, 261, 263
Dante, 235, 256, 261, 265, 295
Daphne, 50
Daphnis, 246-7
Demosthenes, 107
Diana, the goddess, 8, 111
Diaz de Lisla, Ruy, 190
Diocletian, the Emperor, 131
Dionysus, the god, 49
Dives, parable of, 182
Dominic, St., 264
Donatello, 35
Doon, the crusader, 162-3
Duns Scotus, 306
Dürer, Albrecht, 35

Eadberht, King, 277
Ebbe, St., 10
Ebner, Christine, 90

Ecclesiasticus, 12
Ecgbert, St., 277-82
Edward I, King, 48, 154-5
Edward IV, King, 208
Edward VII, King, 155
Edward, the Black Prince, 205
Eleanor of Aquitaine, Queen, 201, 263, 307
Eli, the priest, 93
Elizabeth I, Queen, 48
Erasmus, 81-2, 98, 177
Eros, the god, 297
Estienne, Henri, 34
Ethelbald, King, 85
Eudoxia, the Empress, 11
Eugenia, St., 22
Euripides, 127, 270
Eve, 21-2, 128
Eyck, Jan van, 28, 35

Faidit, Gaucelm, 261
Faulconbridge, Philip, 206
Faventino, Bishop, 91
Fawkes, Guy, 42
Felix, the anti-pope, 269
Ferdinand II, King of Naples, 187
Ferron, Guillaume le, 219
Ferron, Jean le, 219
Filelfo, 269
Flamenca, La, 164-5
Flora, the goddess, 14
Forel, Alexis, 303
Fouel, Guillaume, 70
Fouquet, Jean, 28
Fragonard, 35
Francis, St., 83, 105
Francis I, King of France, 64
Frazer, Sir James, 8
Fredegond, Queen, 248, 286
Frederick I Barbarossa, the Emperor, 236
Frederick II, the Holy Roman Emperor, 235-6, 245
Froissart, Jean, 173
Fulbert, Canon, 78
Fuller, Thomas, 98

INDEX OF PERSONAL NAMES

Gabriel, the Archangel, 9
Galen, 186
Galileo, 265
Galla, 119
Gandolf, St., 251
Gargantua, 187
Gascoigne, Thomas, 186
Gaunt, John of, 186
Geoffroy IV, Lord of Roche-Pozay, 120-1
Germain, St., 248
Germyn, Elena, 98
Giacopo de Henzola, 91
Giacopo de' Vitri, Cardinal, 76
Gibbon, Edward, 299
Giorgione, 35
Giotto, 35
Giovanni da Cremona, Cardinal, 88
Glaber, Ralph, 142
Gnatho, the parasite, 247
God the Father, 9, 18, 25-6, 37, 41, 50, 63, 76-7, 101, 111, 114-6, 122, 124, 128, 176, 182, 192, 195, 203, 214, 251, 270, 274, 278, 302, 304, 309
Godfrey de Bouillon, 163, 241
Godwin, Earl, 88, 94
Goethe, 237, 265
Golet, 69
Golias, Bishop, 47, 253
Gonzalo de Cordova, 187
Gorgonia, St., 10
Gottfried von Strassburg, 251
Gower, John, 291
Gratien, St., 21, 123
Gregory of Tours, St., 181, 247-50
Gregory of Nazianzus, St., 11
Gregory I, the Great, Saint and Pope, 84, 108, 156, 198, 278
Gregory IV, Pope, 108
Gregory VII (Hildebrand), Saint and Pope, 87, 152, 169
Greta, the shoemaker, 137-8
Gromaire, 34
Gros, Jaufré, 257

Grosseteste, Robert, Bishop of Lincoln, 95, 144, 290
Grünbeck, Josef, 191
Grünewald, 35
Guilhem IX, Count of Poitiers, 241, 257-9, 262-3
Guinevere, Queen, 252
Guyot de Provins, 202

Hadrian, the Emperor, 151
Hainselin, the jester, 70
Hamlet, 71
Hardouin V, Lord of Maille, 120
Haribert, King of the Franks, 248
Haroun al Raschid, 165, 185
Hatton, Sir Christopher, 48
Hector, 205
Heine, 254
Heliogabalus, the Emperor, 158
Héloïse, 78
Hemmelin, Canon Felix, 104-5
Henri de Mandeville, 147
Henry II, King of England, 79, 134, 139, 201, 263
Henry III, King of England, 63, 95, 264
Henry V, King of England, 173
Henry VIII, King of England, 260, 299
Hera, the goddess, 43
Hercules, 126
Hermas, 10, 246
Herod Antipas, 48, 111, 217
Herod Philip, 111
Herodas, 126-7
Herodias, wife of Herod Philip and Herod Antipas, 111
Herodias, daughter of Herod Antipas and Herodias, 111
Herrad von Landsberg, Abbess, 41-2
Hesiod, 158
Hilaire, St., 248
Hippocrates, 186, 226
Holy Ghost, the, 9, 304
Honorius II, Pope, 88
Horace, 129, 230, 245

316

INDEX OF PERSONAL NAMES

Horner, Mr., 92
Hort, F. J. A., 111
Hrotswitha, 250-1, 307
Hugo, Cardinal, 144
Huss, John, 104

Ibn Darrach, 238
Ibn Guzman, 260
Ibn Khaldun, 58
Innocent III, Pope, 38, 152, 264, 286, 288, 301
Innocent VIII, Pope, 33, 110, 113
Irenaeus, Bishop, 107
Isabeau of Bavaria, Queen, 42, 70, 208
Isabella of Portugal, 71
Iseult, 251, 259
Isidor of Seville, Bishop, 38
Isis, the goddess, 8, 14

Jacopo della Quercia, 35
Jacote de Chateauvillain, 187
James IV, King of Scotland, 60
Jean, King of France, 205
Jean V, Duke of Brittany, 211, 215, 219-22
Jeanne d'Arc, 109, 211-3
Jerome, St., 9, 10, 116, 132, 156, 306
Jesus Christ, 7, 9, 10, 12, 20, 37, 40, 50, 54, 63, 92, 104, 113, 128, 131-2, 147, 151, 159, 177, 186, 217, 229, 231, 256, 262, 272-4 276, 284, 290-1, 296, 298, 302, 304, 307-8
Joan, the legendary pope, 24
John the Divine, St., 26, 162
John the Baptist, St., 111
John of Salisbury, 63
John XII, Pope, 86, 108, 224
John XIII, Pope, 103-4, 153, 209, 224
John, King of England, 68, 206
Jordan, William, 49
Joseph, St., 22, 48

Joseph, son of the patriarch Jacob, 34
Josephus, 118
Julian of Eclanum, Bishop, 309
Julius Caesar, 15
Jupiter, the god, 188, 294
Justinian, the Emperor, 273, 286, 294
Juvenal, 127, 256, 269

Kenneth I, King of Scotland, 108
Kirchner, 34
Klee, Paul, 34
Kramer, Heinrich (Henricus Institoris), 110

Lactantius, 37
Lafeu, 68
La Fontaine, 101
Lancelot, 161, 252
Lanfranc, 179
Langland, William, 98, 102, 268, 291
La Tour-Landry, 18, 202, 306
Lautrec, Toulouse, 34
Lawrence, D. H., 11, 19, 296
Lazarus, 182
Lea, H. C., 298
Lecky, W. E. H., 308
Leda, 50, 303
Lenard, Pers, 18
Lemaître, Jules, 241
Leo IX, Pope, 87
Leonardo da Vinci, 28, 35, 235
Leoncino, Niccolo, 191
Lesbia, 297
Leudast, Count, 248
Lichtenstein, Ulrich von, 256
Limbourg, the brothers, 28
Lindsay, Sir David, 68
Lisieux, Isidore, 116
Livy, 107
Lizio da Valbona, 267
Longus, Bishop, 246-7
Lot, the Biblical, 34
Louis I, the Emperor, 107 .
Louis VII, King of France, 240, 263

317

INDEX OF PERSONAL NAMES

Louis VIII, King of France, 51, 201
Louis IX, King of France (St. Louis), 65, 79
Louis XI, King of France, 42, 149
Louis XII, King of France, 61, 64
Louis XIV, King of France, 153, 245
Luc, Guiraut de, 240, 261
Lucian, 127
Lull, Raimon, 183
Luther, 45, 94, 118, 306
Lycenium, 247

Macbeth, Lady, 221
Malory, Sir Thomas, 252
Manardi, Ricciardo, 267
Mantegna, 28
Map, Walter, 88, 90
Marcellus Cumanus, 190-1
Marcion, 308
Marco Polo, 152, 243
Marcus Aurelius, the Emperor, 13, 294
Marcus of Memphis, 107
Margot, La Grosse, 270
Marighier, Guillemette, 71
Mark, King, 259
Mark Antony, 57
Mars, the god, 176, 188
Marsan, Arnaud de, 260
Martel, Charles, 233
Martial, 118, 205, 256, 269
Marx, Groucho, 309
Mary of Alexandria, 131
Mary Magdalene, 49, 114, 131, 162, 273
Masaccio, 28, 35
Matilda, Princess, 263
Matthew, St., 92
Maurice, St., 119
Maximin, St., 21
Mechthild of Magdeburg, 90
Meffraye, La, 216
Melbourne, Lord, 294, 301, 306
Mercutio, 68
Merimée, Prosper, 30

Merlin, 111, 118
Merovech, King of the Franks, 275
Mesnil, du, 213
Michelangelo, 32, 35, 36
Michelet, Jules, 180
Mithras, the god, 8, 14
Mohammed, 178, 232
Montfort, Simon IV de, 264
Moreau, Paul, 59
Moschion, 146
Moschus, John, 163
Moses, 186
Murray, Dr. Margaret, 113, 114

Napoleon, 153, 197
Nelson, Admiral, 249
Nero, the Emperor, 268
Newman, Cardinal, 105
Nicholas, St., 33
Nicholas V, Pope, 269
Nicholson, Dr. Brinsley, 110
Nicolette, 266
Nonnus, Bishop, 131
Novaire, Philippe de, 201, 203

Odysseus, 161
Olaf, King, 259
Origen, 8, 9, 11-3, 226
Orpheus, 55
Ory, Messire, 241
Ottar the Black, 259
Otto IV, the Emperor, 145
Ovid, 50, 146

Pan, the god, 14
Pantagruel, 71
Panurge, 64, 71
Paris, son of Priam, 42
Paris, Matthew, 44
Pastons, the, 210
Pathelin, Maître, 268
Paul, St., 12-4, 30, 260, 273, 291, 297
Paul IV, Pope, 32, 36
Pelagia, St., 131
Pelagius, 309

318

INDEX OF PERSONAL NAMES

Penelope, wife of Odysseus, 224
Pernelle de la Bornette, 146
Perrault, Charles, 215
Peter, St., 24, 87, 291
Peter of Aragon, King of Sicily, 236
Peter of Blois, 76
Petrarch, 67, 258, 264, 295
Petronius, 268-9
Philip Augustus, King of France, 67, 145-6
Philip the Fair, King of France, 79
Philip the Good of Burgundy, Duke, 70, 71, 306
Picasso, 34
Pietro Damiani, St., 52, 87
Plato, 118, 151, 297
Plautus, 177
Plutarch, 57
Poe, 67
Poggio Bracciolini, G. F., 99, 100, 170-1, 209-10, 268-9
Potiphar, 34
Pothière, Jeanne, 96
Pound, Ezra, 256
Poussin, 35
Powys, Theodore, 19
Praetextatus, Bishop, 248
Prelati, Francesco, 213-6, 220-2
Priapus, the god, 14, 96, 99, 275
Procopius, 181
Propertius, 259
Purnell, Dame, 98
Pythagoras, 12

Rabelais, 64, 67, 69, 71, 79, 187, 210
Radegunda, St. (Queen Radegond), 84, 179
Raimon VII, Count of Toulouse, 264
Rais, Gilles de, 109, 211-23, 277
Raphael, the Archangel, 116, 287
Raphael, the painter, 197
Rembrandt, 35, 197
Reuben, the patriarch, 307

Richard I, King of England, 68, 201, 206, 257, 261, 263
Richard III, King of England, 18
Robert the Devil, 60
Robin Hood, 66
Roderic, king of the Visigoths, 233
Roger the Norman, Count, 234-5
Roland, 47
Romeo and Juliet, 68
Romulus Augustulus, the Emperor, 14
Roussillon, the Countess of, 68
Rowlandson, Thomas, 23
Rubens, 35

Sacher-Masoch, Leopold von, 110
Sade, the Marquis de, 129
Saladin, 174, 242, 245
Salimbene di Adamo, 91-3
Salisbury, the Countess of, 154
Salle, Antoine de la, 268
Salome, 50
Salome, daughter of Herod Philip and Herodias, 111
Salvian, 262
San Angelo, Cardinal di, 209
Sara, 116, 287
Satan (the Devil), 29, 49, 96, 108, 114-7, 120-4, 126-9, 194-5, 203, 213-4, 217
Saturn, the god, 188
Saul of Tarsus (see St. Paul), 12
Savonarola, Girolamo, 14-5, 309
Scot, Reginald, 110, 112
Scudéry, Mdlle. de, 259
Sebastian, St. 32
Segarello, 92-3
Seneca, 308
Seyny John, 71-2
Shakespeare, 60, 68-9 75, 77, 221, 258
Sinistrari, L. M., 116-8
Siricius, Pope, 291
Socrates, 115, 208
Sordello, 265
Sorel, Agnes, 208

INDEX OF PERSONAL NAMES

Sprenger, Jakob, 110
Stalin, 185
Straw, Jack, 205
Swift, Dean, 194
Swinburne, 230
Symmachus, 119

Tacitus, 260
Taillefer, 47
Tarik, 233
Tennyson, Lord, 194, 259
Terence, 250-1
Tertullian, 9, 45, 118, 264, 291, 300, 308-9
Themistocles, 245
Theocritus, 118, 127
Theodora, wife of the emperor Theophilus, 69
Theodora, wife of the emperor Justinian, 273
Theodoric, King of the Ostrogoths, 178
Theodosius I, the Emperor, 277
Theophilus, the Emperor, 68-9
Thersites, 57
Thévenin, 60
Thomas à Becket, St., 288
Thomas Aquinas, St., 81, 114, 306
Thomas the *trouvère*, 251
Thucydides, 184
Titian, 245
Tobias, 116, 287
Tobit, 116, 287
Torrella, Gaspare, 191-3
Trajan, the Emperor, 294
Triboulet, 64, 67
Tristram, 251, 259
Trotula, 147
Tubal Holofernes, 187
Turold, 73
Tyler, Wat, 134, 205

Urban II, Pope, 87, 239
Ubertinus VIII, Pope, 186

Valentinian I, the Emperor, 277
Valla, 269
Venus, the goddess, 134, 159, 166, 176, 186, 196, 229-30, 253-4, 295, 298
Verena, St., 131
Vertumnus, the god, 14
Vesta, the goddess, 14
Vic, Peire de, 261
Victor of Ravenna, Bishop, 156
Victoria, Queen of Great Britain, 197, 294
Vidal, Peire, 263
Villon, François, 136, 258, 269-70
Virgin Mary, the, 34, 40, 48, 50, 71, 92, 113, 132, 230-1, 233, 256, 259, 265, 270, 296, 304
Voltaire 197, 265
Vreke, St., 131

Waltriquet, 161-2
Walworth, Sir William, 134
Wanamaker, John P., 288
Warton, Thomas, 49
Watteau, 35
Webster, John, 195
Weyden, Rogier van der, 28
William I, the Conqueror, King of England, 69
William IV, King of Great Britain, 294
William of Malmesbury, 257
Wimpherling of Strasbourg, 98
Wolsey, Cardinal, 207
Wright, Thomas, 18
Wycherley, 92
Wyclif, John, 49, 97, 102, 292

Yeats, W. B., 258

Zulma, 121, 124